MOSES

THE REVELATION
AND THE COVENANT

MARTIN BUBER

HARPER TORCHBOOKS / The Cloister Library

HARPER & ROW, PUBLISHERS

NEW YORK AND EVANSTON

MOSES
THE REVELATION AND THE COVENANT
First published in 1946
under the title. MOSES

Reprinted by arrangement with
Horovitz Publishing Co., Ltd., London
Printed in the United States of America

First HARPER TORCHBOOK edition published 1958

Library of Congress catalog card number: 58-5216

PREFACE

IN the year 1906 Eduard Meyer, a well-known historian, expressed the view that Moses was not a historical personality. He further remarked : " After all, with the exception of those who accept tradition bag and baggage as historical truth, not one of those who treat him as a historical reality has hitherto been able to fill him with any kind of content whatever, to depict him as a concrete historical figure, or to produce anything which he could have created or which could be his historical work." It is precisely this, the description of Moses as a concrete individuality and the demonstration of what he created and what his historical work was, that I have made my purpose in this book ; on the, to me, obvious basis of unprejudiced critical investigation, dependent neither on the religious tradition nor on the theories of scholarly turns of thought.

To the best of my knowledge, what has been essayed here is the first comprehensive attempt of this kind. None had been made indeed until the days of Eduard Meyer ; and of the two books which have since appeared on Moses and which deserve scholarly mention,[1] namely, " Mose und seine Zeit ", by Hugo Gressmann (1913), and " Mose ", by Paul Volz (1907, completely revised new edition, 1932), the former did not attempt the task at all, but exhausted itself in an analysis, which frequently led to entirely erroneous results, of the various strata of saga-growth ; while the second, which is valuable and stimulating but too general, and which does not deal adequately with the basic problems of the Biblical text, has conceived the task too narrowly. During the past four decades important contributions have been made to specific problems of research, which have certainly helped to display the historical appearance of Moses and his teaching [2] ; I refer to these in the notes.

Such an account as that attempted here must admittedly renounce one thing. It cannot undertake to submit a consecutive record of

---

[1] That a scholar of so much importance in his own field as Sigmund Freud could permit himself to issue so unscientific a work, based on groundless hypotheses, as his " Moses and Monotheism " (1939), is regrettable.

[2] Ernst Sellin's interesting works, which, following in the footsteps of Goethe, support the untenable theory of Moses' " martyrdom " with an astounding combinative skill, cannot, to my mind, be counted among these.

the course of events ; for what is provided in its sole source, the Biblical narrative, deals for the greater part with only two incidents: the Exodus and the camping at Sinai.   To these are added an introductory legend regarding the previous history of Moses, and a number of more or less fragmentary reports of post-Sinaitic events. It is impossible to produce a historical continuity out of these disparate saga complexes.   Nevertheless, and despite the questionability of Biblical chronology, the following account could endeavour to indicate a certain temporal sequence in connection with Biblical composition.   Though this may not afford any pragmatic connection, it does offer the picture of a sequence of events, in which a great process of the history of the spirit manifests itself as though in visible members.

The introductory chapter, " Saga and History ", deals with some of the guiding lines of the method employed in using the Biblical text for this purpose.   Fuller information will be found in my books, " Kingdom of God " (German, 2nd ed., 1936), and " The Teaching of the Prophets " (Hebrew, 1942).   It may be enough to mention at this point that I regard the prevailing view of the Biblical text, namely, as largely composed of " source documents " (" Yahvist ", " Elohist ", etc.), as incorrect.   Rather do I believe of most of the Biblical narratives that, underlying each single one, there was a reworking of tradition, which, in the course of the ages, experienced various kinds of treatment under the influence of differing tendencies.   To separate the early from the late here, and then to advance, as far as possible, from the reworking of tradition to what may be presumed to be tradition, orally preserved for a longer or shorter period of time, is the task of the Bible scholar as I see it.   The first step towards this can be carried out with relative assurance ; it is necessary to remove, so to say, the supplementary strata which can be identified as such through their language and style, content and tendency, by a process of reduction ; in order to reach those last attainable forms which are left available for a critical investigation of tradition. The second part of this task can scarcely be fulfilled save *ex hypothesi*. But the hypotheses support one another, and what they jointly have to offer, namely, the homogeneous image of a man and his work, confirms all of them together.

I have treated the Hebrew text in its formal constituents more seriously than has become the general custom in modern exegesis. In the course of dealing with this text over a period of many years, I have been ever more strongly reaching the conclusion that the form frequently, as one might say, rounds off the content, *i.e.*, that we are often shown something important by means of it. The choice of words in a given section, and in this connection the original meaning of the words and the changes in meaning, as well as the sentence structure to be found on each occasion, have to be carefully studied. In particular, however, a special function is exercised, in my view, by the principle of repetition. By the fact that the identical sounds, words, and sentences recur, whether in the same passages or in other corresponding ones, our attention is drawn in part to the specific meaning of single motifs, and in part to common analogies and completions of meaning as between them. A more detailed account of all this will be found in the book "Die Schrift und ihre Verdeutschung" (1935), which contains the essays written by my deceased friend Franz Rosenzweig and myself with regard to Biblical problems on the occasion of our translation into German of the Old Testament (of which the first fifteen volumes out of a total of twenty have appeared under the title "Die Schrift").

In view of its subject-matter the present book must deal chiefly with the history of faith. By this, however, something different from the customary meaning of history of religion has to be understood. This latter, in the generally accepted sense, deals with religious teachings, religious symbols and religious practices as such ; here, however, all of them, the theological, the symbolical and the institutional elements alike, have been submerged in the common life-relations of a community. In shaping the common life of that community, with all its social, political and spiritual functions, the faith dealt with here undertook to become flesh in a people. And that is the subject-matter of this book.

It is a fundamental error to register the faith with which I deal as simple "Monotheism". Here may be applied what was written half a century ago by Paul Yorck von Wartenberg to the philosopher Wilhelm Dilthey, his friend and my master : " I should consider it desirable for an attempt to be made to disregard all these categories, Pantheism, Monotheism, Theism, Panentheism. In themselves they have no religious value whatsoever, being only formal and of quantitative character. They reflect views of the world and not views of God, and constitute only the outline of an intellectual attitude ; and only a formal projection even for this." It is not so decisive whether the existence of a Unity exalted over all is assumed in one's consideration, but the way in which this Unity is viewed and experienced, and whether one stands to it in an exclusive relationship which shapes all other relations and thereby the whole order of life. Within the so-called Monotheism the concrete difference of the images of God and the vital relations with God made incisions which are sometimes far more important than the boundaries between a particular " Monotheism " and a particular " Polytheism ". The universal sun-god of the imperialist " Monotheism " of Amenhotep IV is incomparably more close to the national sun-god of the ancient Egyptian Pantheon than to the God of early Israel, which some have endeavoured to derive from him.

What is important for us about this God of Moses is the association of qualities and activities which is peculiar to Him. He is the One who brings His own out, He is their leader and advance guard ; prince of the people, legislator and the sender of a great message. He acts at the level of history on the peoples and between the peoples. What He aims at and cares for is a people. He makes His demand that the people shall be entirely " His " people, a " holy " people ; that means, a people whose entire life is hallowed by justice and loyalty, a people for God and for the world. And He is and does all this as a manifesting, addressing and revealing God. He is invisible and " lets Himself be seen ", whatever may be the natural phenomena or historical process in which He may desire to let Himself be seen on any given occasion. He makes His word known to the men He summons, in such a fashion that it bursts forth in them and they become His " mouth ". He lets His spirit possess the one whom He has chosen, and in this and through this lets him mature the work divine. That Moses experiences Him in this fashion and serves Him accordingly is what has set that man apart as a living and effective force at all times ; and that is what places him thus afresh in our own day, which possibly requires him more than any earlier day has ever done.

Jerusalem, June 1944   MARTIN BUBER

AFTER this work had been finished, in September 1944, Dr. Elias Auerbach of Haifa had the kindness to send me the manuscript of a book he has written on Moses. His work is largely developed on the hypothesis, equally attractive and questionable (and deriving from the viewpoint expressed in Eduard Meyer's study " Die Israeliten und ihre Nachbarstaemme " referred to above), that before the times of Moses there had been a settlement of the tribe of Levi in Kadesh, which had been driven away by the Amalekites until Israel reconquered the oasis under Moses. Auerbach seems more convincing to me when he discusses historical processes, such as the departure from Kadesh to Canaan. In any case all this deserves consideration and testing. The book performs a special service in its attempt to clarify certain fragmentary and obscure reports in the Bible which, for the greater part, have not been taken into consideration in my account. Auerbach has treated the specific elements which belong to the history of religion in somewhat general fashion. With regard to certain points he takes a stand against views which I have already expressed in earlier works ; but it is enough to refer to the relevant sections of the present work, which almost always deprive the criticisms of their point.

I thank my friend Dr. Ernst Simon for reading my manuscript with great attention and for his numerous and valuable remarks.

M. B.

TABLE OF CONTENTS

SAGA AND HISTORY

IN order to learn at first hand who Moses was and the kind of life that was his, it is obviously necessary to study the Biblical narrative. There are no other sources worthy of serious consideration ; comparison of reports, normally the chief means of ascertaining historical truth, is not possible here. Whatever has been preserved of Israel's traditions since ancient times is to be found in this one book. Not so much as the vestige of a chronicle dating from that period, or deriving from the nations with whom the Children of Israel established contact on their journey from Egypt to Canaan, has been preserved ; and not the vaguest indication of the event in question is to be found in ancient Egyptian literature.

The Biblical narrative itself is basically different in character from all that we usually classify as serviceable historical sources. The happenings recorded there can never have come about, in the historical world as we know it, after the fashion in which they are described. The literary category within which our historical mode of thinking must classify this narrative is the saga ; and a saga is generally assumed to be incapable of producing within us any conception of a factual sequence.

Further, it is customary to accept as a fundamental tenet of the non-dogmatic Biblical scholarship of our day the view that the tales in question belong to a far later epoch than the events related, and that it is the spirit of that later epoch which finds expression in them ; or, even more, the spirit of the sundry and various later periods to which are ascribed the " sources ", the different constituent parts of which the story is composed or compiled according to the prevalent view. Thus Homer, for example, to take an analogous case, provides us with a picture of the epoch in which he himself lived rather than of the one in which his heroes did their deeds.

Assuming that to be the case, just as little could be ascertained regarding Moses' character and works as is to be ascertained of Odysseus ; and we would perforce have to rest content with the possession of a rare testimony to the art with which court writers commissioned by the Kings of Israel, or the more popular (in the original sense of the word) prophets of the nation, wrought the image of its Founder out of material entirely inaccessible to us.

The scholarship of our own epoch, however, has prepared the way for another and deeper insight into the relation between saga or legend and history. For example, the philologist Hermann Usener indicated (in 1897) [1] that what finds expression in the saga is not a post-factum transfiguration of a historical recollection but a process which follows on the events, " in their footsteps, so to say ". At a more recent date (in 1933) [2] the Iranologist Ernst Herzfeld observed that " saga and the writing of history start out from the identical point, the event ", and that it is the saga which in particular preserves historical memories, " not of what the consequences show to be ' historical event ', but of that which roused the emotions of the men undergoing the experience ". It is possible to formulate even more precisely the nature of the issue involved. The man of early times met the unplanned unexpected events which transformed the historical situation of his community at a single stroke with a fundamental stirring of all the elements in his being ; a state of affairs properly described by the great Germanist Jacob Grimm (1813) [3] as " objective enthusiasm ". It is a primeval state of amazement which sets all the creative forces of the soul to work. What happens is therefore not a mere recasting of the event perceived by imagination become paramount ; the experience itself is creative. " Periods of a more sensuous religious emotion ", says Usener, " see vast, bright, super-human figures passing before the victorious troops and bringing death and defeat to the ranks of the foe ". Here the emphasis should be put on the word " see ". The historical wonder is no mere interpretation ; it is something actually seen. Even the subsequent comprehension of the flashing lightning-like visions within the consecutive report of the saga is not arbitrary in character. An organic and organically creative memory is here at work.

That this early saga, close as it is to the time of the event, tends to assume rhythmical form, can well be understood. It is not due solely to the fact that enthusiasm naturally expresses itself in rhythm. Of greater importance is the basic idea characterising this stage of human existence that historical wonder can be grasped by no other form of speech save that which is rhythmically articulated, of course in oral expression (a basic concept which is closely associated with the time-old relation between rhythm and magic). This is sustained by the wish to retain unchanged for all time the memory of the awe-inspiring things that had come about ; to which end a transmission in rhythmical form is the most favourable condition.

Occasionally the saga assumes specifically lyrical form ; as in the Song of Deborah, where the bard mocks and curses as from the very battle.

Hence alongside the more registrative forms of historical record, conditioned by the Court and its requirements, which constitute a stage preliminary to the scientific writing of history, and which develop from the Royal Lists of the Sumerians to the well-constructed chronicles of the Biblical Books of Kings, the historical song and the historical saga exist as spontaneous forms, not dependent upon instructions, of a popular preservation by word of mouth of " historical " events ; such events, that is, as are vital in the life of the tribe. It is of importance to investigate the sociological character of these types.

The saga is the predominant method of preserving the memory of what happens, as long as tribal life is stronger than state organisation. As soon as the latter becomes more powerful, on the other hand, the unofficial popular forms are overshadowed through the development of an annalistic keeping of records by order of the governing authority.

If a saga assumes poetic form in its early stage, it remains virtually unchanged for a long time, even when it is transmitted by word of mouth alone ; save that passages may be introduced which describe the course of events subsequent to the initial incident giving rise to the saga. Reminiscences not included in the poem may under certain circumstances condense into a parallel account so that, as in the case of the story of Deborah, prose is found side by side with poetry ; or, more correctly speaking, a loosely cadenced version accompanies the more strictly versified form. If the saga, however, does not assume this strict form at about the time of the event, but remains in its " mobile " state, it will be variously treated by different narrators, without any need to assume a conscious wish to introduce changes. Differing religious, political and familiar tendencies, simultaneous and parallel to one another as well as consecutive, find expression in the treatment, with the result that a product already current in the tradition is " rectified ", that is, supplemented or actually transformed in one or another detail. This continuous process of crystallisation is something entirely different in character from compilation and welding of elements from various sources.

Such a state of affairs invests research with the duty of establishing a critique of tradition. The student must attempt to penetrate to that original nucleus of saga which was almost contemporary with the initial event. The attempt is rendered difficult, *inter alia*, by the fact that the literature of the ages saw fit to round off the saga material by supplementary data ; as, for instance, where it was felt that the unknown or only superficially known birth and childhood story of the hero must not be left untold.

Here the procedure of investigation must necessarily be reductive. It must remove layer after layer from the images as set before it, in order to arrive at the earliest of all.

There can be no certainty of arriving by this method at " what really happened ". However, even if it is impossible to reconstitute the course of events themselves, it is nevertheless possible to recover much of the manner in which the participating people experienced those events. We become acquainted with the meeting between this people and a vast historical happening that overwhelmed it ; we become conscious of the saga-creating ardour with which the people received the tremendous event and transmitted it to a moulding memory. This, however, should certainly not be understood to mean that the only results we can expect to obtain lie in the field of group psychology. The meeting of a people with events so enormous that it cannot ascribe them to its own plans and their realisation, but must perceive in them deeds performed by heavenly powers, is of the genuine substance of history. In so far as the saga begins near the event, it is the outcome and record of this meeting.

The critique of tradition involved in the interpretation of the saga approximates us to the original meeting. At the sight of it we have to stand without being able to educe an " objective state of affairs ". We shall not regain a historical nucleus of the saga by eliminating the function of enthusiasm from it. This function is an inseparable element of the fragment of history entrusted to our study. Yet in every case we can and should test whether and how the narrative can be connected with and incorporated in the historical circumstances. Here history cannot be dissevered from the historical wonder ; but the experience which has been transmitted to us, the experience of event as wonder, is itself great history and must be understood out of the element of history ; it has to be fitted within the frame of the historical. Whether Sinai was a volcano cannot be determined historically, nor is it historically relevant. But that the tribes gathered at the " burning mountain " comprehended the words of their leader Moses as a message from their God, a message that simultaneously established a covenant between them and a covenant between Him and their community, is essentially a historical process, historical in the deepest sense; it is historical because it derives from historical connections and sets off fresh historical connections. When faced by such tales it is wrong to talk of a "historization of myth"; it might be preferable to describe them as a mythisation of history, while remembering that here, unlike the concept familiar in the science of religion, myth means nothing other than the report by ardent enthusiasts of that which has befallen them. And it may very well be doubted whether, in the last resort, the report of an unenthusiastic chronicler could have come closer to the truth. There is no other way of understanding history than the rational one; but it must start off with the overcoming of the restricted and restrictive ratio, substituting for it a higher, more comprehensive one.

However, two factors should be emphasized as having contributed greatly to the strength of the historical content of the Moses saga.

To begin with, the central figures of the Bible saga are not, as in so many hero-tales, merged in or amalgamated with persons belonging to mere mythology; the data regarding their lives have not been interwoven with stories of the gods. Here all the glorification is dedicated solely to the God who brings about the events. The human being acting under the God's orders is portrayed in all his untransfigured humanity. The wonder-working staff in his hand does not transform him into a possessor of superhuman powers; when once he uses that staff unbidden, he is subject to judgment. And when he descends from Sinai with radiant face, the radiance is not a shining forth from his own being, but only the reflection of some higher light. This withdrawing of the human being from the mythical element steeps the tale in an atmosphere of august sobriety, a dry atmosphere, one might almost say, which frequently permits a glimpse of a historical nucleus.

Besides, precise inspection goes to show that the early narrator of the deeds of Moses aimed not at beautiful or instructive individual sagas, but at a continuity of events. It is true that in the report of the journey through the wilderness, for example, we meet repeatedly with episodes; but they are introduced in a connection which obviously derives not from later harmonising literary tendencies (like the Book of Joshua, for instance) but from a powerful primitive emotion which is the passionate recollection of a sequence of unheard-of events. Nor yet does the relation found here appear to show anything of the poetic composition of the epos ; it is the practically related sequence of the itinerary. The latter may possibly have been worked up from an inexact or mutilated tradition to a state of questionable completeness ; maybe the associated temporal sequence has been transformed by didactic aims and number symbolism ; but the origin, the memory of a journey in the course of which the Nation came into being, and the zealous purpose of preserving on record the stations of that journey, has remained unobliterated. In the literature of the world the specifically historical can undoubtedly be found only where the principle of original connection is to be met with ; here it cannot be denied.

All this leads to a threefold critical task which, difficult as it may be, nevertheless seems in some degree to be capable of accomplishment. It is necessary to draw a distinction between saga produced near the historical occurrences, the character of which is enthusiastic report, and saga which is further away from the historical event, and which derives from the tendency to complete and round off what is already given. Therefore it is necessary to establish a further distinction, within the former, between the original components and their subsequent treatment. Finally, it is also necessary to penetrate to the historical nucleus of the saga as far as possible. Naturally it is impossible to produce a coherent historical picture in this way, which is the only one scientifically permissible ; yet we are entitled to hope for the ascertaining of genuine historical outlines. The distinction drawn should not be understood in the sense of elimination ; as we have seen, the saga element too, in so far as it is characterized by closeness to history, is historically important, being a document of the reception of what befell in the minds of those whom it befell. Yet we may go further ; what was added later is also of importance for us. Even the men who round off and supplement do what they do not arbitrarily but under the sustained urge of the primeval impulse. Tradition is by its nature an uninterrupted change in form ; change and preservation function in the identical current. Even while the hand makes its alterations, the ear hearkens to the deeps of the past ; not only for the reader but also for the writer himself does the old serve to legitimize the new. The Moses who had his being long ago is properly expanded by the one who has come into being in the course of long ages. It is our aim to come nearer to the former

by our testing and selective work on the text ; the latter is given to
us directly.   We must hold both in view without confusing them ;
we must comprehend the brightness of the foreground and gaze
into the dark deeps of history.

At the same time we must bear in mind that the forces which
formed the saga are in essence identical with those which reigned
supreme in history ; they are the forces of a faith.   For this faith,
which is in character a history faith, a faith relating largely to
historical time as such, has not subsequently treated a transmitted
material ; it cannot be imagined as absent from this material.   The
transmitted events are steeped in it ; the persons who furthered the
events believed in it, did in it what had to be done, and experienced
in it what had to be experienced.   The research of our day has
reached the point, in the course of its radical doubts and queries, of
providing fresh ground for an old certainty : that the Biblical tales
of the early Israelitic days report an early Israelitic faith.   Whatever
the mixture of fact and legend may be in the events related, the
indwelling story of faith which inheres in them is authentic in all
its main lines.   What we learn of the faith determining the active
and the receptive life of those persons is not, as scholarship supposed
for some time, a " projection " of a later religious development
against the surface of the earlier epoch, but is, in essence, the
religious content of the latter.   And it is this faith which shaped
the saga that was near to history and at subsequent stages also
shaped the more distant saga.

In its character this saga is " sacred legend ", since the relation
to God of the men of whom it tells is a fundamental constituent.
But this history, too, is in its character " sacred " history,
because the people who work and suffer in it work and suffer as
they do in virtue of their relationship to their God.

ISRAEL IN EGYPT

ACCORDING to the Biblical account the entry of the Children of Israel into Egypt, and their departure 430 years later, were brought about by two Egyptianized Israelites. These had both been accepted in Pharaoh's court, one as Grand Vizier and the other as the adopted son of a princess [a]; and both had received Egyptian names, one from a King, the other from a King's daughter. The narrative stresses the connection between the two when it relates how at the Exodus [a] Moses himself brought forth the bones of Joseph, namely the mummy-coffin which is designated in the Hebrew text,[b] assuredly not without intention, by a word bearing the meaning of a coffin nowhere else, but used for that Holy Ark which was the symbol of the covenant established between YHVH and Israel by the words of Moses.

We know of Semites who, at the time when the Tell el Amarna correspondence was being conducted, were high Egyptian officials. One of them was Minister for Syrian affairs and responsible for the granaries. We hear that in time of famine he provided Palestine and Phœnicia with grain. Another, referred to in an inscription on his rock-grave as the "highest mouth of the whole land "[c], is shown on the wall-paintings in the royal grave, receiving the reward of the golden chain [d] and driving through the streets of the residence city in a two-horse carriage.[e] Even at earlier periods we meet with Semitic notables ; especially at the courts of the Semitic Hyksos kings, certain of whom had themselves adopted Egyptian names and, like the legitimate Pharaohs, called themselves sons of the sun-god.

The analogies to motifs of the Biblical narrative are not in themselves of importance, however ; what is important is the historical relationship which finds expression in both sources.

As far as our knowledge goes, Ancient Egypt was not merely the starting point of what we call civilization ; it was also the first and, on such a scale at least, sole successful attempt to chill and congeal, in the most precise sense of the word, the life and spirit of Man, who had already started out on the journey of his history.

The remark made by the Egyptian priests to Herodotus, that Egypt was a gift of the Nile, can be fully appreciated only when

[a] Ex. xiii, 19.   [b] Gen. l, 26.   [c] Cf. Ibid., xli, 40.   [d] Cf. Ibid., 42.   [e] Cf. Ibid., 43.

the tremendous burden which this gift imposed upon those who settled in that country is realized. In order that the risen river might perform its fructifying work in adequate measure, without either harmful deficiency or even more harmful excess, the powers of nature had to be checked and regulated by a comprehensive system of dams, sluices, dykes and water-basins ; a system which could be established and maintained only by dint of nothing less than the uttermost energy of the ages. *Homo faber*, Man as producer of useful objects, was already an ancient when Egyptian history began ; here, however, he for the first time became familiar with the character of a perfectly organized duty of collective work, which ascribed no greater value to the foot of the living human being than to the water-wheel which that foot turned. It is worthy of remark that even the demons, which night by night draw the bark of the sun-god through the underworld, are organized in " troops ". The taskmaster with the whip, whom we meet in the Biblical account of the slave-period of Israel in Egypt and whom, when we now wander down the bank of the Nile, we can still observe above his toiling troop, is only a symbol of this collective duty ; without which the very pyramids would never have come into being. No less a symbol was the Pharaoh himself, who in his own person, as it says in a pyramid text, incorporates " the first wave of the high water ". " Scorpion ", a king of hoary antiquity, is already shown digging an irrigation ditch with his own hands. And just as the King " conducts the supply of all living ", so he exercises a strict, unremittent supervision over all landed property, so that all landed property merges in that of the King. " The land ", as the Bible expresses it in full accordance with the historical reality, " became Pharaoh's " [a] ; and every worker-family was left with just as much of the yield of the soil as was required for bare subsistence. As the pyramid culminates in its apex, so the Egyptian state culminates of almost mathematical necessity in the Crown, the " red flame ", which is addressed in the pyramid texts as living Godhead. In the last resort everybody received from the King the function which made him a man. All customs were bound up with the strictly regulated rites conducted daily by the King, through which the life of the country was maintained ; it was therefore vitally important to preserve the customs unaltered. Here, unlike the no less conservative China, State did not stand vis-à-vis village community with its own customs and institutions.

[a] Gen. xlvii, 20.

The State tolerated here the family, to be sure, since the latter submitted and adapted itself entirely to the State and its needs ; but it did not tolerate society by the side of the State. The perfect economic and political centralization which characterized Ancient Egypt has led certain students to speak of it in terms of State socialism. In his fine book, " The Dawn of Conscience ", Breasted has shown how the first ideas of social justice developed in Egypt. This, however, was also a centralized justice, which took up the whole field for itself and left no room for individual freedom.

The tendency to persist was operative in Egypt with a degree of exclusiveness which has been achieved by no other civilization. In its double expression—the wisdom of knowing what should persist, and the art of ensuring that it should persist—it produced a gruesomely consistent world in which there was every kind of ghost ; but in which each ghost carried out the function assigned to it. Stupendous as the technical achievement is in economy and politics, this civilization creates most where it errs most ; where, reaching beyond the limits of the human, it aspires even to the conquest of Death. The most precious spoil of decay has to be won back. In order that the genius of the dead King might be retained for the benefit of the land instead of roaming about and producing evil, the people fashion him his never-decaying abode, the mummy ; and in order to shelter it from any body-snatcher, hundreds of thousands of toilers raise the pyramids in the course of decades of effort. The pyramid, so to say, links the royal soul with the heaven-world into which it of all souls is taken up. This, however, is not sufficient assurance either. Since the genius in its new home may still feel itself threatened, a statue is carved for it out of the granite and diorite as a second dwelling ; and there it enters. Of these statues the seated figures are far and away the most striking ; these persons clearly sit never to rise again ; nowhere else has Art ever achieved such a sitting. Anybody who sees it learns the greatest effort made by human beings to give secular duration to a spiritual substance by introducing form into a material substance.

Yet even this is not everything. The soul must face certain dangers in the spheres of the gods ; and in order to do so successfully it is armed with magic. But in the history of Mankind there are two differing kinds of magic to be found. By this I do not mean " white " or " black " magic ; that is a distinction which does not touch the root of the matter. On the one hand there is a magic of spontaneity, where a person goes out to meet the chaotic element with his full collected being, and overpowers it by doing what is unforeseen and unforeseeable to himself, even though he may use transmitted utterances for the purpose and with sovereign freedom. On the other hand, there is a magic of formula ; fixed formulas, fixed rhythms, fixed gestures are all prepared, and nothing more is necessary than their correct application. This second kind can be described as technical magic. It was the kind which, in Egypt, was given to the dead to accompany his journey to the heaven world or the underworld. Obviously no spontaneous behaviour, no improvisation could be expected of him. All he had to do was to recite the requisite incantations, and he was secure ; in fact it was enough to write the formulas on the mummy-coffin or, at a later date, to insert a copy of the " Book of the Dead ", and the deceased in the Beyond was protected from the Powers that might menace him there. The texts read themselves, as it were, thus providing the dead with what is desired therein on his behalf or reported about him.[5] Sometimes they demand nothing less than that the King equipped with them should supplement the sun-god himself, and rule the world in his stead. That this can be required by one King after the other, without their interfering one with the other, is an important feature in this logic of the absurd. Here all contradictions continue : yet the completeness of a technique which fixes every detail takes the sting from the contradiction, and everything is compatible with everything else.

It would be incorrect to contrast this civilization, based as it is on the maintenance of fixed forms, with the Semitic element as such. The latter obviously played a part in the origins of the Egyptian nation during the prehistoric period after a fashion unknown to us but, as can be concluded from the Semitic components of the Egyptian language, to no small degree ; and the civilization of Babylon, Egypt's great rival, a civilization little less conservative though pointing in quite a different direction, developed largely through the combination of Sumerians and Semites. The factor, with whose singular contact, now attractive, now repellent, yet in the last resort antithetical, with Egypt we are concerned here, comprehended only part of the Semites on the one hand, and on the other shows not irrelevant non-Semitic constituents. This factor is found in those hordes known by the designation Habiri or Khapiru, whom we find mentioned in numerous documents between the middle of the Third and the end of the Second

Millenium B.C.E. They are found in varying social structures and
political constellations, first in Southern Mesopotamia, thereafter
amid the peoples of Anatolia, then in Syria and Palestine, and
finally in Egypt.[6] It has justly been pointed out that the migration
—which took place assuredly not as a direct mass-migration but as
one of numerous advances and withdrawals, and certainly not in one
definite mass movement after the other, but more frequently in an
uncertain and wavering groping and adaptation of large and small
groups—corresponds geographically in some measure to the route
of that clan whose history is related in the Book of Genesis as the
story of the " Fathers " of Israel. The suggestion that the Hebrews,
to whom this clan belonged, are more or less identical with the
Habiru, has come to be regarded as highly probable by the over-
whelming majority of students ; it has even become for them a
virtual certainty. It also seems likely that an association between
the two names may be assumed, no matter whether Habiru—in this
regard opinions differ—means unsettled, rovers, or (less probably)
comrades, confederates (both of which would apply to the hordes
equally well), or something else ; nor whether *Ivrim*, Hebrews,
means wanderers or yondermen, those who come from beyond the
Euphrates or the Jordan ; nor yet whether the relation between
the two names derives from actual relationship or only from a
Hebrew or Canaanite folk etymology which adapted the foreign
names to the local language. It is more important to compare the
report of Archæology during recent decades on the Habiru with
the Bible narrative of " Abraham the Hebrew " [a] and his immediate
descendants. Certain essential characteristics are found to be
common to both ; but we must never forget the high level of
civilization represented by the " Fathers " of Israel within the
development of semi-nomadism.

Habiru means not a tribe or a people but a human type, in
accordance with its particular way of life and peculiar relation with
the surrounding world ; yet the name has a decided tendency to
evolve into an ethnic designation.[7] This human type is composed
of members of various groups of nations, among which the Semites
(who presumably gave the first urge to the migrations) are for the
greater part dominant. They are people without a country, who
have dissociated themselves from their national connections and
unite in common journeys for pasture and plunder ; semi-nomadic
herdsmen they are, or freebooters if opportunity offers. They

[a] Gen. xiv. 13.

seemingly (we have to use analogy in order to complete what is known to us) wander to and fro in the wilderness with their flocks of sheep and goats, they hunt wherever they can do so ; they conduct a fleeting form of cultivation with primitive tools wherever they find suitable sites ; they pitch their tents near towns with which they exchange their produce ; but they also endeavour to establish themselves more securely. If they succeed in any enterprise of this kind, the leaders of the band may quite conceivably rise to ducal rank ; or they may temporarily become so powerful that the Egyptian administrative officials in the province of Syria and Palestine, for example, have to consider whether to make common cause with them against the Canaanite city-states or *vice versa*. If a warrior band cannot advance on its own, it temporarily becomes a mercenary body for some party waging war. If it is broken up, the individual members gladly accept service in public works as overseers, scribes, etc. ; they are given preference on account of their qualifications and achievements, and rise to leading positions. What this type of life requires is a " particular combination of the pastoral with the military virtues " [8] ; but it also calls for a peculiar mixture of adaptability and the urge to independence. The civilizations into which they penetrate are their opportunity ; they are also their danger.

The view the great civilizations held of the nomads, whom they apparently did not differentiate from the semi-nomads, can be seen, for instance, in a Sumerian hymn (dating from about 2000 B.C.E.) to the god of the West, wherein reference is made to the Amorite of the Western hills, " who knows no submission, who eats raw flesh, who has no house in his lifetime, who does not bury his dead kinsfolk ". In an Egyptian document, presumably centuries older, we read " Here is the miserable stranger. . . . He does not dwell in the same spot, his feet are always wandering. From the days of Horus (*i.e.* since time immemorial) he battles, he does not conquer, and is not conquered ". Here can be heard the deep animosity of the settled State form of life towards the unstable elements of the wilderness, yet also the knowledge of their indomitability. And soon after the period of the king with whom this record deals, we read in the " Admonitions of a Sage ", that describe the troubles of a period of decline (meaning the middle of the Third Millenium B.C.E.) : " The alien people from without are entered into Egypt ; the aliens are skilled in the works of the land of the marshes (the delta)." The sense of antithesis can develop to a metaphysical dualism among the settled population, as in ancient Iran, where they saw the Powers of Light on their side, and the Powers of Darkness on the side of the Turanians (which, like Habiru, is no ethnic term); and who believed that the war which had flamed from the first progenitors of both would end in the complete victory of the good principle over the evil one. Unhappily we do not know how the Turanians regarded the situation. Still, we do know that the nomads are accustomed to look down upon " the peasant tied to his clods, and the cowardly townsfolk, who seek to protect themselves behind walls and who serve a lord as slaves " [9].

The relationship between the nomad and the settled civilizations is a recurrent one in human history. In the Babylonian kingdom in the last quarter of the Third Millenium B.C.E., the " Wall of the West " was erected as protection against the nomad Amorites. In Egypt the " Wall of the Ruler " was erected at the beginning of the Second Millenium B.C.E., " in order not to permit the foreign hordes to come down again to Egypt, so that they should beg after their fashion for their cattle to drink " (clearly an ironical description, implying that they might begin in that way but would afterwards expand). So in China during the Third Century B.C.E., the Great Wall was erected to protect the Central Empire from the irruption of the nomads. The name Hiung-Nu (Huns) applied to the latter resembles the terms Habiru and Tura in having no ethnic character. It is extended to the nomadic bands of the north in general. Related to them are those Khirgis Kazaks whose original structure shows a particular resemblance to that of the Habiru, as appears to be indicated by their name. " Khirgis " means apparently something like " wandering, roaming ", while Kazak means, according to an etymology that seems convincing to me,[10] " separated from the tribe, from the horde, outlier "; it is the name given to both human beings and animals who have left their community. The union of such freebooters produced the clans one of which founded the Ottoman Empire. They are condottieri, who, as we know of the Habiru, may become conquerors and kings or else have to negotiate and submit to some State system as vassals, wardens of the marches or mercenaries.

We find a striking analogy to the name Khirgis Kazak in the Bible. The prayer [11] to be recited on the occasion of offering first fruits begins [a] with a formula which appears to me even older than

[a] Deut. xxvi, 5.

the remaining archaic constituents of the prayer. Its alliterative form is clearly intended to impress it on the generations of the Nation as particularly important : *arami obed abi*, "a straying Aramean (was) my father". This, like the word Kazak, is "stock-raising" language. The same word "obed" is used for describing the sheep which has wandered from the flock ; in which connection it must be borne in mind that when it is desired to vilify a Habiru he is called a runaway dog.[12] In a corresponding fashion Abraham, using what appears to be an ancient formula, tells the Philistine king in the Genesis narrative [a] that the Elohim, the Divine Powers, had "made him stray from his father's house", that is, had made an *obed*, a Kazak, out of him ; though his cultural type stood incomparably higher than that of the average Khirgis. In the same fashion, although in a different sense, might have spoken the grandfather of a North Syrian King of the middle of the Second Millenium B.C.E., who had apparently raised himself from freebooter leader to town lord and whose name "Tettish the Habiru" has justly been compared to the Biblical "Abraham the Hebrew" ; which is found, characteristically enough, in a chapter retaining wellnigh chronicle style, where Abraham appears as the leader of a band trained in war and battle. It seems that the Habiru also had their *ilani*, their gods. To be sure, it is probable that the term *lani Ḥabiri*, which is met with in Hittite documentary sources, means not "Gods of the Habiru" but "Habiru gods" ; that is, a special category of gods [13] who constitute in the divine world of the gods exactly what the Habiru constitute on earth, namely, nomadic gods, a wandering god-host. Yet since the express designation "gods of the Habiru folk" also occurs, it may be assumed that the gods which were so designated in the Hittite cultural world into which the Habiru penetrated were the ones which the latter honoured in their *ilani* : gods who themselves wandered, and who led the wanderings of the human bands dependent on them. The Biblical Abraham certainly had no plurality of gods in mind when, in order to make himself quite understandable to the Philistines, he used the word *Elohim* in the plural sense, which the form of the word retains. In the religion of Israel the term *Elohim*, as expressed in our own range of concepts, means the totality of divine forces or the divine substance, regarded as a single person. Abraham's god, however, is a wanderer like himself. He has no fixed spot, no "house" ; he wanders hither

[a] Gen. xx, 13.

and thither ; he takes his folk and leads them wherever he will ;
he moves on with them from one place to another [14].

Certain geographers view the countries in which the early
civilizations developed as vast oases ; and this certainly applies to
Egypt. That the wanderers of the wildernesses or steppes should
yearn to penetrate thither at the sight of such an oasis is as understandable as the fact that the settled populations endeavour to repulse
them. But the emotion of the peasants is simple, while that of
the nomads is ambivalent. They desire to settle here ; yet something within them feels that their freedom, their independence, the
social forms suited to them, their highest values, are all threatened.
Historically considered this is not a struggle, as one tends lightly to
assume, between a higher and a lower stage of development ; for
as compared with hoe cultivation and as an *indirect* exploitation of
the products of the soil, the domestication of animals is a no less
important advance than the economy of the plough. The stable
oasis society, however, with its State trends and closed culture,
fights against a fluctuating cultural element which, its small units
linked by a strong collective solidarity, organizes itself in closer
tribal association solely for war or cult activities, and recognizes
personal authority solely in so far as the bearer of the latter evinces
it by his direct effect. It has correctly been said [15] that this " fluid "
character of the social constitution is the main prerequisite for the
well-being of a nomad people, and that it is this " which leads
them to an inevitable conflict at every contact with a settled people ".
Here the dynastic principle faces the charismatic one ; a thoroughly
centralist principle faces one of primitive federalism. State law
faces tribal law ; and beyond this a civilization established in rigid
forms faces a fluid element which rarely condenses into a comprehensive structural form of life and work. The tradition of the
pyramid faces that of the camp fire. It is precisely when the
nomads or semi-nomads receive the alien State form in their power,
and take possession of leadership, that they fall most rapidly under
its sway. A daring student [16] has endeavoured to identify the great
Egyptian queen Hatshepsut with the princess who, according to
the Biblical account, saved and brought up the infant Moses.
Long after the driving out of the Hyksos (who, again like the Habiru,
were composed of varying ethnic elements, though in this case
partly non-Semitic, and containing strongly nomadic constituents)
she praises herself for having restored what they destroyed, and
accuses them of having overthrown what had been established.

Such a charge is assuredly not based on arbitrary deeds of destruction, but on the heavy battles which ended with the retreat of the invaders to Palestine and Syria. To all appearances the Hyksos had in general adapted themselves to the Egyptian civilization, and proceeded with its development. But after the foundering of their undertaking they were not in a position to renew their own form of existence, and obviously collapsed into their component units.

Where the nomad peoples persist in their independence and their separate manner of life, they constitute a singular and important cultural element, which exercises a reviving and renewing effect on the surroundings. It has been justly remarked already of the cattle-raisers of ancient times [17] that their historical function can scarcely be over-estimated. Likewise where part of a nomad people becomes settled and thus establishes stable forms, as in the great South Arabian city civilizations, the fluid element seems to continue to lave them with a force that preserves their vitality. Nomadism has the effect of producing culture in the precise sense where it neither needs to fit itself into a dominant civilization nor overruns one after the other, but gains room and time enough to establish one of its own. Under such conditions they, the nomads, continue to develop traditional elements, deriving from their period of wandering, in notable fashion. The descendants of the Berbers, it is true, raised Spanish agriculture to a high level ; but in their art they developed motifs which they had already been employing in the carpet weaving of their nomad days. The essential inner cultural development of the nomad peoples sometimes falls [18] during the specific period before they enter history. The tradition is expanded to a great cultural series only after the decisive conquests and, as is demonstrated by the Saracenic civilization, the greatest example during the Christian era, with an extensive co-operation of the defeated indigenous inhabitants. Yet the elemental forces finding expression therein derive from the nomads who, after the conquest in this as in analogous cases, continue to maintain an inner nucleus at least of the hereditary forms of life and society. The Greeks, whose forefathers came to Hellas " as a nomad or semi-nomadic shepherd people ",[19] should not be taken as an example to the contrary. The particularism of the small States, which was the weakness of the Greek commonwealth and the strength of the Greek culture, permitted no small proportion of the essence and structure of the original clans to persist.

A renowned sociologist has justly pointed out [20] that in all these peoples their way of life is more than a form of livelihood ; it is a kind of faith.   This makes it possible to understand the problems they must face when they penetrate into lands of stable civilizations. We must regard Israel's sojourn in Egypt against this background in order to comprehend the special importance of the events. Though they were already something more than the typical nomads, the Israel of the period of growth, viewed from the viewpoint of world history, nevertheless shared the structure and fate of the nomadic element.

In the remarkable fourteenth chapter of Genesis, which was long regarded as a late product of fantasy but in which the strong nucleus of tradition is again beginning to be recognized, Abraham, hitherto a peaceful semi-nomad, takes the field against invaders or marauders at the head of a band of warriors.[21]   The band which he commands consists in part of allies and in part of " initiated " [22] who have grown up in the community led by him, and who were trained for peace and war alike.   They are called " bondsmen " too, but also appear to bear to Abraham, who in other tales is regarded by the natives [a] as one " exalted by God " or a " godly leader ", the relation of a cult community to their chief.   Certain students tend to regard the Abraham of this chapter as a different person, because he appears in so different a fashion here.   Yet this unit of livestock raisers and condottieri, this band who journey to and fro with their tents and herds but are always capable and ready for battle, clearly correspond to the type of the Habiru.   The Biblical report, however, lays special stress on two particular characteristics, assuredly with the purpose of contrasting Abraham and his folk with the normal type.   Abraham finds it important not to be regarded as a mercenary [b] ; and he finds it important to identify the God of his community, who leads their wanderings, with that particular one among the gods of the settled people who is recognized by them as the " Most High God " [c].   There, as here, this God is the " founder " or " procreator " [23] of Heaven and Earth ; and both here and there he is likewise the one who places the foes of his faithful ones in their hands, who remains present to them in their campaigns.   Both of these facts, the warlike co-operation with the natives without mercenary submission and the effort to

[a] Gen. xxiii, 6.   [b] Gen. xiv, 23.

[c] *Ibid.*, verse 22, which repeats the name of God given in verse 19, but extends it emphatically.

induce the natives to recognize the God accompanying him as the one they themselves mean, while simultaneously, by giving Him the name unknown to' them, preserving his own superiority—these two facts together produce that singular maintenance of distance which we also meet in the other tales of Abraham. It is in this identical manner that he negotiates [a] with the Hittites to purchase the grave, which should under no conditions be acquired otherwise than at the full value of the land ; while naturally not forgetting even for a single instant that " this land ", the whole of it, has been promised him by his God.

The same is indicated by the thrice-repeated account [b] of the abduction of the tribal mother. It derives from the conception that the particular blessing power or blessing substance,[24] which had descended from Heaven to Earth, rests not only on the heads of the fathers but also in the wombs of the mothers. The fathers must transfer the blessing specifically to the sons ere they die, whereas the mothers transmit it naturally to those born of them. It is this that the alien rulers, Egyptian and Philistine, vainly endeavour to make their own. And for this reason it is so strongly insisted on here [c] that women of one's own tribe must be espoused in order to concentrate the blessing power and enhance its potency ; whereas during the ensuing period Judah marries a Canaanite woman, Joseph an Egyptian and Moses a Midianite without Scripture finding any cause for censure in their doing so. The sacral distance maintained in ancient times, a tradition of which has been preserved in the stories of the patriarchs, grew less and less rigid.

What such tales preserve is the memory of a phenomenon which has played an important part in the peculiar existence of Israel. The apparently instinctive tendency of semi-nomads, to settle without sacrificing tribal freedom and tribal faith, has crystallized here after a remarkable fashion in the history of the " Fathers ", of whom Isaac already shows strong peasant tendencies whereas Jacob again reverts to the semi-nomadic type. What is it that marks out this single Ḥabiru wave, or whatever else we may wish to call it, from all the others ? Presumably the fact that this " Israel " understood as a divine charge something that was potential within him, and that it felt this too realistically to be able to satisfy its conscience through a purely symbolic fulfilment of that

[a] Gen. xxiii.   [b] Gen. xii, 12-20 ; xx ; xxvi, 1-17.
[c] Gen. xxiv, 3 f., cf. xxvii, 46.

charge. This is the deep-seated sentiment which finds poetic expression in Balaam's prophecy [a] : " Behold a people ('*am*) that dwells alone and amid the nations (*goyim*) is not accounted " ; which should perhaps be understood in the sense that it is predominantly a people in the social sense, a community of people who live with ('*im*) one another, and as such stand over against all the others, who are predominantly people or nation in the physical sense (the word *goy* deriving from a root meaning " body "). The story of Joseph tells something analogous, since according to it Joseph takes steps for his brethren to receive a more or less autonomous separate territory for settlement. The individual may be a vizier ; but the clan remains closed and separate. This one band among the wandering " Hebrews " enters the Egyptian land of culture as a unit. It receives and moulds the Egyptian influence as a unit ; it suffers slavery as a unit ; and as a unit it departs from slavery to freedom. This part of the " fluid " element enters into the sphere of set forms and maintains itself there, apparently not without a measure of degeneration. Yet under the surface of this degeneration it grows to a might which begins to manifest itself in the liberation and after.

Towards the end of the speech summing up the Exodus, which is set in Moses' mouth in the first section of the Book of Deuteronomy, we find [b] : " Or has (at any other time) Godhead endeavoured to come to take Him a people from the midst of a people ? " This " from the midst ", which might more precisely be rendered " from the bowels ", characterizes the situation accurately. As the " Children of Israel ", as a congeries of clans, they came to Egypt [c] ; in the midst of the Egyptian people they grew into a people whose God " comes to take him ". Here the word *goy* is used for " people ". Scripture is concerned here with the very body of the people. Yet when the God of this people speaks of it for the first time as his own at the Burning Bush, as told in Exodus,[d] he uses the word '*am*. In this word '*ammi*, " my People ", recurring at the beginning and the end of God's words, which unites the " with " of human community with the heavenly " my ", the mystery of the nature and charge of Israel has found its most elemental formulation.

[a] Num. xxii, 9.   [b] Deut iv, 34.   [c] Gen. xlvi, 8.   [d] Ex. iii, 7, 10.

LEGEND OF THE BEGINNING

WE do not know when the tribes of Israel (or, as many scholars think, part of them, as against whom the balance remained in Canaan) came down to Egypt and settled in the Land of Goshen in the eastern part of the Delta ; nor when they departed and whether they did so in more than a single wave. Correspondingly we do not know when the Exodus took place. Chronologies both Biblical and non-Biblical, archæological findings, and computations on the part of the historians all contradict one another. Various periods between the middle of the fifteenth and end of the thirteenth centuries B.C. come into consideration. The two named are available for narrower choice ; but our knowledge is inadequate for decision. In the course of modern Biblical studies first one and then the other view gains the upper hand. For a long time it was believed that Rameses II, who reigned during the first three-quarters of the thirteenth century, had to be identified with the Pharaoh " who knew not Joseph ",[a] which is supported *inter alia* by the name of one of the " store cities " built by the Israelites.[b] More recently [25] there has been a tendency to give preference to the earlier period, which again has been replaced during the last few years [26] by a renewed preference for the later epoch. There is much that speaks for an arrival of the tribes in Egypt as early as 1700, that is, even before the Hyksos rule ; and despite all objections certain historical factors seem to me to point to Thutmose III, the spouse and rival of Hatshepsut, who reigned in the first half of the fifteenth century, as the " Pharaoh of the Oppression ". In that case the Exodus would belong to the time of his successor. It seems probable that the change in the attitude of the Egyptians to Israel commenced in the period following the overthrow of the Hyksos. Yet it is impossible to deny considerable weight to the arguments in favour of the later date, which are drawn from the historical changes in the relations between Egypt and Palestine. In any case there can be no doubt as to the historicity of the servitude of Israel. It has justly been pointed out,[27] that no people would care to invent so ignominious a chapter of its own history.

[a] Ex. i, 8.   [b] *Ibid.*, 11.

33

Moreover, the report of the Enslaving [a] is unmistakably maintained at an exalted poetic tone. " And as they oppress him the more so does he increase and so does he spread forth " [b] is not chronicle but poesy ; and the same is indicated by well-weighed repetitions, like the rhyming reiteration " with rigour " [c] or the fivefold repeated and hammered " servitude, bondage " in the same two verses. Here the ignominy has obviously been raised to a theme of folksong, as prelude to the story of the Exodus, ever enchanting the audience ; the story which is constructed round the recurrent leitmotif that the God of Israel has liberated his people from the " servitude " of Egypt in order to take them into his own " service ". " Go, serve ", cries Pharaoh for instance to his Hebrew overseers [d] ; and in the course of the same speech, after his mind has begun to waver, he repeats to Moses three times,[e] and yet again at the decisive hour,[f] that they should go and serve YHVH. This epic with its repeated transition into hymn must be grasped after its own fashion and according to its own impulses, in order to understand what this legend of tribulation has meant for the generations of the people from those who composed it down to those who, in our own later day, recount it at the Passover Evening, that most historical of all historical festivals of the human race.

It is evident that the report grew into a legend in the mouths of the reporting generations. The motif of the slaying of the children has nothing to do with the story of the hard labour ; it bluntly contradicts the logic of the narrative (slave economy naturally aims at an increase in the number of working hands) ; it has clearly come into being through the motif of the saving of the boy Moses. And this as well is truly a motif of legend. We know a similar case in the often-quoted cuneiform text wherein the great Semitic king Sargon of Akkad (about 2600 B.C.E.) relates that his mother bore him in hiding and placed him in the stream in a reed box, the door of which she sealed with pitch ; that the stream had not risen and he was afterwards taken out of it by an irrigator and brought up as a gardener, until the goddess Ishtar came to love him and brought him to the throne. Of Sargon we know the fact that he was a gardener in his youth. Comparative mythology can adduce a whole series of motifs analogous to that of Moses,[28] and even permits the conclusion " that there is no

[a] Ex. i, 11-14.　　[b] *Ibid*, 12.　　[c] *Ibid*, 13-14.　　[d] Ex. v, 18.
[e] Ex. x, 8, 11, 24.　　[f] Ex. xii, 31.

justification for believing that any of these heroes were real persons, or that any stories of their exploits had a historical foundation ".[29] Instead it should be realized how the passion of tradition, which is a passion for reshaping, fills gaps in a transmitted biography by carefully drawing on the treasury of legendary motifs common to early humanity.

Yet what is most important of all here, as in all forms of comparative study in the humanities, as far as these wish to give their due to concrete historical facts, is, after having analysed the common elements, to restore the individual elements to their relationships, and thereafter to inquire into the meaning to be attributed to any special linking of the common and the singular elements. In the Biblical narrative of the saving of the boy Moses the meaning is obvious : in order that the one appointed to liberate his nation should grow up to be the liberator—and of all analogous legends this is the only one containing this historical element of liberating a nation—he has to be introduced into the stronghold of the aliens, into that royal court by which Israel has been enslaved ; and he must grow up there. This is a kind of liberation which cannot be brought about by anyone who grew up as a slave, nor yet by anyone who is not connected with the slaves ; but only by one of the latter who has been brought up in the midst of the aliens and has received an education equipping him with all their wisdoms and powers, and thereafter " goes forth to his brethren and observes their burdens ". The Biblical narrative sets this clearly historical motif against that other of Joseph sold to Egypt as the one sent ahead " to a great deliverance ".[a] A Semitist [30] concludes from the Egyptian loan word that the mother really chose to make the " box " of papyrus,[b] in which the child was exposed, in the shape of one of those shrines wherein pictures of the gods floated on the Nile during festivals, in order to be certain of rescue. If this was so, we may be permitted to consider it as symbolic ; he who must immerse himself in the innermost parts of the alien culture in order to withdraw his people from thence is hidden as a child in the seat of the foreign gods.

That Moses bears an Egyptian name, no matter whether it means " born, child (of somebody) " or something like " seed of the pond, of the water ",[31] is part of the historical character of the situation ; he seems to derive from a largely Egyptianized section of the people. Whoever wishes to make an Egyptian of him on

---

[a] Gen. xlv, 7.   [b] Ex. ii, 3.

that account deprives the tale of the foundation on which it rests.
The narrative itself sets out to explain the name on the basis of Hebrew etymology as meaning " he who is drawn (out of the Nile) ".
But the form of the Hebrew verb (which with the exception of
this passage is not found save in a Psalm [a]) can only mean " he who
draws forth ".   And as it seems to me, it was the covert purpose
of the etymology to indicate this : the intention was to characterize
Moses as the one who drew Israel forth from the flood.   I gather
from a never hitherto understood passage in Scripture that there
must have been a tradition to this effect.   In a remarkable hymn
which was included in the Book of Isaiah [b] it is told of God : " He
remembered the days of old ", whereupon follow the words
mosheh ammo.   At first sight this can scarcely mean anything but
" Moses his people " ; which, however does not offer a satisfactory
sequence. . The meaning becomes clear when we notice that the
words may also be interpreted as : God remembered " the drawer-
forth of his people ", the man who had withdrawn the people of
God from the flood.   Then follow, and with obvious intention,
the words indicating God's co-operation with Moses : " Where
is He who brought them up from the sea with the shepherd of
His flock ?   Where is He who set His holy spirit in his midst ? " [32]
The narrative of the manner in which Moses went forth to his
brethren,[c] which is the beginning of the essential life story, is
composed in true Biblical fashion on a thrice-recurring " he saw ",
and a rhymingly repeated " his brethren " ; the Biblical epic
frequently indicates the more important elements in this particular
fashion without forsaking its own style.[33]   The point brought home
here is that Moses now came to " see " his brethren.   How did
he, who had grown up as an Egyptian at the Egyptian Court,
know that the Hebrew slaves were his brethren ?   We are not told ;
and this is also characteristic of the Bible style, with its unique
mixture of frankness and reticence.   What we have to know is
that he " goes out " from the Royal Court yonder where the
despised slaves toil ; and that he goes out because he wishes to see
his brethren.   And now follow the three moments of the action.
First he sees the weary slave labour.   Then he sees a single incident ;
an Egyptian taskmaster beats a Hebrew man, one " of his brethren ".
Now he looks round, yes, he actually looks round, driven to action,
yet clear-headed.   He aims not at becoming a martyr but a liberator ; and he slays the Egyptian.   That " beating " and this

[a] II. Sam. xxii, 17 ; Ps. xviii, 17.   [b] Is. lxiii, 7-19.   [c] Ex. ii, 11-15.

" slaying " are conveyed in precisely the same word in the Hebrew ;
Moses does what he saw done to the one who did it. Now, however,
the narrative blossoms forth remarkably. On the next day Moses
goes there again ; it is his place, it is his affair, he must go there
afresh. And now he sees one of his brethren beating another.
What a discovery ! Taskmasters are not alone in beating slaves ;
one slave beats the other. And when Moses upbraids him, the man
answers with a growling burst of passion, the meaning of which
is betrayal, and which serves to foreshadow the ever-latent restive-
ness that a liberator has to expect from the liberated : " Who hast
set thee as chief and judge over us ? " And then louder, barking
rather than growling, " dost thou think to slay me as thou hast
slain the Egyptian ? " Now Moses is alarmed, but he does not
flee yet. Only when Pharaoh " seeks to slay him " (the expression
sounds more like Semitic blood vengeance than Egyptian justice)
does he flee " before Pharaoh ".

What follows, the scene of Moses at the well in the land of the
Midianites (irrespective of whether the latter like Mount Sinai has
to be sought on the Sinai Peninsula, in North-West Arabia or
elsewhere) ; how he protects the seven daughters of the tribal
priest, among whom is his own future wife, from the bad shepherds
and helps them to water their flock ; is sometimes regarded as an
idyll. Unlike Jacob's meeting with Rachel at the well, with which
it is often compared, it is not an idyll. It serves, possibly on the
basis of a tradition preserved by those Midianites or Kenites who
joined Israel in the Exodus from Egypt, to demonstrate how a
basic principle of Mosaic legislation, the protection of the weak
from the power of the strong, was applied by the legislator himself,
both at home and in foreign parts ; that is, as a universally valid
norm. The fact that the girls took Moses for an Egyptian [a] is
not without weight, no matter how casually the motive is introduced. The narrator stresses the fact that Moses had not already
become part and parcel of his brethren before his flight but retained
Egyptian costume and manners until he came to the Midianites
and accepted their customs together with their society. He had
not passed through the degrading forms of life involved in the
slave status, like the other Hebrews. He came directly from the
lofty culture of the Egyptian Court to the proximity to Nature of
the semi-nomad existence which the tribe of his father-in-law
continued to maintain until a late period, even in the midst of

[a] Ex. ii, 19.

settled Israel.[a] Something of fundamental importance is to be
found here. Whatever may have been the relationship between
Israel and Midian,[b] Moses came back to his forefathers by way of
his flight. For the customs and order of life in the tribe which he
entered closely resembled in their character the customs and order
of life of the " fathers " of Israel. A man of the enslaved nation,
but the only one not enslaved together with them, had returned to
the free and keen air of his forebears.

At this point a biographical and historical truth, which is fundamental for the understanding of all that follows, emerges from the
midst of the legend.

[a] Jer. xxxv, *cf.* I Chr. ii, 55.   [b] *Cf.* Gen. xxv, 2.

THE BURNING BUSH

THE section which deals with the Revelation at the Burning Bush [a] cannot be regarded as a compilation from varying sources and documents. All that is needed is to remove a few additions, and there appears before us a homogeneous picture ; any apparent contradiction can be accounted for by the fact that the text has not been fully understood. The style and composition of this section show that it is the fruit of a highly cultivated dialectic and narrative art ; but certain of the essential elements of which it is composed bear the stamp of early tradition.

Moses, tending the flocks of his father-in-law, leads them out of the accustomed steppe on one occasion ; just as we hear of the Bedouins of the same district moving with their flocks into the hills, where the animals find pastures that are still green. There Moses suddenly finds himself at the " Mountain of God ", Mount Horeb or Sinai. " Mountain of God " (or " of gods ") had been its name since time untold, presumably because mysterious phenomena, either of volcanic or other character, take place on it and local tradition therefore claims that divine beings reside there.[34] Here Moses sees the " burning bush ". Just as the mountain is described as " *the* mountain of God ", that is, the mountain known as " a god-mountain ",[b] so is the bush described as " *the* thornbush ", that is, the specific bush which is known to grow upon Sinai. The name *seneh*, which is peculiar to it (no other kind of bush is called so) echoes the name of the mountain, which is omitted of set purpose at this point. The word *seneh* repeated three times in the same sentence suggests the name Sinai, that is used only [c] when the nation reaches the mountain in order to receive the revelation.

The bush burns, the blaze flares up, and in the blaze the " messenger of YHVH " is seen by Moses. Such " messengers " (which we call " angels ") are always recorded in the earlier Scriptures without personal names, and, so to say, without personal character. They are nothing save the perceptible intervention of the God in events ; which is sometimes made even more plain by the fact that they and YHVH Himself are alternately named as speakers.

[a] Ex. iii, 1-iv, 17.
[b] Only after the revelation to the people in Numbers x, 33, is it called " the Mountain of YHVH ".   [c] Ex. xvi, 1.

The flame does not consume the bush. This is not a consuming fire that nourishes itself on the material it has seized, and is itself extinguished in the destruction of that material. The bush blazes but is not consumed : and in the blaze shining forth from it, Moses sees the " messenger ".

Certain scholars take the story to mean that " on Sinai there was a holy thorn bush which was considered by the residents of the region to be the seat of the mountain divinity ", and they draw the conclusion that YHVH " is also regarded here as a tree god ".[35] They find support from the fact that in the " Blessing of Moses " [a] the god is designated *shokhni seneh*, which is translated as " He who dwells in the thorn bush ". The verb, in question, however, did not originally mean to dwell but to take up residence ; to sojourn, no matter how temporarily. Further, the apparition is seen not in the plant but in the fire ; and accordingly the voice which [b] calls Moses " from the midst of the bush " should be understood as coming from the fire which blazes throughout the entire bush. YHVH, to be sure, can just as little be regarded here as mountain god, he who attacks Moses on the way to Egypt [c] and orders Aaron in Egypt [d] ; and in our story he already states the deeds which he would perform there in support of Moses. All these are characteristics the like of which are not reported of any of the mountain gods, and which (apart from the fact that YHVH himself says [e] that he has " come down " from heaven) speak against the view that Moses had " discovered the seat of YHVH ".

There are some who tend to " draw a distinction in principle " between the calling of Moses, which commenced with this apparition, and the calling of the prophets ; " for whereas the latter undergo a psychological experience which takes place in dream or vision, there is a mythical event in the case of Moses, since the divinity appears to him corporeally " [36] This is a distinction in categories which finds nothing in the Bible text to support it. Isaiah says,[f] apparently in a memorial written many years after the event reported, that his eyes had seen " the king YHVH of Hosts " ; which is not less but rather more corporeal than the apparition described in the story of the summoning of Moses. For it is made perfectly clear here that Moses saw no form. After the messenger permitted himself to be seen " in the blazing fire ", what Moses sees is expressly stated : " and there, the bush was

---

[a] Deut. xxxiii. 16.   [b] Ex. iii, 4.   [c] Ex. iv, 24.   [d] *Ibid.*, 27.
[e] Ex. iii, 8.   [f] Is. vi, 5.

burning with fire, but the bush was not consumed ". That it was this he saw and nothing else is also stressed by the fact that he says to himself : " Let me go across, and see this great sight—why the thornbush is not burnt up ". Nobody who had seen a divine form in the fire could talk in that way. Moses actually sees the messenger *in* the blaze, he sees nothing other than this ; when he sees the wondrous fire he sees what he has to see. No matter how we explain the process as being natural, this at least is what the narrative tells us and wishes to tell us ; and whatever this may be, it is clearly not " mythology ".

As against this the difference between the literary categories of saga and prophecy is indicated in scholarly quarters, and the explanation is given [37] that literary history must " ab initio protest at the obliteration of this saga-like character " ; no scientific investigator, it is claimed, would even dare " to derive the legends of Hellenic heroes, whose eyes so often saw divinities, from psychological experiences ". Yet with all the deference to literary categories, their scientific dignity is not great enough to decide the character and dimension of the content of truth in an account of a revelation ; it is not even enough to ensure the correct formulation of the question. Instead of the legends of Greek heroes let those of Greek thinkers be taken, say that of Pythagoras, which appears to have influenced the late Alexandrian version of Moses' life story [38] ; and it will immediately be seen that we are face to face with the problem of a transmitted nucleus of personal experience contained in it—naturally without even thinking of being able to extract that nucleus. How much more so when it comes to a vision so singular, so characteristic, despite certain external analogies, as that of the Burning Bush, followed by such a conversation as the one which follows. It compels us to forsake the pale of literature for that singular region where great personal religious experiences are propagated in ways that can no longer be identified.

YHVH sees Moses approach to look ; and " God " (here of set purpose not " YHVH " appears as the acting one, as previously, but " God "), in order to establish the connection with the " messenger ", calls to Moses from out of the bush. It has correctly been remarked [39] that such a calling by God from a specific place occurs only three times in the story of Moses, and that each of them is made from a different one of the three sites of revelation : once, in our text, from the bush, once [a] from the mountain, and once [b]

[a] Ex. xix, 3,   [b] Lev. i, 1.

at the Tent of Meeting. The Biblical work of redaction indeed shows wisdom and art of a rare kind. The passage now under consideration differs from the others by the fact that Moses is called on by name. That is the fashion in which divinity establishes contact with the one chosen. The latter, not conscious yet aware of the one whose voice is calling him, places himself at the service of the God by his words " here I am " ; and the God first orders him not to come closer (the restriction on the " approach " to the divinity is one of the basic provisions of Biblical religion) and to remove the sandals from his feet. The reason may possibly be because being holy ground, it should not be trodden by any occupy- ing and therefore possessing shoe.[a] [40] It is only now that God tells him who he is ; he who communicates with him, Moses, here in strange parts, is none other than the god of his forefathers, the God of the Fathers ; and hence, as we may suppose, the God of whom Moses must have heard yonder in Egypt when he went forth every day " unto his brethren ".

The favoured " Kenite " hypothesis explains that YHVH was unknown to Israel until then, being a mountain, a fire or maybe a volcanic god and simultaneously the tribal god of the Kenites (who are often assumed to have been wandering smiths) and that Moses had " discovered " this god at his seat of worship on Sinai. This hypothesis is unfounded.[41] There are not the faintest indications that any god of the name was ever honoured in that district. No more than suppositions are possible with regard to the character and qualities of a, or the, putative Kenite god. For this reason the hypothesis has not unjustly been described [42] as " an explanation of ignotum ab ignoto ". We know of YHVH's connection with Sinai only from the Bible ; and what we know is that at the time of the Exodus of the Children of Israel from Egypt YHVH had selected Sinai as the seat for his manifestation. The Song of Deborah, which is referred to,[b] does not bring YHVH, as is sup- posed, from Sinai to the Galilean battlefield, it only ascribes the name " a Sinai " to Mount Tabor, from which [c] the God who had come in storm clouds out of the south revealed himself in the glorious victory over his foes. And Elijah, who is thought to have made a pilgrimage to Sinai when he wished to " speak per- sonally to and seek an audience of YHVH ", [43] really wandered defeated and weary of life to the mountain in order to lay himself down and perish in " the cave ",[d] that is, in yonder cleft in the rock,[e]

[a] Cf. Ruth iv, 7.   [b] Jud. v, 5.   [c] Jud. iv, 6.   [d] 1 Kin. xix, 9.   [e] Ex. xxxiii, 22.

familiar to the wanderers, from which Moses had once seen the God passing by. YHVH never appears in the tales of his revelations to Moses and Israel as " fixed " on Sinai ; he only comes down thither on occasion, descending from heaven to do so.[a] Comparative religion, too, is familiar with mountains not merely as the divine seat, but also as the place where gods manifest themselves.

And just as this does not make him a mountain god, so the fact that in the course of the revelation he often makes use of the element of fire, the heavenly origin of which is frequently referred to in the Bible, does not convert him into a fire god. For our purpose, however, the most important fact is not the traits of the nature gods which he has absorbed (criticism of these particular characteristics is offered in the story of the Sinai revelation to Elijah [b]) but what he is to begin with. Is he an alien god whom Moses meets, and through Moses, Israel, and who is made the national god of Israel by Moses ? Or is he a " God of the fathers " ?

The Bible permits us to ascertain this. All we have to do is to compare the peculiarities of the God of Moses with those of the God of the Fathers. More precisely, it is our concern to reveal the peculiar divine likeness, first in the constituents of our tale which, beyond all question, lead back to early tradition, and then in the corresponding elements of the other, a likeness, that is to say, which it is impossible simply to classify by some type or other of the pre-Mosaic religious history of the Ancient East, for despite all its relationships with one or another of these types, it shows a character differing from them all. Thereafter we must compare the two divine likenesses with one another.

If the material in the Bible is subjected to such an examination, the two likenesses will be found to differ in a special manner ; namely, just as a clan god in non-historical situations might be expected to differ from a national god in an historical situation. Yet at the same time it can be observed that both depict the identical god. To begin with the former, the clan god : we immediately observe two main characteristics which are both demonstrated in his relation to the men chosen by him. One is that he approaches these men, addresses them, manifests himself to them, demands and charges them and accepts them in his covenant ; and the second, closely connected with the first, that he does not remain satisfied with withdrawing them from their surrounding world

[a] Ex. iii, 8 ; xix, 18, 20.　　　　[b] Cf. 1 Kin. xix, 11 f.

and sending them on new paths, but wanders with them himself and guides them along those new paths ; meanwhile, however, remaining invisible insofar as he does not " make himself seen " by them. Taken both together, these cannot be compared with the attributes of any other divinity in the history of religion, despite certain analogies of detail. The prerequisite assumption for both is that this god is not bound to any place, and that the seats of his manifestations do not restrict him ; above them open the gates of heaven,[a] through which he descends and returns to his inaccessible realm.

We find all this once more in the second likeness, in the national god ; but here it has the vivid colour of a historical driving force. The new and supplementary characteristics, striking as they may appear, nevertheless seem peripheral to us when compared with the central power of the common element. Once again the God makes his great demands of his men, commanding and promising, establishing a covenant with them. But now he no longer turns to single persons but to a people, and that people too he leads forth and himself conducts along the new way. Once again the invisible one becomes manifest from time to time. Once again heaven and earth are joined, and the God utters his words from heaven unto earth.[b]

This is no alien god " discovered " by Moses on Sinai ; it is the God of the Fathers. And yet it is in his eyes none other than the God of whom his wife's kinsfolk may have told him, saying that he dwells on this mountain. When Moses came to the Midianites, he entered the range of life of the Fathers ; and he senses the apparition he now sees as being that of the God of the Fathers. As Yhvh had once gone down with Jacob to Egypt,[c] so has he now gone from Egypt to Midian ; possibly with Moses himself, who was obviously under his protection like Jacob of old. At all events Moses perceives who it is that appears to him ; he recognizes him. That was what had happened in the days of the Fathers too. Abraham had recognized Yhvh in the El 'Elyon of Melchizedek, Yhvh had permitted himself to be seen[d] by Abraham's concubine, the Egyptian maid, Hagar, as the spirit of a desert spring—seemingly one of those divinatory springs at which something can be " seen " during sleep. What happens here, as it had happened there, is, from the point of view of religious history, an identification. The God brought with and accompanying a

[a] Gen. xxviii, 17.   [b] Ex. xx, 22.   [c] Gen. xlvi, 4.   [d] Gen. xvi, 7, 13.

man is identified with the one known as previously to be found at this spot ; he becomes recognized in him. From Babylonian and Egyptian religious thought we know the tendency to give full expression to the faith in the supremacy of a single god by inter-preting the other gods as his forms of manifestation. But with the exception of the short-lived imperialistic theology of Amenhotep IV, no serious attempt in this direction was or could be made in the great Pantheons. Only in the religious atmosphere of a solitary exclusive God outside the Pantheons, claiming and leading his own men, could any such identification become a living reality.[44]

Attention deserves to be given to the fact that YHVH addresses Moses not merely as the God of the Fathers, but first as the God of his (*i.e.* Moses's own) father. Later on this was, at times, no longer understood, as can be seen in the text of the Samaritans which knows only of a " God of thy fathers ". But the Biblical narrative lets Moses [a] say when naming a son : " the God of my father was my aid ". Only Jacob before him in the Bible spoke of himself both personally and yet in relation to past generations.[b] Nobody spoke in that way after him. Here too can be felt the peculiar relation with the world of the patriarchs. And, whatever may be the position in disentangling the sources, the redactor knew well what he was doing when he introduced those passages ; in which the man who had grown up in his own father's home is shown to be conscious of his God as the God of his own father.

After the God tells his chosen one who he is, he reveals the cause and purpose of the message with which he wishes to entrust him. The sentence with which this partial address begins, and that with which it ends, balance one another like the members of a building, through the two key-words *ammi*, my people, and *Mitsraim*, Egypt. These are repeated in both, and denote the subject and the aim of the act : " I have indeed seen the sufferings of my people who are in Egypt ", and " lead out my people the children of Israel from Egypt ". To attribute the two sentences, as is so often done, to different sources, constitutes a misunder-standing of the entire form and sense of the speech. With this repeated " my people " at the commencement and close of the passage, YHVH recognizes Israel in a fashion more powerful and unequivocal than would have been possible by any other verbal means. To be sure, he has not yet designated himself their God. He will become the God of Israel as a people solely through the

[a] Ex. xviii, 4.   [b] Gen. xxxi, 5, 42 ; xxxii, 10.

revelation to the people ; now he wishes to be known only as the God of their forefathers, to whom he had once promised the land whither he would lead Israel. But since he so stresses the naming of Israel as his people, he shows that the bond uniting them had been established of old. No new, no alien god talks in such a way. This likewise indicates the hopelessness of the attempt sometimes made to attribute this first speech, which refers to the patriarchs, to some later stratum of the text. Try to insert at this point the phrase assumed to have been in the original, namely " I am the god ", *i.e.* " I am the god of this mountain ", and the message, flaming with historical revelation and historical faith, shrinks, one might well say, to a private remark which conveys nothing.

And now begins the great duologue in which the God commands and the man resists. As we have it before us, it is clearly disfigured by supplements, inserted by editors, which should not be considered as sections of a source. To begin with, something is introduced between the two first objections of the resisting man, namely his inadequacy and his inability to tell the people what they would demand to hear of the name and hence of the character of the God, on the one hand ; and the final passage which returns once again to his inadequacy, on the other. In the interpolated passage Moses asks how he can demonstrate the reliability of his message to the people and is instructed to perform wonders. Here later narrative motifs are introduced in evidence, largely in order to link the story of the revelation with that of the negotiations with Pharaoh ; but by this both sections are impaired. The style differs here from that in the undoubtedly genuine parts of the narrative of the burning bush ; it is more loose, more expansive, more wordy. Here necessity does not hold sway as it does there ; the purposeful repetitions are replaced by casual ones ; and finally a rhetorical note is to be heard. The hard rhythm has become a thin absence of rhythm, the firm composition has become negligent ; even the structure of the sentences is careless. The contents do not resemble those of the genuine parts ; questions and answers move at a lower level. In the genuine part every reply gives some essential information as to the will and work of the God ; but here there is, so to speak, a technical atmosphere. The clearest sign of the difference, however, is that the word " sign " is used here in a sense differing entirely from the one in which it is used there. In the genuine parts it is used in accordance with prophetic terminology. (For instance, compare Isaiah, xx, 3, where the Prophet's nakedness appears as a sign, or Ezekiel, iv, 3, where the erection of an iron wall which separates the Prophet from the city of Jerusalem has the same function). It is a symbolization, a sensory presentation of a manifested truth, a perceptible reality which, no matter whether it is more or less "wondrous", always reminds people once again of that truth. In the same sense, after Moses says [a] : "Who am I that I should go to Pharaoh and that I should lead the children of Israel out of Egypt?" YHVH provides the assurance "Indeed I shall be present with you", and He promises Moses a "sign" which at first seems strange to us : that the people would come to this same mountain, where they would engage in the service of their God ; and this is what must serve Moses as a sign that it is this same God who has sent him. We have to understand this as meaning : what is now only existent in words will then take on real existence. Then Moses will experience the mission of this God as an expression of His being ; not as a spiritual mission, as now, but as a reality apparent to the senses. Unlike this, the word "sign" in the supplement [b] appears as a proof of reliability produced by way of supernatural arts, which have no inner relationship with the truth intended ; a meaning which is alien to the prophetic sphere. (The case of Isaiah, viii, 8, 11, for example, is not concerned with a proof ; the "sign" proposed there is not a proof).

If we omit this supplement, however, together with the seven final verses of Chapter III, all written in a later and rhetorical style (reminiscent of the late parts of Deuteronomy), which were also clearly introduced in order to link the passage with the following events, we are left with a narrative religious document of almost incomparable purity ; in which every word is evidence of its derivation from the hands of an early prophet, who worked up elements offered to him by tradition in the light of his own basic experience. The resistance offered to the mission, which was opposed to all the natural tendencies of the one charged, and the breaking down of this resistance by the Divine Power, belong, as shown us by the autobiographical notes of Jeremiah and the paradigmatic little book on Jonah (the nucleus of which may derive from the eighth century B.C.E.) [45] to the most intimate experience of the prophetic man.

[a] Ex. iii, 11.   [b] Ex. iv, 8 f.

The first objection, that of his own smallness compared with the vast task, corresponds precisely, after eliminating the supplements, to the third [a], in which Moses stresses his difficulty of speech. And once again, after YHVH responds that He, the God of Creation,[46] makes the mouth of man to speak or be dumb, and therefore made Moses himself as he is, and sends him just as he is, YHVH continues : " Go, I myself shall be present with your mouth and shall instruct you what you should say ". Here ends the original wording of the narrative. (Verses 13-16, repeating the motif, " I shall be present with you " once again, but without inner necessity, are formed on a variant to Chapter VII, verse 1, and have clearly been inserted in order to introduce Moses' brother Aaron, " the Levite ", the forefather of the Priesthood, at this early point, as fellow-carrier of the Divine Will. This complement actually has a later stamp than the original tale, but an earlier than the supplements. Verse 17 derives from the author of the second supplement.)

It is necessary to bear in mind the two promises of the speaking God which begin with the word *ehyeh*, " I shall be ", I shall be present, assuring that he would remain present amid his chosen, in order properly to understand the central part of the duologue, the central question and the central response, framed by these two pillars.

The point at issue here is not Man but God, the name of God. The words of Moses are generally taken to mean that he wished to learn the answer which he would have to give the people if they asked him to tell them the name of the God whose message he brought. Understood in this sense, the passage becomes one of the chief supports of the Kenite hypothesis, since it is scarcely possible to imagine that any people would not know the name of the God of their fathers. If you wish to ask a person's name in Biblical Hebrew, however, you never say, as is done here, " What (*mah*) is his name ? " or, " What is your name ? ", but " Who (*mi*) are you ? ", " Who is he ? ", " Who (*mi*) is your name ? ", " Tell me your name ". Where the word " what " is associated with the word " name ", the question asked is what finds expression in or lies concealed behind that name.

When the " man " with whom Jacob wrestled at the ford of Jabbok asks him [b] " What is your name ? ", the point at issue is that this name can be given the reproach of an interpretation as " Heel-sneak ".[c] Now, however, the new name Israel is intended

[a] Ex. iv, 10.   [b] Gen. xxxii, 28.   [c] *Cf.* Gen. xxvii, 36 and Hos. xii, 4.

to take away the reproach of the old : " Not Jacob, heel-sneak, should any longer be uttered as your name ". That is the change which is to be introduced through the mention of the old name by the one who bears it. In simpler form, and without dialogue, this takes place again when God fulfils the promise.[a]

The phrase, " What is his name ? " appears once more in a gnomic saying [b] ; but here the question asked is certainly not the name of the one who " has established all the ends of the earth ". The speaker is presumably well aware of that ; the subject of the question is not sound but mystery. Moses expects the people to ask the meaning and character of a name of which they have been aware since the days of their fathers. Which name ? From the answer of the God it can be seen that the question refers to YHVH.

In a later manifestation,[c] YHVH informs Moses that he was seen by the forefathers " in El Shaddai ", that is, in the quality of a Shaddai God ; but " By my name YHVH I did not make myself known to them ". What Shaddai is can only be guessed from the word and the circumstances under which it is used in the stories of the patriarchs ; yet the name clearly means the Divinity as Power ; and, as seems to be indicated by five of the six passages in Genesis where the name is found, as the power making the human clan fruitful. Therefore the term can be taken to imply the power founding the tribe. Here, indeed, the issue is the biological development of Israel, which is understood as a divine work. The name YHVH, it is true, is introduced only once in the Genesis narrative in the form of a direct revelatory speech placed in the mouth of the God,[d] and in the identical form of phrase with which the revelation to the people begins.[e] But Abraham proclaims the name when he comes to Canaan as might a herald, at one spot after another (which should not be understood as a calling in prayer),[47] and his clan knows the Name. Is it likely that the author of Exodus vi, 3, did not know this ? Here, however, what is said is not that the patriarchs made no use of the name of YHVH, but only that they did not know him in the quality characterized by this name ; and that this had now been discovered. What can that mean ?

Of all the various suppositions regarding the prehistoric use of the name YHVH there is only one [48] the development of which makes all this understandable without contradiction. To the best

[a] Gen. xxxv, 10.　[b] Prov. xxx, 4.　[c] Ex. vi, 3.　[d] Gen. xv, 7.　[e] Ex. xx, 2.

of my knowledge it was first expressed nearly half a century ago by Duhm in an (unpublished) lecture at Goettingen : " Possibly the name is in some degree only an extension of the word *hu*, meaning he, as God is also called by other Arab tribes at times of religious revival—the One, the Unnamable ". The Dervish cry Ya-hu is interpreted to mean " O He ! ", and in one of the most important poems of the Persian mystic, Jelaluddin Rumi,[49] the following occurs : " One I seek, one I know, One I see, One I call. He is the first, He is the last, He is the outward, He is the inward. I know no other except Yahu (O He) and Ya-man-hu (O-He-who-is)." The original form of the cry may have been *Ya-huva*, if we regard the Arabic pronoun *huwa*, he, as the original Semitic form of the pronoun " he " which, in Hebrew as well as in another Arabic form, has become *hu*. " The name *Ya-huva* would then mean O-He! with which the manifestations of the god would be greeted in the cult when the god became perceptible in some fashion. Such a *Ya-huva* could afterwards produce both *Yahu* and *Yahveh* (possibly originally *Yahvah*) ".[50] Similar divine names deriving from " primitive sounds " are also known in other religions, but in, say, the Dionysos cult the cries developed into corresponding nouns, whereas the Semites preserved the elemental cry itself as a name. Such a name, which has an entirely oral character and really requires completion by some such gesture as, for example, the throwing out of an arm, is, to be sure (as long, at least, as the undertone of the third person still affects the consciousness of speaker and listener) more suitable for evocation than for invocation. As an invocation it appears in the story of the patriarchs only in a cry [a] which strangely interrupts the continuity of the blessings of Jacob. This may also explain why during the pre-Mosaic period scarcely any personal names are recorded as having been formed with this divine name. The only known exception, as it would appear, is the name of Moses' mother, Yochebed, which apparently means " YHVH is weighty ". If so, it might possibly be regarded as a sign of some specific family tradition, which prepares the way for a new relation to the Divine name.

Certainly it is more typical that in the course of the ages, particularly at an epoch of increasing religious laxity, as the Egyptian period appears to have been for Israel, the element of excitation and discharge connected with the calling of the name did not merely ebb away, but the name itself degenerated into a sound simultaneously

[a] Gen. xlix, 18.

empty and half forgotten. Under such conditions an hour might well come when the people would ask this question of a man bringing them a message from the God of their fathers: " How about his name ? " That means : " What is this God really like ? We cannot find out from his name ! " For as far as primitive human beings are concerned, the name of a person indicates his character.

But there is also something else included in the question, namely the expression of a negative experience which the enslaved people had had with this God of theirs : " After all, he never troubled about us all this while ! When the Egyptians require their gods, they invoke them by uttering their ' true ' names in the correct fashion, and the gods come and do what is necessary. But we have not been able to invoke him, we cannot invoke him. How can we be certain of him, how can we bring him into our power ? How can we make use of his name ? What about his name ? "

The " true " name of a person, like that of any other object, is far more than a mere denotative designation for men who think in categories of magic ; it is the essence of the person, distilled from his real being, so that he is present in it once again. What is more, he is present in it in such a form that anybody who knows the true name and knows how to pronounce it in the correct way can gain control of him. The person himself is unapproachable, he offers resistance ; but through the name he becomes approachable, the speaker has power over him. The true name may be entirely different from the generally familiar one which covers it ; it may also, however, differ from the latter only in the " correct " pronunciation, which would also include the correct rhythm and the correct attitude of the body while engaged in the act of pronouncing it ; all things which can only be taught and transmitted personally. And since the true name phoneticises the character of the object, the essential thing in the last resort is that the speaker shall recognize this essential being in the name, and direct his full attention upon it. Where that happens, where the magical work requires an aiming of the soul at the being meant, that is, when the " person " aimed at is a god or a demon, the fuel is provided into which the lightning of a religious experience can fall. Then the magical compulsion becomes the intimacy of prayer, the bundle of utilisable forces bearing a personal name becomes a Thou, and a demagisation of existence takes place.

As reply to his question about the name Moses is told : *Ehyeh asher ehyeh*. This is usually understood to mean " I am that I am " in the sense that YHVH describes himself as the Being One or even the Everlasting One, the one unalterably persisting in his being. But that would be abstraction of a kind which does not usually come about in periods of increasing religious vitality ; while in addition the verb in the Biblical language does not carry this particular shade of meaning of pure existence. It means : happening, coming into being, being there, being present, being thus and thus ; but not being in an abstract sense. " I am that I am " could only be understood as an avoiding of the question, as a " statement which withholds any information ".[51] Should we, however, really assume that in the view of the narrator the God who came to inform his people of their liberation wishes, at that hour of all hours, merely to secure his distance, and not to grant and warrant proximity as well ? This concept is certainly discouraged by that twofold *ehyeh*, " I shall be present ",[a] which precedes and follows the statement with unmistakable intention, and in which God promises to be present with those chosen by him, to remain present with them, to assist them. This promise is given unconditional validity in the first part of the statement : " I shall be present ", not merely, as previously and subsequently, " with you, with your mouth ", but absolutely, " I shall be present ". Placed as the phrase is between two utterances of so concrete a kind that clearly means : I am and remain present. Behind it stands the implied reply to those influenced by the magical practices of Egypt, those infected by technical magic : it is superfluous for you to wish to invoke me ; in accordance with my character I again and again stand by those whom I befriend ; and I would have you know indeed that I befriend you.

This is followed in the second part by : " That I shall be present ", or " As which I shall be present ". In this way the sentence is reminiscent of the later statement of the God to Moses [b] : " I shall be merciful to him to whom I shall be merciful ". But in it the future character is more strongly stressed. YHVH indeed states that he will always be present, but at any given moment as the one as whom he then, in that given moment, will be present. He who promises his steady presence, his steady assistance, refuses to restrict himself to definite forms of manifestation ; how could the people even venture to conjure and limit him ! If the first part of the statement states : " I do not need to be conjured for I

---

[a] Ex. iii, 12 ; iv, 12.   [b] Ex. xxxiii, 19.

am always with you ", the second adds : " but it is impossible to conjure me ".

It is necessary to remember Egypt as the background of such a revelation : Egypt where the magician went so far as to threaten the gods that if they would not do his will he would not merely betray their names to the demons, but would also tear the hair from their heads as lotus blossoms are pulled out of the pond. Here religion was in practice little more than regulated magic. In the revelation at the Burning Bush religion is demagicized.

At the same time, however, the meaning and character of the Divine Name itself changes ; that is, from the viewpoint of the narrator as well as from that of the tradition given shape by him, it is unfolded in its true sense. By means of the introduction of an inconsiderable change in vocalization, a change to which the consciousness of sound would not be too sensitive, a wildly ecstatic outcry, half interjection half pronoun, is replaced by a grammatically precise verbal form which, in the third person (*hqvah* is the same as *hayah*—to be—but belongs to an older stratum of language) means the same as is communicated by the *ehyeh* : YHVH is " He who will be present " or " He who is here ", he who is present here ; not merely some time and some where but in every now and in every here. Now the name expresses his character and assures the faithful of the richly protective presence of their Lord.

And it is the God Himself who unfolds his name after this fashion. The exclamation was its hidden form ; the verb is its revelation. And in order to make it clear beyond all possibility of misapprehension that the direct word *ehyeh* explains the indirect name, Moses is first instructed, by an exceptionally daring linguistic device, to tell the people " *Ehyeh*, I shall be present, or I am present, sends me to you ", and immediately afterwards : " YHVH the God of your fathers sends me to you ". That *Ehyeh* is not a name ; the God can never be named so ; only on this one occasion, in this sole moment of transmitting his work, is Moses allowed and ordered to take the God's self-comprehension in his mouth as a name. But when, shortly before the destruction of the Northern Kingdom of Israel, the prophet Hosea, in order to give concrete expression to the impending crisis in national history, calls his new-born son *Lo-ammi*, not my people, he justifies this name [a] with the Divine word : " you are not my people and I am not *ehyeh* for you ". One expects to hear : " . . . and I am not your God ",

[a] Hos. i, 9.

but what is said is : " For you I am no longer *ehyeh*, that is, ' I am present ' ". The unfaithful people lose the presence of their God, the name revealed is concealed from them once again. Just as the Lo-ammi refers to the *ammi* of the Burning Bush episode, so does this *ehyeh* refer to that.

Again and again, when God says in the narrative : " Then will the Egyptians recognize that I am YHVH ", or " you will recognize that I am YHVH ", it is clearly not the name as a sound, but the meaning revealed in it, which is meant. The Egyptians shall come to know that I (unlike their gods) am the really present One in the midst of the human world, the standing and acting One ; you will know that I am He who is present with you, going with you and directing your cause. And until the very close of the Babylonian Exile, and later, sayings such as " I am YHVH, that is my name ",[a] or even more clearly, " Therefore let my people know my name, therefore on that day, that I am he who says ' Here I am ' ",[b] cannot be otherwise understood.

However, it appears that the message of the name never became actually popular in Biblical Israel. It seems that the people did not accept the new vocalization. The interpretation, to be sure, hovers around the name in their consciousness ; but it does not penetrate it. In the innermost nucleus it remains the dark, mysterious cry, and there is evidence in all periods until the days of the Talmud that an awareness of the sense of the pronoun " he " hidden in it was always present. The prohibition against pronouncing the name only raised an ancient reluctance, which was rooted in the resistance against rationalization, to the power of a taboo. Nevertheless a tremendous vitalization in the relation of the people to the name clearly took place on Sinai ; the boys are given names containing it, and just as its proclamation combines with the moving and stopping of the crowd, so it also finds place in the life of the tribe and in that of the individual ; the certainty of the presence of the God as a quality of his being began to possess the souls of the generations. It is impossible properly to grasp such a process independently of the actually unaccepted yet so effective message contained in the meaning of the name.

The meaning of the name is usually ascribed to the " Elohist ", to whose source this section of the narrative is attributed. But quite apart from the fact that there was no Elohist in this sense and that, as has been said, if we eliminate complements and supple-

                    [a] Is. xlii, 8.   [b] Is. lii, 6.

ments, we find a uniform and firmly constructed narrative—such discoveries or conversions are not born at the writing desk. A speech like this *ehyeh asher ehyeh* does not belong to literature but to the sphere attained by the founders of religion. If it is theology, it is that archaic theology which, in the form of a historical narrative, stands at the threshold of every genuine historical religion. No matter who related that speech or when, he derived it from a tradition which, in the last resort, cannot go back to anybody other than the founder. What the latter revealed of his religious experience to his disciples we cannot know; that he informed them of what had happened to him we must assume; in any case, the origin of such a tradition cannot be sought anywhere else.

At his relatively late period Moses did not establish the religious relationship between the Bnei Israel and YHVH. He was not the first to utter that " primal sound " in enthusiastic astonishment. That may have been done by somebody long before who, driven by an irresistible force along a new road, now felt himself to be preceded along that road by " him ", the invisible one who permitted himself to be seen. But it was Moses who, on this religious relationship, established a covenant between the God and " his people ". Nothing of such a kind can be imagined except on the assumption that a relation which had come down from ancient times has been melted in the fire of some new personal experience. The foundation takes place before the assembled host; the experience is undergone in solitude.

DIVINE DEMONISM

WHILE Moses makes his way to Egypt with wife and child at the divine behest, something strange, according to the Biblical narrative, happens to him ; something which apparently runs counter to the mission. In the night-lodge YHVH attacks him and wishes to slay him. Thereupon his wife, Zipporah, takes a flint, cuts off the foreskin of her son with it, and then touches [52] his legs and says : " Thou art *a hathan–dammim* unto me ". Thereupon " he ", the assailant, lets " him ", Moses the assailed, be. The story is told with archaic stiffness, but its sense can in some measure be comprehended ; particularly when it is noted that the narrator is interested in the term " *hathan–dammim* ", which is clearly stressed by a gloss at the end ; thereby Zipporah coined the designation which has been customarily applied since then to boys who have just been circumcised. Here a singular and untranslatable play of words can evidently be found ; in Arabic the word *hathana* means to circumcise ; and since among the ancient Arabs as among certain tribes to the present day, the adolescent youngster was circumcised shortly before his wedding, the bridegroom was a *hathan*, a cut one. At the moment of peril Zipporah carries out the bloody ceremony on the child ; that is, she replaces the Midianite custom by that of the Israelites, which, in accordance with the story in Genesis, can be regarded as having been the practice of the latter since the earliest times. We feel entitled to assume that it had already replaced the general Semitic circumcision of the adolescent. Thereafter she touches his legs, an act which apparently has a symbolic meaning resembling the setting of the hands on the head of the animal sacrificed ; an identification of the one performing the action with the creature touched by him.[53] Zipporah's purpose is to have the child represent and personify the entire clan, and she adds the protective words that for her, the clan mother, and hence for the clan, he has already become a *hathan* through the shedding of blood (*dammim*). By this action she places her clan, both the born and the unborn, under the God of Israel and thus conciliates him.

Modern historians and exegetes,[54] basing themselves on the word " unto me ", have converted this remarkable but not inconceivable process into a scene of fantastic " primitiveness ". According to them the incident happened during the bridal night in the original story. The god or demon had disputed the *jus primæ noctis*, the " prerogative of the gods ", with Moses. Zipporah had thereupon cut off the foreskin of her spouse and thrown it at the sexual organs of the " lustful nocturnal monster ", while at the same time repeating a " magic formula " by which she " simulated that he had had access to her ", and " was bloody from it " ; whereupon he turned away satisfied and let Moses be. The following is added by one of the scholars. " A period which invented such stories can be considered to have had the corresponding customs ". This is an almost incomparable example of the devastation which the excessive enticement and allure of ethnology has effected in the history of religion.

But the full implications of this too brief story go far beyond the problem of origin and metamorphosis of rites. It is usually regarded as an " erratic block of the oldest tradition, in which not YHVH but a demon was the actor on the stage ". [55] The view that YHVH had " absorbed everything demonic " very early, and that since then " no demons were required any more in Israel " [56] leads further. But it is of decisive importance to realize that this process had its origin in the message of Moses, and that this in turn had derived from Moses' own experience. We can choose between three alternatives : Either YHVH has been made to replace the original demon in the already-fashioned account of the nocturnal terror ; or this correction had already taken place in the tradition ; or else the tradition had already found YHVH here as the active party, and did not dare to make any change even for the honour of their god. This third assumption is the only one which reveals the whole significance of the tale for the history of faith.

It is part of the basic character of this God that he claims the entirety of the one he has chosen ; he takes complete possession of the one to whom he addresses himself. It is told of him [a] that once in the early days of the human race a human being (Enoch) was allowed to accompany him in his wanderings ; this human being had then suddenly vanished, because the God had taken him away. Such taking away is part of his character in many respects. He promises Abraham a son, gives him and demands him back in order to make a gift of him afresh ; and for this son he remains a sublime " Terror ".[b] His character finds even more direct expression when he first tells the son of that son to return from

[a] Gen. v, 22 ff.   [b] Gen. xxxi, 42.

Aram to Canaan,[a] and thereafter attacks him or causes him to be attacked and dislocates his hip while wrestling. At this point the tradition is not yet fully interested in ascribing everything to YHVH himself, and so the one who performs the action is " a man ", but that the God stands behind cannot be doubted.[b] Unlike the narrative of the attack on Moses, the motif of the " dread night ", which is merely hinted at there, is expanded in repeated keywords. By the nocturnal struggle with the divine being,[c] by holding the " man " fast until a blessing is obtained, Jacob passes his test. His leading God had ordered him to wander, the same God who had once [d] promised him : " See, I am with you, I shall protect you wherever you go, and shall bring you back to this land ". And now that he had returned to this land, the wanderer had to face the perilous encounter before he enjoyed the final grace of God.

The strange episode in the Exodus story is associated and yet different. YHVH attacks the messenger whom he has just sent, clearly because the man's devotion to him after his resistance has been surmounted does not appear full enough. Here it cannot be a question of the person, but of the clan. For this reason it is the woman who plays the leading part. She performs the action by which, from the Israelite point of view, the clan as such makes its covenant in the flesh with the God and renews it again and again. It is because the clan is concerned that the " sign " is made on the organ of generation. In this way the woman obtains the conciliation.

We know from the life of the founders of religions, and also from that of other souls who live in the deeps of faith, that there is such an " event of the night " ; the sudden collapse of the newly-won certainty, the " deadly factual " moment when the demon working with apparently unbounded authority appears in the world where God alone had been in control but a moment before. The early stage of Israelite religion knows no Satan ; if a power attacks a man and threatens him, it is proper to recognize YHVH in it or behind it, no matter how nocturnally dread and cruel it may be ; and it is proper to withstand Him, since after all He does not require anything else of me than myself. The words of the prophet of exile [e] " Who makes peace and creates evil, I YHVH do all this ", have roots that go very deep. In the account of the manner in

---

[a] Gen. xxxi, 13.

[b] In view of the connection between Gen. xxxi, 28 f. and Gen. xxxv, 10.

[c] Gen. xxxii, 29.   [d] Gen. xxviii, 15.   [e] Is. xlv, 7.

which YHVH meets Moses as a demon one of these roots has been uncovered. Here is the unmistakable language of a tradition which also points to the obscure yet perceptible threshold of experience.

It may be that a further step has to be taken, and that something more than a metaphor should be recognized in the figure of speech with which the Bible in the identical words twice repeats [a] Moses' remark as to his heaviness of speech : " For I am uncircumcised of lips ". This is a kind of uncircumcision which cannot be eliminated by any circumcision, an absence of liberation which is clearly not organic but penetrates to the core of the soul, an absence of liberation and an impossibility of liberation ; not a mere defect in the instruments of speech but a fundamental inhibition of expression. Sent as bearer of the word, intermediary between heaven and earth through the word, Moses possesses no mastery over freely coursing speech. He has been created thus and has been chosen thus. By this a barrier is raised between him and the human world. He who has to establish the covenant between the people and YHVH is, so to speak, not accepted fully into the covenant of his tribe. Teacher, prophet, law-giver ; yet in the sphere of the word he remains insurmountably lonely ; alone in the last resort with the word of heaven which forces itself through inflexible soul into inflexible throat.

Yet to me even this does not seem to be the most decisive thing. In a supplement to the story of the Burning Bush,[b] which, however, clearly preserves an early prophetic spirit, Moses is made a " god ", an inspiring power, in regard to Aaron, who is to be his " mouth ". Consequently, when the God who himself speaks his word into him uses him as a " mouth ", it is a stammering mouth. And in this way the tragedy of Moses becomes the tragedy inherent in Revelation. It is laid upon the stammering to bring the voice of Heaven to Earth.

[a] Ex. vi, 12, 30.   [b] Ex. iv, 16.

MOSES AND PHARAOH

FROM the legend of Moses' childhood, to which we owe the item of information that he was closely connected with the inner circles of Egyptian power and culture, we have advanced into an atmosphere of tangible biographical motifs. These are well suited to the actual course of life of the leader and founder, yet in our opinion do not appear to belong to any typological pattern. Instead they seem to be records of concrete events that may be assumed to have happened once.

We found four such motifs. The first is the flight, characteristic of the liberator of a nation who must go to alien lands in order to return full-grown, fully equipped, and capable of doing whatever he has been called to do. Nevertheless the flight is given an individual and unschematic character; first by the slaying of the Egyptian, and even more by the sojourning in the desert which follows.

After this comes Moses' reception by the Midianites, with their manners and customs so resembling those of the " Fathers " of Israel; and his service as a shepherd, which is once again something of a representative character—for Semitic religions at least. (Tradition reports a saying of Mohammed that nobody becomes a prophet who was not first a shepherd.) The association of the above two traits, however, gives the story a unique stamp.

Then follows the Vision and Audition, so familiar throughout the religious sphere, yet elevated above all analogously patterned accounts by the circumstances and manner of manifestation, even more by the vital urge of the duologue, and most of all by the content of the Divine Utterance.

Last of all comes the demonic encounter, without which the path of the religious can scarcely be imagined; and which, though barely indicated here, is nevertheless vivid enough to be unique, by reason of that awesome encompassing of the demonic by the divine, which nips any dualistic tendency in the bud.

Although these four stages of a man's path cannot be reconstructed in their historical dimensions and order of sequence, each of them can be grasped in its own place and according to its own basic character.

The situation is different when we come to the section with which we must now deal ; namely, the measures leading to the fulfilment of the Divine Mission. The main contents of this section, consisting of the negotiations between Moses and Pharaoh and the associated plagues, can scarcely, when assessed in accordance with the historical approach followed, be fitted into place, even under their fundamental aspects, as recording any historical reality. In the Egypt known from history the negotiations between the King and the representative of the slaves cannot possibly have assumed any such forms as those recorded ; not even when the former accounts of the relations between that representative and the Court are given all due consideration. Further, the story of the plagues does actually link with natural phenomena of a kind that is, for the greater part, peculiar to Egypt. Yet how is it possible to enucleate a historical kernel from this breathless accumulation of extraordinary events, magnified immeasurably ?

Yet even here, in this fantastic popular narrative, intended as it is to bring to later generations of the nation a sense of the one-time passage of their history from wonder to wonder, we feel the breath of some distant event of which there is no longer any clearcut recollection. Only the might of a metamorphosing mytho-pœic remembering bears witness identifiable throughout all its fantastic work. There are two recognized approaches in this regard ; that of the person accepting traditions entire, holding that everything written here records something that has happened in fact in some specific place at some specific time ; and that of the self-assured professional scholar who proposes to treat everything recorded here as literature pure and simple, and believes that he can equate it all to, and comprehend it by, literary categories. Between these two there must be a third, which is our own.

We must adopt the critical approach and seek reality, here as well, by asking ourselves what human relation to real events this could have been which led gradually, along many bypaths and by way of many metamorphoses, from mouth to ear, from one memory to another, and from dream to dream, until it grew into the written account we have read. It is certainly not a chronicle which we have to work on, but it is equally not imaginative poesy ; it is a historical saga. But that is a concept the employment of which should not calm the scientific conscience ; it must stir it up. From this starting-point we shall, as used to be said deprecatingly, proceed along " rationalist " lines (we admit our rational search for reality). In the best of cases we shall not attain more than an outline of a *possible* historical process, but this we deem a gain.

A starting-point and a finishing-point are afforded. The starting-point is provided in the story of Moses' life, as we have already indicated along general lines. It is the return of Moses to Egypt, where meanwhile, as the Bible reports [a] in order to join the heavenly by the terrestrial motif, all his adversaries had perished. We find the finishing-point in the historically indisputable fact of the Exodus. What lies between these two? How did the Exodus come about, and what was Moses' share in it? Naturally we cannot seek more than the kernel of tradition round which the growing material of legend developed. How can we penetrate it? How can we separate kernel from husk?

The starting-point provided informs us what it is we have to ask in order to find the answer to this question. What we first need to know is : As what was Moses summoned in the original account of the Revelation at the Burning Bush? If we wish, in other words, to adumbrate a historical Moses who, feeling himself summoned and given a mission, returns to Egypt, what can his purpose be and how can he set about its execution?

Our question is not identical with the current one of the " type " to which Moses belonged. All we are concerned with here is the hour and its purpose. If our distinction between original tale and supplements is correct, it is plain that Moses was summoned as a *nabi*, a " prophet ". This, of course, does not mean that Moses was simply a *nabi*, but only that the service on which he returned to Egypt was in essence analogous with that reported by those prophets of Israel whose existence is historically incontestable. Hosea, one of the earliest prophets whose writings have come down in the Bible, declares,[b] " By a *nabi* did the Lord lead Israel out of Egypt ". He certainly did not wish to imply that Moses was nothing more than one of the *nebiim*, but that he had done what he had done as a *nabi*. It was a historical action ; Hosea, a man filled with a passionate zeal for history, was thinking of the historical function of Israel's prophets ; and we think of it with him. The issue here is not that of the ecstatic experiences which characterize the *nebiim* from early times until late. That would mean a diversion of the centre of gravity from the events that happened to the nation into the personal religious life. It can just as little be

[a] Ex. iv, 19.　　　　　　　[b] Hos. xii, 14.

a question of miracles, such as are related of Elijah and to an even greater degree of Elisha ; for that would mean exchanging history for legend, and of necessity not finding the historically possible kernel which we seek. (I suppose that the expansion of tradition into the legendary cycle of the Egyptian Ten Plagues took place among the disciples of Elisha, who sang the legends of the Father of the *nebiim* together with those of their own master.) What is essential here, however, can only be that historical situation which recurs again and again from Samuel to Jeremiah, a situation in which the *nabi* penetrates into history again and again and operates therein. It is the great refrain in Israel's history : prophet versus king. What appears in this picture is not myth-making or stylization, but the flesh and blood of history.

For the rest, we are not concerned here with the origin of the *nebiuth* (I personally am of the opinion that it evolved in Israel's prehistoric days from primitive Semitic sources) ; and we are certainly not concerned with the origin of nomenclature and concept, but only with that of the historic function of the *nabi*. What one prophet after another did on the stage of history at his-torically determinable times was to stand forth against the ruler with words and signs of rebuke. The word was a demand in the name of God and His " Justice ", a warning of the penalties and an indication of the disastrous events which must sooner or later follow in case of refusal. The sign was an incarnation of the word ; the process must indeed be extraordinary, though not necessarily in any way supernatural, in order to have an effect as sign. Wonders as such, purely as a production of credentials, are not performed by the prophet in front of the king ; nor does the former soothsay. He announces the fateful development proceeding or impending at that hour, and proclaims it to be bound up with the given or prospective decision of the king ; and he points to the impending disaster as being a consequence of the false decision or absence of decision. If we may permit ourselves (as I think we may) to seek commencement of this historical phenomenon with Moses, and if his appearance before Pharaoh is regarded as the first in this series of prophetic incursions, there must remain a firm kernel of fact, after the dispersion of all the wonder-working which the Biblical account ascribes to Moses and his God. Disaster cannot indeed be directly induced, but it can be threatened, even though in general terms only, and such disasters as befall can be accounted for as an outcome of " stiff-neckedness ". What is remarkable, yet still

worthy of credence, is the fact that this process which mostly failed
in later ages in the case of the kings of Israel, caused Pharaoh to
fulfil the demand made of him.

The historical Moses who returned to Egypt is neither a magician
nor a visionary. He knows precisely who Pharaoh is ; he knows
precisely what it means to talk to Pharaoh in the way that he,
Moses, will have to talk to him ; and he has resolved to do so.
As far as concerns the historical situation he is no " national
liberator " ; he has nothing more to offer than the Word ; yet
since the Word came to him on the mountain he is certain that it
will suffice, for when he utters it, the " Present One " will be with
him. Apparently the Word does not prove effective, for the king
responds with contemptuous condescension to this alien godling
which imagines that he will be able to intervene in the affairs of
Egypt. Nevertheless it does prove effective, for some (no matter
how long) time afterwards Pharaoh releases the hordes of slaves. In
between lie events which Moses regards as a fulfilment of his
(conditional) warning of calamity ; events which, however,
extraordinary if by no means supernatural admit of such an interpretation according to their time and sequence. Each of these
events occurs between one prophetic utterance and the next,
words of warning and words of interpretation, although each is
separated from both warning and interpretation by longer and
shorter periods of time. The important thing is that each of the
events admit of easy inclusion within the causal nexus announced
by the word of the prophet.

Why does Pharaoh permit himself to be convinced ? We
find ourselves face to face with a historical mystery ; one, however,
which is historical and not literary in character. A historical
mystery always means a relation between a super-personal fate
and a person, and particularly that which is atypical in a person ;
that by which the person does not belong to his type. The task
given to Moses is prophetic in character. But the fact that Moses
fulfils it, tremendous as it is ; that what has to be achieved is
achieved ; that unlike the later prophets of Israel he proves victorious in wrestling with the king ; all this is clearly due to a
large degree to the fact that he is something more than a prophet.

Though it may not be possible to determine with any measure
of certainty what part of the " Plagues " belong to the kernel of
truth and what is later crystallization of legend, it nevertheless
seems to me that the four final plagues, as well as the second,

retain a trace not only of actual events, but also of events that belong to this period. The seventh and eighth plagues bear the clearest signs of literary treatment, yet both contain parallel verses which, as it seems to me, constitute an early tradition. One of them [a] (following an account of Moses raising his staff, which is not an integral portion) reads as follows : " YHVH gave thunderbolts and hail ; fire fell to the earth ; YHVH rained down hail upon the land of Egypt. There was hail and within the hail a fire taking hold of itself, exceedingly grievous ; the like had not been in the land of Egypt since it was held by a nation." Behind this passage stand both direct observation and an intention to describe the event as natural, and only its force as something unheard-of. Corresponding to this, but transferred from the description to the warning, the narration [b] gives the following account of the locusts, ." They cover the surface of the earth ; the earth cannot be seen ; and they eat the residue of that which is escaped, which remaineth unto you from the hail, and eat every tree which groweth for you out of the field . . . which neither thy fathers nor thy fathers' fathers have seen since the day that they were upon the earth unto this day." Here, too, is the same direct observation and the identical purpose ; and in addition comes the express linkage with the previous plague. Hereupon follows [c] the sign of darkness, remarkable once again for words which show direct observation, " Then there will be darkness over the land of Egypt, one will feel darkness ". That is no actual plague but apparently either a transition to or, more correctly, the background of the final one, the factual kernel of which we may assume to have been a plague which slew even the first-born son of Pharaoh.

This is indicated by an assuredly early fragment, which now stands shortly before the account of the Divine Attack [d] ; " Thus said YHVH, my first-born son is Israel. I said to thee, ' let my son go that he may serve me ' ; but thou has refused to let him go, so behold I slay thy first-born son." That is not a forecast of things to come, no demand or threat, but the words of the hour of destiny itself, suited precisely to the immediate moment breathing of inevitability. And the matter under consideration here lies not between YHVH and Egypt, but between YHVH and Pharaoh alone. Although the sonship of Israel implies not a mythical procreation but a historical act of adoption, it must be understood as a true

---

[a] Ex. ix, 23 f.   [b] Ex. x, 5 ff.   [c] Ibid., 21.   [d] Ex. iv, 22 f.

state of sonship in order wholly to grasp the meaning of the words. It is one father speaking awesomely to another father.

The kernel of the story of the deeds of Moses in Egypt seems to me to be somewhat as follows :

Moses, accompanied by his brother and helper Aaron,[57] comes to the slave people, informs them of his mission, and wins their belief. The deliberations, however, soon arouse the suspicions of the authorities, and in order to restrict the " freedom of assembly " of the aliens, they subject the latter to more stringent working conditions. Thereupon the people turn away from Moses and refuse to hearken unto him any more. Flung back to the feet of the God who had spoken to him from the flame, Moses tells of his woe and accuses Him. What the narrator places in his mouth here,[a] namely the question, " Why indeed hast thou sent me ? ", and the repetition in critical fashion of the motif of *ammi* (my people), " While as for delivering, thou hast not delivered thy people at all ! ", echoes the language of the earlier part of the Revelation at the Burning Bush. These too are words of a kind which are not born of literary devices. Words of the identical genuineness are found in the response which is made to the violent suppliant [b] : " I am YHVH (He-Who-Is-Here, the Present One) and I lead you out from the burdens of the Egyptians. . . . I take you to me for a people, and I will be to you a God ; and ye shall know that I, YHVH, am your God."

He who has hitherto been only the " God of the Fathers " and whom the tribes, " the Children of Israel ", have regarded only as such, wishes to become the God of them as a people, as His people ; and thereby to make them genuinely a people. Only now, in the hour of disillusion at finding the people not yet truly a people, and most certainly not a people of YHVH, only now does the thought come to Moses of the Covenant ; which shall simultaneously unite the tribes into a people and bind the people to their God ; not merely religiously but in their living substance. Now they do not listen to him by reason of " impatience of spirit and hard work ". Then when they will be free yonder on the mountain, in the free air of God, they will hearken unto that to which they have to hearken.

This thought of the Covenant makes Moses—who has meanwhile become an old man according to our ideas if the Biblical data [c] are correct, but we are reluctant to follow them—feel himself

---

[a] Ex. v, 22 f   [b] Ex. vi, 6 f.   [c] Ex. vii, 7.

strong enough to go forth and meet Pharaoh ; and as it appears, he seeks him " on the banks of the Nile " [a].   In the name of " the God of the Hebrews " he demands of Pharaoh to let God's people go in order that they " may serve Him in the wilderness " ; in accordance with that " sign " which YHVH had given Moses at the Burning Bush.   Moses proclaims the catastrophe which will occur in case of refusal, possibly pointing in sign as he does so to the river ;   which was red, as was frequently the case, particularly before the Nile begins to rise.

And the catastrophe does not fail to come.   Some time later it begins to announce its arrival, seemingly through abnormal phenomena originating in the same Nile.   This is presumably the place for the story of the masses of small frogs which come out of the river (it is summer and the season for the flood) ; and which, impudent as never before, penetrate everywhere.   It is here that we find, in the account of the Plagues, a passage showing the same youthfully intensive power of vision as those already quoted [b] : " Frogs shall swarm from the river ; and they shall go up and come into thy house, into thy bedchamber, upon thy bed . . . into thy ovens, into thy kneading-troughs ; upon thee, upon thy people, upon all thy servants shall the frogs go up." This, however, is no more than a grotesque prologue.   At Court it is reported that those disgusting Asiatics are standing around again and fitting interpretations of their own to the incident.   That the Levites, who promote the state of unrest, are not interfered with is apparently due to the uncanny air of power which the Egyptians scent as emanating from Moses.

Many doubtless still have tales to tell of his singularities at the time he was associated with the Court : he had indeed absorbed all the " wisdom of the Egyptians ".[c]   But that he has, apart from this, foretold the incident and, unlike the usual magician, has done so without any magical conjurations (which I assume to be the historical truth) ;   and that he further knows how to interpret the signs of the incident ;   these facts have a somewhat weird atmosphere not inviting any too close contact.   The unwieldy words, with which a strange God jerkily moves his throat, only serve to enhance the weirdness.

And now things move further.   In one winter there comes the hailstorm ;   in the same one (or the next) comes a swarm of locusts ;   between them they devastate the agriculture and thereby

[a] Ex. vii, 15.   [b] Ibid., 28 f., found in Authorized Version as Ex. viii, 3 f.
[c] Ex. vii, 22.

the life of Egypt. While ever and again the uncanny man appears and speaks his words, occasionally standing in the way of Pharaoh himself. He is mocked at more and more ; and he is feared more and more.

And then, one spring, a sandstorm of hitherto unknown fury bursts out. The air is black for days on end. The sun becomes invisible. The darkness can be felt. All and sundry are paralysed and lose their senses. In the middle of all this, however, while a pestilence, a children's epidemic, begins to rage and do its work, the voice of the mighty man sounds through the streets of the Royal City ; unaffected by the driving masses of sand. The signs have persuaded his people. Massed around him, their hope is stronger than the darkness ; they see light.[a]

And then, after three days of the furious storm, the first-born son of the young king perishes in the night. Disconsolate in his innermost chamber, bowed over the little corpse, no longer a god but the very man that he is, he suddenly sees the hated one standing before him ; and, " Go forth " ! he cries.

[a] Ex. x, 23.

THE PASSOVER

ACCORDING to the Biblical narrative,[a] Moses spent the interval between the announcement of the death of the first-born and its fulfilment in ordering the preparations for the Passover meal. A widely-spread view denies this text, even in its older part,[b] any importance in elucidating the period of the Exodus, and regards it as nothing more than an " ætiological legend ", the intention of which was to explain the festival rites as having been ordained by Moses. It is true that the linking of the ordinances with the legend of the death of the first-born, in which YHVH " leapt over " the houses of the Israelites, which were smeared with blood,[c] interferes with attempts at understanding what happened from the historical viewpoint. Nevertheless it appears to me that the historical approach, which endeavours, despite all obscuration of the original content, to penetrate to the men acting in a given situation, should not be renounced here either. We must maintain the conclusion that, for times about which we have nothing more than reports impregnated with material of an obviously legendary character, it is necessary to assume the same fundamental forms of historical behaviour as we know in periods which have found more sober chroniclers.

Favourable circumstances have, within a relatively brief period, provided a man possessing the character and destiny of a leader with the external prerequisites for the fulfilment of his immediate task, the leading of a group of semi-nomadic tribes out of a land of " bondage ". The geographical and political conditions under which the impending wandering has to take place are tremendously difficult, no matter whether that wandering already aims at landed possession and settlement or, for the time being, at the resumption of a nomadic life. The human groups whom he proposes to lead out are only loosely associated with one another ; their traditions have grown faint, their customs degenerate, their religious association insecure.[d] The great thought of the man, his great impulse, is to establish a covenant of the tribes in the purer and freer atmosphere of the desert, which had once purified and

[a] Ex. xii, 1-14, 21-27.   [b] Ibid., 21 ff.   [c] Ibid., 12-13, 23, 27.
[d] Cf. Ezek. xx, 7, and xxiii, 8.

freed him himself, and to establish that covenant on the basis of
their common covenant with a common divinity who had been
neglected for generations. However, the degree of inner unity is in-
sufficient even for the way to this initial goal. The extraordinary
events, to be sure, had their effect ; but the sense of unity, unity
of destiny and of road to be taken, was not yet ripe enough. At
such times, as we find at all historical periods, what is required is a
common symbolic act in which the joint existence is converted
into a sensory experience. But this cannot be brought about of
set purpose ; any astutely calculated steps injure the basic root of
eventuation. Even though promoted by the words and deeds of
a man, it must evolve out of whatever has existed from times immemorial. And so Moses reintroduces the holy and ancient
shepherds' meal, renewed in meaning and form.

It may be supposed on the basis of the known customs of Arabs
in Moab [58] and other lands, that the early Semites annually dedicated the first-born of their flock of sheep and goats (which was
regarded as a unity), and that they marked those first-born as
being dedicate. When it reached the age of about a year, at the
time of the full moon, a meal was prepared of it which served
as a festival of peace and common joy to the tribe and united
it with its blood-brothers and outliers, who came from other
places to be present. The blood of the animal was smeared on
the tent supports in order to keep the demonic element, apparently
consisting originally of the revengeful forefather of the species
of animal, at a distance ; particularly from the human first-born
whom he menaced.

A short while before the Exodus, when Moses is quite certain of
its impending fulfilment without knowing the exact hour, he
orders that the holy meal should be eaten on the evening prior to
the Departure ; when he recognizes that what he is awaiting is
immediately due, he gives the signals. He takes over the old
customs, but what had been distributed over a number of days by
the various clans is now concentrated into a single evening. The
clans slaughter the preordained animals at the same time. Each
family eats of its own, each in its own house, which nobody may
leave [a] ; but they all eat at the same time, a single meal unites
them into a community. Blood is smeared on the portals and
lintels of the houses ; but the demons are now replaced by Yhvh,
to whom all the tribes jointly devote themselves in blood, and

[a] Ex. xii, 22.

thereby simultaneously redeem the debt of the human first-born, which they owe him.

The process is a preliminary form of the blood covenant which the people as such was to conclude with YHVH on Sinai.[a] What is now being prepared in the form of diversity will be completed there in that of unity. "It is a passover for YHVH" which, though called an " offering ", does not resemble anything referred to in the Bible as sacrifice ; it is a sacramental meal. This should not be understood as meaning that the God partakes of it (none of the rites indicate this) nor that divine substance dwells in the animal or is consumed with it. The essential thing to realize is that here a natural and customary human activity, that of eating, is elevated by the participation of the whole community to the level of an act of communion ; and as such is consecrated to the God. It is eaten " for him ". We do not know what the original meaning of the term pessah, translated Passover, may have been. The interpretation of the " leaping over " the houses of Israel by YHVH or the " destroyer " during the night of the death of the first-born [b] is, in any case, secondary ; even though at the time of Isaiah this supplementary meaning of the verb, to pass over and spare, had already become established.[c] The verb originally meant to move on one foot, and thereafter to hop. It may be assumed that at the old nomad feast a hopping dance had been presented, possibly by boys masked as he-goats. It should also be added that the word hag, festival, originally meant to dance in a ring. " It will be a song for you ", says Isaiah [d] of YHVH's coming judgment on Assyria, in the likeness of the Passover judgment on Egypt, " as in the night when the ring dance is hallowed ", that is, when the holy ring dance is danced. It is obviously a mimetic game which is meant, a later transformation of the old shepherd round-dance. " And so you shall eat it ", are the instructions : " your loins girded, your shoes on your feet, your sticks in your hands ; and you shall eat it in haste, it is pessah for YHVH ". " The Exodus was, so to say, performed ", it has been correctly said of the Passover feast,[59] and possibly a hopping beating of time by those standing round the table was part of the performance. But this fresh mimetic character may have been given to the feast at the historical moment itself. Just as there are war dances in which the desired event is portrayed and simultaneously trained for until the mime suddenly becomes a reality, so, it may well be imagined, a symbolic

[a] Ex. xxiv, 6-8.   [b] Ex. xii, 23, 27.   [c] Is. xxxi, 5.   [d] Is. xxx, 29.

representation of the Exodus may have passed into the Exodus itself.

If our assumption is correct, Moses transformed the clan feast of the shepherds (the *matzoth* too, the unleavened flat cakes, are the bread of the nomads) into the feast of a nation, without its losing its character of a family feast. And now the families as such are the bearers of the sacramental celebration ; which, however, unites them into a national community. Moses did not change the custom of the ages into a cult ; he did not add any specific sacrificial rite to it, and did not make it dependent on any sanctuary ; but he consecrated it to YHVH. He transformed the already-existent Passover by introducing a new sense and symbol, as Jesus did later by the introduction of a new sense and symbol. The question as to whether his instructions already applied to the annual ceremony, or were only subsequently extended to it,[a] must be left open. The new character of the feast is explained by a phrase of early coinage [b] ; " A night of watching was it for YHVH, to lead them out of the land of Egypt ; and that is this night unto YHVH, a watching of all the children of Israel throughout their generations ". The words may very well derive from a period before the legend of the death of the first-born children had developed : YHVH watched over his people, who are preparing and executing their flight out of the " house of bondage ".

The *pessaḥ* underwent a vast transformation in Israel. The domestic blood rite was apparently less and less observed ; despite the fact that it is, strikingly enough, still the practice of the Samaritans to-day, though in attenuated form. The domestic meal became a great sacrificial feast, a general tribal pilgrimage to the Jerusalem Temple ; where the clans jointly, as once in Egypt, experienced the living reality of their communion. After the destruction of the Second Temple the Passover naturally became a domestic family feast again ; and this it has remained until the present day. It may be said that the Jewish people who celebrate the Passover have again drawn close to the meal of the Egyptian Exodus, despite their dispersion. The Passover was and has remained a spring festival, first of the shepherds and then of the peasants ; and it is still celebrated by those who have become entirely landless, who no longer have even a common wilderness to wander in. By celebrating the memory of their liberation they glorify the unfettering power whose activity in Nature

[a] *Cf.* Num. ix.   [b] Ex. xii, 42.

manifests itself every year in the likeness of the spring. Yet since the night of the Exodus it has become a history feast, and indeed *the* history feast par excellence of the world ; not a feast of pious remembrance, but of the ever-recurrent contemporaneousness of that which once befell. Every celebrating generation becomes united with the first generation and with all those that have followed. As in that night the families united into the living people, so in the Passover night the generations of the people unite together, year after year.

What was established then, found expression in the introductory sentence " Let this month be the head of the months for you ", which does not appertain to the message to the people, and which therefore seems to be of an esoteric character. The sentence may be belated ; a reform of the calendar which made the year begin with the spring, a reform of the kind which in one or another fashion seems to be associated with the foundation of religions, may not have taken place then. But the establishment of the Passover in any case means a regulating of the time of Nature by means of the time of history ; the foundation of a new beginning.

THE WONDER ON THE SEA

A SONG dating back to the time of Moses is preserved in Exodus xv, 21. Hymn-like in tone, in the Hebrew text it contains no more than nine words : " Sing to YHVH for He has raised Himself high, horse and charioteer He flung into the sea ". Even radical critics recognize that this " can have been born only of the situation itself ".[60] The sensuous power of an event has streamed into it and lives on. In the history of Israel no other event can be identified whose hymnic expression it might be, save that central incident of the Exodus, the great miracle of delivery on the sea. The song does not give any ample picture of a historical reality, but it gives enough ; a sea, on its shore a mounted force inimical to Israel—cavalry or chariots—and their downfall in the waters for some reason which could not be ascribed to human power. For this stage of the Exodus the passage affords us what was not available as regards the earlier stages : a document recording the definite fact to which the crystallizing, shaping memory of the people has attached itself, a memory both true and transforming.

The song is placed in the mouth of Miriam, the sister of Moses,[61] who is described as a *nebia* (a " prophetess "), a woman proclaimer or spokeswoman, probably on account of this very poem ; for by it she fulfilled the second of the two basic prophetic functions, of bearing God's words to the community and bearing the words of the community to God. She chants this song to the women of the community, plays it and dances it to them. The chorus of the women respond with song, drum play and round dance ; and all this is directed towards YHVH and devoted to Him. This is a process which we can well imagine as deriving directly from the situation ; if not in all its details, at least in essential elements.

The situation itself cannot be reconstructed from the narrative. In order to gain a historically possible picture for all that, we must very much reduce the figures given about the departing of the tribes [a] ; which naturally does not affect the actual importance of the event ; for the inner history of Mankind can be grasped most easily in the actions and experiences of small groups. Further, it may be assumed that the frontier guards set out in pursuit of the fugitives, or those regarded as such, whether they had received

[a] Ex. xii, 37.

no special instructions from the capital, and hence acted in accordance with standing orders, or whether [a] the government did not propose to interpret a cry of the stricken Pharaoh as a binding order, and in the morning sent out the necessary orders by special couriers. We do not know where the pursuers caught up with the fugitives ; whether in the neighbourhood of the present Suez or, if the Gulf of Suez was then differently shaped from its contemporary form, further north at one of the bitter lakes or the other inner lakes, most probably at the Sirbonian Lake—or even, as some suppose, only at the Gulf of Akaba (though in that case it is hard to understand why the pursuing chariots should not have caught up with them sooner). Wherever it may have happened, however, there begins a natural process, or a series of natural processes (whether a combination of tides with unusual winds which raised them tremendously, or the effect of distant volcanic phenomena on the movements of the sea [62]) which, together with a daring advance on the part of the Israelites and a destruction of the Egyptians, whose heavy war chariots are caught in the sand or the swamp, leads to the saving of the one and the downfall of the other.

What is decisive with respect to the inner history of Mankind, however, is that the children of Israel understood this as an act of their God, as a " miracle " ; which does not mean that they interpreted it as a miracle, but that they experienced it as such, that as such they perceived it. This perception at the fateful hour, which is assuredly to be attributed largely to the personal influence of Moses, had a decisive influence on the coming into being of what is called " Israel " in the history of the spirit ; on the development of the element " Israel " in the religious history of humanity.

The concept of miracle which is permissible from the historical approach can be defined at its starting point as an abiding astonishment. The philosophizing and the religious person both wonder at the phenomenon, but the one neutralizes his wonder in ideal knowledge, while the other abides in that wonder ; no knowledge, no cognition, can weaken his astonishment. Any causal explanation only deepens the wonder for him. The great turning-points in religious history are based on the fact that again and ever again an individual and a group attached to him wonder and keep on wondering ; at a natural phenomenon, at a historical event, or at both together ; always at something which intervenes fatefully in

[a] Cf. Ex. xiv, 5.

the life of this individual and this group. They sense and experience it as a wonder. This, to be sure, is only the starting-point of the historical concept of wonder, but it cannot be explained away. Miracle is not something " supernatural " or " superhistorical ", but an incident, an event which can be fully included in the objective, scientific nexus of nature and history ; the vital meaning of which, however, for the person to whom it occurs, destroys the security of the whole nexus of knowledge for him, and explodes the fixity of the fields of experience named " Nature " and " History ". Miracle is simply what happens ; in so far as it meets people who are capable of receiving it, or prepared to receive it, as miracle. The extraordinary element favours this coming together, but it is not characteristic of it ; the normal and ordinary can also undergo a transfiguration into miracle in the light of the suitable hour.

The historical reality of Israel leaving Egypt cannot be grasped if the conception of the accompanying, preceding, guiding God is left out. This is the " God of the Fathers ", with whom the tribes have now established contact. He has always been a God who wandered with his own and showed them the way. But now he has been revealed to them afresh through the secret of his name, as the one who remains present with his own. He leads them by a way differing from the customary one of the caravans and armies.[a] He has his own ideas of guidance, and those who follow him find welfare. Carrying with them, as a symbol of the rescue of the whole of Egyptized Israel, the mummy of Joseph, which has not to be left in Egypt, they go along the road where YHVH precedes them. A passage in poetic rhythm and style [b], either a fragment of a poem or a lyrical rise in the narrative, relates : " And YHVH went before them/ by day in a pillar of cloud/ to lead them the way/ and by night in a pillar of fire/ to give them the light/ to go by day and night. /Aside turns not/ the pillar of cloud by day/ nor the pillar of fire by night/ before the people." Quite irrespective of whether volcanic phenomena have or have not exerted any influence here on either the nucleus or the development of the tradition, it is to be felt that the primæval phenomenon which has found optical expression in the clearly native, unique picture is the belief of the man Moses in the leadership of the God whose voice he heard from the fire ; and that this belief, though in a far slighter measure and in varying degrees, is also transferred to the people. Moses himself, at least, follows when he leads a leader ingenuously and

[a] Ex. xiii, 17 f.   [b] Ibid., 21 f.

undauntedly. We may call it intuition or whatever we like. He
calls it obedience, and if we wish to understand him we must take
cognizance of his view and build upon it. Following his leader,
Moses comes to the shore, he steps on sands that are barely covered
by shallow water ; and the hosts follow him as he follows the God.
At this point occurs whatever occurs, and it is apprehended as a
miracle.

It is irrevelant whether ‧" much " or " little ", unusual things
or usual, tremendous or trifling events happened ; what is vital is
only that what happened was experienced, while it happened, as
the act of God. The people saw in whatever it was they saw " the
great hand ",ᵃ and they " believed in YHVH ", or, more correctly
translated, they gave their trust to YHVH.

We have found that the permissible concept of miracle from
the historical approach means, to begin with, nothing but an
abiding astonishment. In order to arrive at the completeness of
the miracle from this concept we must add something which
proves to be essential. We may ascribe what gives rise to our
astonishment to a specific power, which therefore requires no other
content than that of being the doer of this miracle or this kind of
miracle, than to be, so to say, the subject of a miracle. That does
not do away with the astonishment, the event is not included in a
general chain of cause and effect apt to explain it adequately ;
but for the performance of the miracle a particular magical spirit,
a special demon, a special idol is called into being. It is an idol
just because it is special. But that is not what historical consideration means by miracle. For where a doer is restricted by
other doers, the current system of cause and effect is replaced by
another, less adequate, lacking sequence and connection. The real
miracle means that in the astonishing experience of the event the
current system of cause and effect becomes, as it were, transparent
and permits a glimpse of the sphere in which a sole power, not
restricted by any other, is at work. To live with the miracle
means to recognize this power on every given occasion as the
effecting one. That is the religion of Moses, the man who
experienced the futility of magic, who learned to recognize the
demonic as one of the forms by which the divine functions, and
who saw how all the gods of Egypt vanished at the blows of
the One ; and that is religion generally, as far as it is
reality.

ᵃ Ex. xiv, 31.

At a later time the song of Miriam gradually, presumably first in the days of Samuel, and afterwards in the days of Solomon,[63] was expanded into a long hymn.[a] In the proclamation with which it closes, " Yhvh will reign in time and eternity ", can be heard a feeling which had its origin in Moses himself. Whoever recognizes the one effective power on every given occasion must desire that the whole life of the community should be made subject to that power. The verb which we translate with " will reign ", or " be king ", *malak*, is to be understood from the Assyrian *malaku*, to counsel, to resolve, to decide ; and *melek* originally meant the one whose opinion is decisive. For that reason we find that certain West Semites, clearly of the pre-state period, use the substantive *malk*-*melek* as a designation of the tribal god,[64] which characterizes him as the actual and supreme head of the tribe. There are weighty reasons for assuming that this also applied to Israel.[65] As a result, however, of the intensity of religious experience which flowered in this way only here, and particularly as a result of the singular development of the prophetic spirit, but most of all thanks to the personal influence of Moses, the basic view assumed a seriousness and concreteness not to be found anywhere else. Yhvh has led Israel from Egypt with miraculous power, with miraculous power He leads them on their way to their goal, miraculously He precedes them ; where uncertainty and anxious questionings arise at one of the stations of the road, His is the miraculous wisdom by which the *nabi* gives his counsel. In this way He is the heavenly and yet present leader and decider, the only effecting power restricted by no other, to whose leadership and decision must be subjected all fields of common life ; the lord of wonder, the everlasting *melek*.

The *melek* proclamation stands with full meaning at the close of the hymn which deals with the miracle on the sea. Under the echo of this miracle the children of Israel learned to understand that they had a God who, and who alone among all the protective gods of the peoples, could really perform miracles,[b] [66] whereas all the neighbours who had no such lords and leaders are gripped with fear when He acts.[c] So Israel renders homage to Him as being the One to whom alone kingship is due.

I have apparently just treated Nature and History as being equal in relation to the miracle ; but they are not really so ; not, at least, in the Biblical, which is a history religion. Here there is no Nature in the Greek, the Chinese or the modern Occidental sense.

[a] Ex. xv, 1-19.   [b] *Ibid.*, 11.   [c] *Ibid.*, 14 ff.

What is shown us of Nature is stamped by History. Even the work of creation has a historical tone. Certainly during the historical period Nature always points to History, and from the Biblical viewpoint History always contains the element of wonder. Prophets and psalmists praise the deeds of Yhvh at the Red Sea with the same images of cosmic battles and victories in which the divine works of Creation are extolled and glorified. The defeated Egyptian " dragon " grows into a symbol as vast as the world in the drama of rescue which serves as prelude to the revelation, but which in itself is also already revelation. For here the miracle is revelation through the deed, which precedes revelation through the word.

THE SABBATH

IN a section [a] which is apparently independent, and is composed of various traditions which have converged and been repeatedly reworked, the tale is told of the manna (a secretion of a cochineal insect, tasting like crystallized honey, which covers the tamarisk bushes at the time of the apricot harvest, drips to earth by day and becomes hard at night [67]). "Something fine, scaly, fine as the hoar-frost on the earth", it was greeted as a heavenly gift by the hungry desert wanderers who yearned to return to the fleshpots of Egypt. Woven into this is an order of Moses not to pick it up on the Sabbath, as that day is "a time of rest" (shabbaton), a resting (shabbat) consecrated to YHVH. In this order Moses refers to a word uttered by YHVH which is not, however, to be found in the preceding narrative. Thereafter, YHVH himself speaks: "See that YHVH has given you the Sabbath". The gift of the manna is the occasion for remembering the greater gift; the latter, however, was given not now but earlier. In this way the actual Sabbath command is anticipated with unmistakable intention. It is first found recorded in the Decalogue, then in various forms, and with various reasons given for it on each occasion. (Together with the passage on the manna in this section there are ten express commandments.) The Sabbath is not introduced for the first time on Sinai, it is there already; the believers are only ordered to "remember". However, it is not introduced for the first time even in the wilderness of Sin, where the manna is found. Here, too, it is proclaimed as something which is already in existence. And the strange narrative motif which leads to this announcement, namely, that there was a double portion on the sixth day but none on the seventh, indicates something connected with it. Sabbath does not exist exclusively in the world of human beings; it also functions outside their world.

Here traces of a definite fact seem to me to have been preserved in a singular fashion and in a singular connection. Moses does not introduce the Sabbath as something new, but renews something old, probably very old indeed; he simultaneously extends and condenses it, he endows it with a new and vast meaning; the renewal of the name of God and of the Passover has a third chord,

[a] Ex. xvi, 2-36.

the renewal of the Sabbath. And here as well the renewal ensues as an unravelling of something pre-existent. In the Sabbath Moses recognizes not merely a human law but a universal law, which has only to be discovered and separated out. That is how it always was with the founders. They desire not the new but the time old and eternal, that which has always and everlastingly been there, part and parcel of the inner essence of the world ; where they beheld it and from which they have revealed it. They do not regard themselves as the inventors of the order of life which they bring, but as those who find it. Moses should not be regarded as more primitive than this, despite his early period. The now wide-spread shifting into the primitive is no less capable of blurring the historical figure than did the once popular shifting into the mystagogical.

From Babylon we are familiar with the term *shabattu*, as applied to specific days in the year, which are likewise designated as " calming of the heart ", that is as days of penitence and thus of the mollification of the anger of the gods. A similar name is applied to the mid-month day, which would be identical with that of the full moon. In addition four of the " evil days ", or " days of wrath " of the month, fall on the seventh, fourteenth, etc. Among the Babylonians, it should be remembered, the seven was not merely a holy number, which it was among the Semites in general as well as other peoples, but it also included the concept of the comprehensive whole in space and time. Hence underlying those critical days may have been the idea of the restoration of a violated integrity, the idea of rectification.[68] The Israelite Sabbath cannot be derived from the whole of this approach. It has not been possible to prove that it was originally the feast of the full moon.[69] (Similarly the existence of an early Israelite moon cult has not left the stage of hypothesis. On the contrary, the patriarchal religion seems to have been a renunciation of the cult of the " planet of way for the wayfaring Semitic race ",[70] and a going over to the cult of the *invisible* leader.) The Sabbath is mentioned together with the New Moon because both of them together mark the festive rhythm of the year in weeks and months. It has been just as little possible to expose a day of penitence and atonement behind the festival of joy [a] for the whole community, from the fathers of the households to the servants and cattle. We read of the Babylonian unlucky days that on them the king, the

[a] Hos. ii, 13.

priest of the oracle and the physician should cease their most important activities ; naturally because on those days they would produce only misfortune. Certain practices of a mournful nature are also prescribed for the king. In Israel, on the other hand, it is impossible to find any sign that here the Sabbath rest of the entire people, and, indeed, of everything created, was ever caused by a negative motive.[71]   Babylon and Israel had the word in common. We do not exactly know whether it means " to cease ", or " to cause to cease ", or something else, in the former place. On the other hand the Hebrew word *shabat* means exclusively to be finished with an action or a situation, not to do or not to be something any more ; it does not mean to rest or to leave something undone. What is involved here is in essence the completion of an activity or a function, its no-longer state.

All this taken together in no way justifies the assumption that the Israelite Sabbath is borrowed from the Babylon culture. Here and there the material indicates a common origin, a common Semitic conception of some qualitative difference between the whole six days on the one hand and the seventh on the other ; and in addition the name of a day which is, however, not dependent on but independent of that conception. Out of the original content it seems that two almost opposed developments took place in Babylon and Israel respectively. There the seventh day, which is not called Sabbath, is the day of instability, the day of dire peril, of the pressing need for immediately propitiating the angry gods ; here it is the day of stability, of untroubled serenity, of utter peace between Heaven and Earth. And this state of serenity, this achievement of peace in the creation, is regarded as a rhythm running uniformly through the whole year and through all the years of time. In Israel and, as far as we know, in Israel only, the seven-day week developed as the ever-returning passage from toil to appeasement and from discord to harmony.

Moses clearly found the Sabbath in Israel in some already existent elementary form. Presumably he had already met related customs in Midian ; and as shepherd he himself may have observed certain rites there on every seventh day. He took hold of something that was already in existence, in order to create what was necessary for the beginning of his initiatory work ; a holy order of time. The men whom we call founders of religions are not really concerned with founding a religion, but wish to establish a human world that is subject to a divine truth ; to unite the way of the earth with that of heaven. And it is an important factor in this that time, which is itself articulated only by the cosmic rhythms, by the changes of the sun and the phases of the moon, has to be set firm and stabilized in a higher holiness that extends even beyond the cosmos. In this way Moses establishes the Sabbath, and with it the week that flows into the Sabbath, as the divine measure that regulates the life of human beings. But the God, whose measuring-rod it is, is the same God who takes care of human beings, who supports them, who liberates them, who aids them to achieve salvation. And so the Sabbath week cannot be merely an " absolute metre of time " [72] ; it is likewise and of necessity the ever-recurrent way of God's peace.

The decisive step is : The seventh day, which had even pre-viously been regarded as " holy ", that is, as something excepted from the general series of days, and which accordingly enjoyed taboos peculiar to itself, was now to belong entirely to YHVH. It was to be " holy unto YHVH ". Just as on the Passover the shepherds brought the first-born of every flock to the God, so should they now bring a tribute of their time : the seventh day. Henceforward it was no longer " holy " in itself, no longer some-thing uncanny, charged with magic, a day for dread and caution, to be treated with all kinds of negative and positive rites. It was hallowed by the very fact that it was hallowed unto YHVH : it was hallowed through him and through the contact with him. This God had indeed absorbed everything demonic in himself, but whoever established communion with him was liberated from all demoniality ; and the seventh days hallowed unto him were times of joy. The hallowing of the day led to a certain limitation of work, such as is possible even under nomadic conditions. In order to be there for YHVH it was necessary to change the cus-tomary working habits as far as possible. Nothing more than the absolutely necessary minimum was done. People washed them-selves, put on festival clothing, gathered round holy emblems, and, by coming to YHVH, came to one another. We have no clear idea of the Mosaic celebration of the Sabbath, but this is obvious : here again a great step had been taken towards unifying the people, towards bringing the national community into being ; and, once again, by means of an institution which served to gather Israel round their God.

With the establishment of the Sabbath as the day of YHVH and of his community, two things were germinated that could

develop in due course : something cosmic and something social.
The results of the dual development are to be found in two passages [a] which closely bear a relation to one another. Their present
form (or that, at least, of one of them) has been influenced by the
fact that they were intended to complement one another, and that
the reader of the one is intended to be reminded immediately of
the other. In one passage a command is given to celebrate the
seventh day " in order that your ox and your ass may rest, and the
son of your maid servant and the stranger (ger) may breathe
freely ". In the other YHVH describes the Sabbath as a " sign "
between himself and the Children of Israel, a bodying forth and
visualization of the fact that " in six days YHVH made heaven and
earth, and on the seventh day he rested and breathed freely ".
Israel, who are repeatedly commanded to go in the way of their
God, are thus told to " do work " six days and to celebrate the
Sabbath on the seventh day.[b] The first of these two passages, in
its character as part of the " Book of the Covenant ", is usually
regarded as very early if not necessarily as Mosaic ; whereas the
second, which is attributed to the " Priestly Code ", is regarded as
very late. The early origin of the first seems beyond all doubt to
me as well ; but the second, which clearly developed under its
influence, obviously derives from a time which had no fear as yet
of daring anthropomorphisms, if they were found necessary to
bring something of basic importance to direct apprehension in this
way. And that was what was necessary here. The extremely
rare verb meaning regaining one's breath or breathing freely is
used for YHVH's resting after the erection of the world, in order
to make that first passage even more impressive by setting God, so
to say, on the same level as the most dependent and least protected
of human beings. Even the slave admitted into the household
community, even the ger, the stranger admitted into the national
community, must be permitted to share in the divine rest ; they
also must be allowed to celebrate the day of YHVH together
with him. The Sabbath is the common property of all, and all
ought to enjoy it without restriction.

No matter when the one passage or the other may have been
written down, the spirit of Moses speaks out of both. It is impossible to gain any adequate idea of the man if we do not bear in
mind that from the very beginning he strives for the coming of
justice ; the reign of his God and a just order between men are one

[a] Ex. xxiii, 12 ; xxxi, 17.   [b] Ex. xxxi, 15.

and the same to him ; as legislator, too, he wishes to help the unfree, the exposed ones, to gain their rights. It is an inseparable part of his great conception of Sabbath rest that all are united, free and unfree, those who derive from Abraham's seed and those strangers who have joined them. On that one day in every week, on the day of communion with YHVH God's leisure and God's joy must reign among all members of the community.

But the doctrine of the relation between the Sabbath and the creation of the world likewise seems, to me, inseparable from Moses. If the Sabbath week is really to articulate universal time, it cannot enter it at a certain moment, but can only be discovered and revealed at that moment as something which has always been in existence ; that is, it must be rooted in the very beginnings of the world itself, and the very creation of the world must be such a week and flow into such a Sabbath. Whatever may be the period to which we attribute the writing of the first chapter of Genesis (and it unquestionably bears the stamp of a period of ripe structural art) the idea of the work of creation itself belongs to the early days of humanity. The Egyptian myths, in whose atmosphere Moses grew up, know it as well as the Babylonian, which may have had a direct or indirect influence on the " Fathers " ; and the priest of Midian doubtless also had something to tell of this.

If we take away all the legendary traits of Moses we must still recognize him as the spiritual force in which the Ancient Orient concentrated itself at its close and surmounted itself. In the silence of the steppes he may have tested all the myths against his own awareness of God, finally arriving at his own view. He may have commingled the conception of the Sabbath week, which was already maturing within him, with this view of his. The God who " makes " heaven and earth and in addition man, in order that man may " make " his own share in the creation ; the God who rests on the completion of his work and wishes man to rest with him throughout the future, Sabbath after Sabbath ; that God is no concept of a late priestly speculation. The vital sap of an early, elementally alive humanity is in this vision, and no less a person than Moses was necessary in order to bring it into the world of the word.

THE MURMURERS

WE are told that even in Egypt at the first lack of success, shortly after the people came to believe in Moses' mission and bowed down before Yhvh,[a] the elders of the people assailed the divine messengers and threatened them with divine judgment.[b] At the Red Sea, when the people see the Egyptian war chariots approaching, they cry to Yhvh, to be sure ; but then they complain against Moses in a little speech artistically composed by the narrator,[c] which, in genuine Biblical style, brings out the antithesis of Egypt and desert by closing five of its seven members with the word " Egypt " and two with the word " desert ". The life of servitude in Egypt appears preferable to death in the desert as far as they are concerned.

After the great wonder they believe again " in Yhvh and his servant Moses " ;[d] but scarcely have they passed through the desert without water for three days than they " murmur " again ;[e] and this time without crying out to Yhvh. Instead it is Moses who does so on this occasion on their behalf,[f] and who is heard. But this is only the first of three stations between the sea and Sinai where they murmur. The second is that at which they demand the " flesh-pots " again.[g] Promptly thereon follows the third,[h] where once again the wrangling is increased through shortage of water. " Yet a little and they will stone me ! ", says Moses to God. And so it goes on steadily until the great revolt after the report of the spies, where the people say that they wish to choose themselves a new chief and to return to Egypt[i] ; with all that follows thereon.

It is probable that certain of these narratives are only " doublets " and can be attributed to varying traditions of the same event. In addition, the genuine traditional material has certainly been supplemented by all kinds of fictions, partly popular and partly literary in character. Only in a restricted degree is it possible to distinguish here between what is close to history and what is far from history. Yet the basic description of the process bears a strong stamp of reality. To its shaping some later prophetic experiences with the " stiff-necked " people may have contributed ; yet it is the frequent repetition of such experience, known to us from

[a] Ex. iv, 31.   [b] Ex. v, 20 f.   [c] Ex. xiv, 11 f.   [d] Ibid, 31.   [e] Ex. xv, 24.
[f] Ibid., 25.   [g] Ex. xvi, 3.   [h] Ex. xvii, 2 f.   [i] Num. xiv, 4.

elsewhere, which justifies the assumption that the repetitions in question began very early.

Nevertheless, there is clearly a basically important historical difference, quite apart from all the other differences, between these "men of the spirit" and Moses. They are powerless, officeless spokesmen of Heaven, whereas he, although sent from above as they are, is sent not merely to speak, but also to perform ; he is the commissioned leader of Israel. In the case of the prophets, the actual conflict is not with the people, but with the persons wielding power ; and naturally the people, even though they may secretly maintain and support those who call for justice, ostensibly stand with the authorities. The hidden covenant existent between the oppressed classes of the people and the demanding spirit proves here ineffectual, as is so frequently the case ; and the "stiff-neckedness" may find expression not only in the palace, but also in the market place without restriction.

The situation of Moses is entirely different. He himself possesses the power, but his power is a doubtful one. He is the leader who demands no dominion for himself, and evidently by reason of a sentiment in which different motives converge. We can trace one such motive if we remember the resistance of Bedouin tribes, even in pre-Islamic time, to the granting of unlimited authority to an individual, and in particular to every stabilization of the power ; if we remember their tendency towards a "commonwealth without authorities" as Wellhausen once called it in a noteworthy address.[73] We tend to assume that in Midian Moses was strongly influenced by this basic attitude, and that a, in view of his biography, quite understandable anti-pharaonic sentiment was favourable to its further development.

The other motive, which I have already indicated, and which will yet engage us, is rather more difficult to grasp genetically. It is the passionate wish to make a serious political issue of the faith in the earthly dominion of the god, such as is met with in varied forms and situations in the Ancient Orient, including Southern Arabia.[74] The stern and deep realism of Moses, which could not bear that, as elsewhere, a sacred symbolism should replace or supplant the factual realization of his faith, determines the type, the order of the power. Power lies in the hands of the "charismatic" leader who is led by God ; and, for that very reason, this wielder of power must not engage in any transformation to dominion, which is kept for the God alone. Hundreds of years

later Gideon refuses the crown offered to him *a* with the words,
" I shall not rule over you nor shall my son rule over you, Yʜᴠʜ
will rule over you " ; an expression which to me carries an unquestionably historical scent.[75]

Those words seem to me to have their origin here. There are
early Arabic parallels to this as well.

But the double tendency of which we speak conceals dangers
which militate against its fulfilment. The unbridled craving for
independence, which was common to semi-nomadic Israelites of
ancient times and to the Bedouins, leads again and again to a
singular misapprehension with regard to the charismatic idea.
Only as long as the leader is successful is he regarded as equipped
with the authority of Heaven. As soon as something goes wrong,
or unsatisfactory circumstances ensue, people are swift to detect a
rift between him and the God, to whom appeal is made against his
unworthy because unlucky representative ; if indeed they do not
prefer to draw the conclusion from the mishap that it is impossible
to depend on the favour of Yʜᴠʜ, or even on his loyalty.

Always and everywhere in the history of religion the fact that
God is identified with success is the greatest obstacle to a steadfast
religious life. In the Biblical narrative of the Exodus and the
wanderings in the desert this identification becomes particularly
acute. Moses has to engage in a never-interrupted, never-despairing
struggle against the " stiff-neckedness " of Israel ; that is, against
this permanent passion for success. Certainly, the unfamiliar and in
themselves excessive privations of the journey are a cause of great
suffering to the people, but historical deed always means the surmounting of suffering, the suffering inherent in human being.
The majestic Moses of Western art tradition should not cause us
to forget the one suffering with the people. In a fashion which
no narrator could invent do we observe him suffering all that the
people suffer, and far more deeply than they do ; and we see him
wrestling to overcome the evil.

Assuredly he sometimes speaks in a petty fashion, " Yet a little
and they stone me " ; but he rises with the needs of the hour. And
in the ultimate moment when, following the great sin of the people,
he permits himself to remind Yʜᴠʜ of his faith as Abraham once
reminded him of his justice, he utters the bold words *b* : " And
now, if you will bear with their sins . . . ! But if not, blot me
out of your book ! " And the fact that he has said this, that he has

a Jud. vııı, 23.   *b* Ex. xxxii, 32.

done this, permits him soon after to mount still higher and to address his God with words that cannot be surpassed, words of the most intimate knowledge and the most intimate daring [a] : " Indeed, a people stiff of neck are they—forgive then our transgression ! " Because the people are stiff-necked, God ought to forgive them. This can certainly be explained in the sense that where and when a person or a people are just what they are, nothing, so to say, is left except for God to forgive them. Yet might it not be understood otherwise, as arising out of the deeps of the situation ? According to its current exterior character, stiff-neckedness means permanent passion for success and a rebellious mind. Yet hidden therein is a kind of secret virtue, which only rarely comes to light. This is the holy audacity which enables the people to do their deeds of faith as a people. Here Moses and Israel become one, and he genuinely represents his people before YHVH.

Granted, all these are obvious literary attempts to retrace footsteps that have almost entirely vanished. Yet this state of affairs is enough to permit us to use them, with careful hand, for the picture.

[a] Ex. xxxiv, 9.

THE BATTLE

THE weary hosts passing through the wilderness are suddenly attacked by a wild tribe of Bedouins, presumably in order to prevent any entry into the pasture of the latter by means of a well-timed attack ; yet the desire, on such occasions, to increase one's own herds and flocks is also part of the reason. These Amalekites, who apparently called themselves the " first-born of the peoples ",[a] and were therefore regarded as such, were certainly a very old people. Like the Bedouins of that district to this day, they jealously guarded the approaches to their territory but willingly entered other people's lands and took away their harvests.

Thanks to their strategy of surprise, they now succeeded in cutting off a part of the army which wearily followed the main body ; and they destroyed them. Such a proceeding was generally regarded as against the " fear of God "[b] ; that is as against the custom of the nations whose practice it was to spare those who could not fight and were left behind. In the night, while they share the booty and do not think for the time being of further undertakings, Moses, who promptly grasps the situation, orders Joshua [76] his " servant " (as Elisha is called in relation to Elijah), meaning his adjutant and personal representative who is mentioned for the first time in this narrative, immediately to call out an experienced band in order to attack the Amalekite camp early in the morning.

At the moment when Moses' men have succeeded in approaching the enemy unnoticed, Moses himself appears on a neighbouring hill with the " staff of God " in his hands ; and as long as his strength permits, he holds his hand aloft. " And it came to pass that as Moses held his hand up Israel prevailed, but when he rested his hand, Amalek prevailed."[c] When his hand becomes heavy it is supported. The plural " hands " which appears at this point for the first time and implies that not only the right hand holding the staff was supported but also the left, can be recognized as a change by an editor who mistakenly assumed the position to be one of prayer. And now his hand remains *emunah, i.e.* firmness, staunchness, until at sunset victory is won. According to a supplementary report Moses builds an altar ; and the cry which, as was the

[a] Num xxiv, 20.   [b] Deut. xxv, 18.   [c] Ex. xvii, 11.

practice after completing the building of an altar, he utters over it is [a] : "Yʜvʜ is my banner"! The raised staff was a flagpole, but the true banner is the name Yʜvʜ, which inspirits and puts power into the staff by its pledge of the divine presence.

Moses' staff is not originally a magical one. It is the shepherd's staff which was in his hand at the time he found the Burning Bush. (We hear of it only from the supplement, but the motif can be attributed to the oldest stratum of tradition.) And it became a "staff of God" when it touched the "holy ground"; at the time when Moses became a "man of God".[b] That magical powers were ascribed to it even at the time of Moses is likely enough. But the main source of this was probably in its actual use for signalling or giving orders, which is what seems to have been its purpose in the account of the battle with Amalek.

The belief in the supposed power of a man over inanimate things has its deepest root in the actual power of that man over living beings; and that is also true of the instrument which the person uses for making signs, or which represents the contact of power. The staff has become "the symbol of the simplest dominion in its primal form among nomadic steppe dwellers, such as those who still wander to and fro in the highlands of Asia"; [77] not merely, as Lobeck thinks, because the relation of the shepherds and their flocks was symbolically transferred to that of the ruler and the ruled, but to a far greater degree because the staff is the natural instrument in which the effect of the power of a man on a human group is most strongly concentrated. Such a man raises the staff over the group set in motion; and all eyes turn to it as do those of the musicians to the baton of the conductor. But the musicians feel themselves directed and strengthened even when they do not look there; the fighters do not need to see the baton of the commander in order to be led by him to victory. The commanding soul-substance which streams into it streams out of it again across the distance and into their hearts. Even when the banner is carried by somebody nameless, it waves over and inspires the strong army; a sign and manifestation of that power which moves the leader.

And here a time-old aspect of the symbolic function is active. Raising the staff rouses the elementary will to be uppermost, to "prevail", to bear away the victory; and even the capacity to achieve this. This is also the way in which to understand the

[a] Ex. xvii, 16.　　　　[b] Deut. xxxiii, 1.

statement that the hand of Moses is *emunah*. It was the firm and fixing organ of the manifestation, of the command of power, of endowment with power. Here *emunah* means, precisely, reliable signal.

According to the order of events, the story of the victory over Amalek, the historical kernel of which cannot be doubted, should certainly come at a later point, since the approach to Kadesh was clearly the objective fought for here. But the point at which the account stands is fraught with meaning. The intention of the narrator was to place the battle at the identical station where that increasing murmuring of the people was reported. Greatly as they may have murmured—that is what we are told by implication— the true relation between them and Moses is nevertheless as tremendous, as is shown in this picture of the raised hand and the victorious troops.

It is told of an East Jordan tribe of modern times [78] that they are always accompanied in their forays by a " knowing man ", who is asked for counsel before the battle, who advises the leaders of the favourable moment for attack and who, during the battle, often draws lines with his staff which the foe must not be permitted to cross. The tribe might thank him for a number of victories. In Moses we find one of those cases, rare in the whole history of the world, in which the " knowing man " is also the leader.

At the end of the section we are told that after Moses has cried out over the newly-built altar, " YHVH is my banner ", he adds a further sentence. Translated literally, it appears worded as follows [79] : " Hand on throne, Yah ! YHVH wars with Amalek for age on age ! " It is YHVH's own war because, as far as we can conclude from those apparently early words of Deuteronomy, this tribe transgressed against the most primitive " fear of God " by attacking the defenceless. And without that fear of God no nation should or can exist. Previously, YHVH himself had declared, and had committed to both written and verbal transmission : " Yea, I shall indeed blot out the memory of Amalek from under the heaven ". And so by that sentence Moses enters into an alliance with YHVH, in the name of Israel, for the execution of his word ; and we know how the war with Amalek flared up again and again afterwards until the victories of Saul and David. According to the text before us, Moses calls on YHVH (the latter's abbreviated name Yah, which occurs almost exclusively in songs and verse-like sayings, still echoes the ancient cry-character of the divine name) and summons him to place hand on throne and swear the oath in which Israel shares. Yet, even when we ignore the fact that the word which is translated as " throne " occurs in this form (*kes* instead of *kisse*) only here, and that the concept of the hand placed " on throne " is queer, this sentence, like other such cases, is clearly intended to supplement the preceding cry, the giving of the name to the altar " YHVH my banner " ! ; and flag-pole or banner is called in Hebrew *nes*. The two Hebrew letters corresponding to K and N can easily be confused ; and so there is good reason to agree with the generally-accepted emendation and to read the passage : " The hand on the flagpole of Yah " ! Moses sets his hand on the divine staff, which had become the flagpole of God in the course of the battle, and takes oath. On behalf of Israel he takes oath to fight, following the God whose name is the true banner. The knowing man knows what is given him to know. The leading man leads where he is told to lead.

JETHRO

AND Jethro, the priest of Midian, the father-in-law of Moses, heard . . . And Jethro, the father-in-law of Moses, took . . . And Jethro, the father-in-law of Moses, came . . . The lofty three-fold arsis of the story does more than merely indicate the importance which it has in the eyes of the narrator. Jethro is referred to in this section as Moses' father-in-law ten times more, yet never again does his priestly title recur. It seems as though the narrator wished to obviate that view of the event which has become widespread in modern Biblical criticism ; namely, that when Israel made a covenant with the Kenites, it also adopted the god of the latter " in the person of Aaron and all the elders of Israel, who here took part for the first time in their lives in a solemn offering to Yahveh " ; and that in this way took place the most ancient example of conversion to another religion which is known to us.[80]

This view cannot base itself on the Biblical narrator. The latter tells us in his own impressive fashion that Jethro came to Israel not as the priest of Midian but as Moses' father-in-law ; and in addition the further facts that are told can be used for the Kenite hypothesis only by exploiting the text in a kind of exegesis that puts the text to work more than it explains it.

That the incident is found here and not at a later point,[81] since it takes place " at the mountain of God ",[a] once again appears to evince specific purpose on the part of the redactor. He wishes to show here, immediately after the battle with the Amalekites, how clear a distinction has to be drawn historically between the Amalekites and the Kenites, in view of the fact that this tribe or part of it afterwards united temporarily with the former.[b] But it seems that the narrator himself is interested in describing the meeting in strong and awe-inspiring colours, possibly because he wishes to explain why it was that in the days of the kings the Kenites were zealous for YHVH.[c] At the same time he stresses the family motive, once again by a three-fold emphasis on the fact that Jethro brings to his son-in-law the latter's wife and sons ; he or the redactor clearly takes it for granted [d] that Moses had previously sent his family back to Midian, presumably from Egypt. After

[a] Ex. xviii, 5.   [b] Cf. I Sam. xv, 6.   [c] II Kin. x, 15 f., 23.   [d] Ex. xviii, 2.

94

a shrewdly described greeting the two of them, the widely-ex-
perienced sheikh and his daring disciple, enter the tent ; and Moses
tells what there is to tell, the news of which has already reached
Midian. Jethro praises YHVH for that which he has done in
Egypt—once again a striking three-fold naming of Egypt as the
common foe— and states *ª* : " Now do I know that YHVH is
greater than all the gods ". The word *Elohim,* which means both
gods and God, now becomes the motif, repeated three times
immediately and seven times later, which is clearly intended to
show that in spite of everything the Kenites and the Israelites
were then united only in the *Elohim* concept, which was common
to the peoples ; but not as yet in the knowledge of YHVH. Jethro
offers up cattle, apparently brought by him, " for *Elohim* ", and afterwards he eats the offering and covenant meal " before *Elohim* ",
together with the elders of Israel. The fact that only at this point
is a report made of an offering in Israel to *Elohim* instead of, as
elsewhere, to YHVH, serves to illuminate the uniqueness of what
happened.

" This action ", declare the supporters of the Kenite hypothesis,[82]
" is incomprehensible except on the assumption that Yahweh was
the god of Jethro and his tribe, the Kenites, and that Jethro himself
was Yahweh's priest. " Actually, what happened becomes something beyond understanding on this assumption. Jethro's praise
of the God is interpreted [83] as meaning that he gave expression to
his proud joy because his own god had proved himself mightier·
than all the others. Something different, however, is found in the
text. Jethro says : " Now have I known . . .", or " Now I
know. . . ." By this, if he were the priest of YHVH, he would
be saying that hitherto he has not known his god to be the greatest ;
whereas now that Israel had been saved and Egypt beaten by him,
he, the priest, does know this. Never, it seems to me, has the
priest of a god spoken in such a way to a community which is not
his own ; he could scarcely say such a thing to his own community
unless—which, of course, cannot be the case here—the god has
hitherto occupied a subordinate or uncertain position in the
pantheon.

At this point, however, it is asserted that it is after all Jethro
who offers up the sacrifice. " How does a strange, even though
related and friendly priest, come to take the place of the native
one ? " [84] Further, the absence of Moses from those mentioned as

ª Ex. xviii, 11.

participating in the meal cannot, it is claimed, be considered an
accident ; while he was resident among the Kenites he had " long
earlier participated in the YHVH service and therefore no longer
required acceptance in that community ".[85]

This argument, however, also runs counter to the wording of
the text. Jethro does not conduct the sacrifice but " fetches " it
or has it fetched ; and it is incorrect that this " does not recur anywhere and has no understandable meaning " and must therefore be
amended.[86] The initiator of an offering in Biblical terminology,
either " brings " the animal or alternatively " fetches " it.[a]

And the reason why Moses is not mentioned is—as rabbinical
exegesis [87] recognized—very simply that the spot where the sacrifice
is brought " before God " lies at the entrance to the leader's tent,
to which Moses had led his father-in-law, and which Aaron and
the elders now enter as well. This tent is the real " tent of meeting " ;
its entrance is the place " before God ", at which the communal
offerings are brought.

The days of Moses did not know private offerings but only
communal offerings and communal feasts ; and those only under
particular conditions.[88] The person making the offering is naturally
the possessor of the tent and leader of the community, without the
need for making any special mention of the fact ; which, incidentally, leaves him just as little of a priest (as some scholars claim) as
the offerings brought by Samuel or by Elijah. As a result of this,
no part of the text can be taken to mean a " conversion of Israel ".

Nevertheless, it would be an equally unsatisfactory simplification of the problem if we were to reverse the statement and speak
of a conversion of the Kenites. What happens here is rather that the
" identification ", which Moses had once made in the presence of
the burning bush, is now resumed in a new dimension, in the
relation between two communities ; that is, in the field of history.
Jethro's words of praise " Blessed be YHVH who . . . " are reminiscent of those of that other priestly leader, Melchizedek, in his
greeting to Abraham [b] : " Blessed be El 'Elyon who. . . ".
There Abraham responds (in words which were obviously originally directed to Melchizedek) by identifying the El 'Elyon, the
Most High God, with his own God YHVH.

This is not to be regarded as a political action despite the fact
that it certainly has a political side as well. The inner nature of
the event is appreciated only when it is understood that the

[a] Lev. xii, 8.   [b] Gen. xiv, 19.

" monolatrous " believer in a god—that is, a man devoted only and exclusively to one single god and opposed to any construction of a pantheon—when experiencing divine action directly or indirectly elsewhere than in his own society, will always ascribe such action to his own god, will claim it for him and will, therefore, be inclined to identify the god brought along and the god already present. The Biblical narrative does not tell us how Melchizedek received Abraham's declaration, which meant more or less : " The divinity to whom you refer as the Most High God is none other than YHVH whom I serve, and this is his correct name ; hitherto you have only known his epithet". And so at that stage the subject does not enter the historical dimension.

With Jethro matters are different. He comes and professes. Once, when Moses returned home with the herds, he may have told his father-in-law, and presumably instructor, that the God who really appears on the " mountain of God ", is none other than the God of the forefathers of his brethren. How is Jethro likely to have received this report ? Surely in the way of a wise priest and accustomed to receive such things in that cultural milieu, and possibly elsewhere as well ; he certainly had no doubt of the reality of the phenomenon itself, but would have reserved judgment in respect of the real meaning of the words ; and for the rest he is likely to have preserved a, so to say, expectant memory of the happening as possibly being likewise directed to him and to his own.

We do not know how far Sinai lay from the customary pastures of the Kenites, from which Moses had strayed on that occasion. Yet even if it was at a great distance we have to assume that they ascribed to their own god those divine messages of which they heard. We know nothing of this god, but we may regard him in a tribe which participated in the early Midianite exploitation of the copper mines of the district,[89] and part of whom were also apparently smiths by calling,[90] as having been a mountain and fire god. It is therefore reasonable to suppose that Jethro now waited attentively to hear whether the God had kept the promise, given to Moses, of liberating " His people ".

If the God did this, one may suppose the line of thought of the Midianite priest to have been, then the name announced by Moses might be recognized as the correct one, and union must be established with those favoured by the God ; that is a demand of religious discernment. It would also admittedly be a demand of political understanding, particularly if the Exodus, as is now mostly assumed, took place at a period when the foreign power of Egypt was growing steadily weaker.

And when Jethro now received information of the successful Exodus, he may also have come to remember that it would be advisable to direct these tribes, who are admittedly favoured by so mighty a god, away from the Midianite pastures to other more distant ones ; yet at the same time to give them a section of Kenites as companions in order to ensure participation in their good fortune. What appears to have been decisive, however, for the clearly priestly Jethro was not the political consideration but the kernel of message which was brought to him. It meant that the god himself had left Sinai and now went before the tribes.

That, it seems to me, must have been the decisive factor for the old man who may have experienced all kinds of things with gods ; this dazzling picture of the Lord who dwelt high above the mountains, in the deeps of heaven itself, and who chose from thence a people, descended to them and wanders with them as their guide. " Yes ", he may have weighed matters to himself, " the Hebrew spoke the truth ; among us the god only took his seat here and there, but he has attached himself to them and has revealed his name to them."

So he then comes and states : " Yes, we now know that the god whom you rightly call the one who is present because he is with you and supports you, your god, who has done all this for you yet whom we have also known, is the greatest of all gods ". That does not mean : " I have now become aware that my god is the greatest ". It means : " I have now come to know that your god is the greatest, but have also recognized in him the true form and the true name of my god, the fiery gleam of the middle whose rays have illuminated me ".

By this the identification enters the historical dimension. The holy communal meal of the Covenant takes place on this basis. " At Sinai Israel does not go over to the god of the Kenites, yet equally the Kenites do not go over to the god of the Israelites." Israel has seen that their national god also directs the forces of Nature. The Kenites have seen that their fire and mountain god rescued the tribes he has chosen and leads them. " The concept of god possessed by each is growing." [91]

On the day following the Covenant meal, continues the narrator, Jethro observed how Moses is surrounded all day long by the people who demand the divine decision on great and small issues, as well as in all their daily uncertainties, both public and private ; obviously because many people either do not wish to trust the understanding of the elders, or appeal from the latter's decision to that of the man of God. Jethro warns his son-in-law, that this is too difficult for him to continue to take upon himself ; and advises him to entrust all subordinate matters, that is, those in which only the general law and legal custom need be applied, to reliable men, each of whom should be appointed over a fixed part of the people, one over ten, one over a hundred, and so on. He should keep himself only for important matters in which nobody can take his place ; that is, those matters for the decision of which it is not enough to know what the law is, or which are not merely individual cases of a general rule but each of which is different, a different life and a different problem, and therefore demands a comprehension of its particular content and the decision of its particular request. Only in such a limitation of his own personal responsibilities would he be able adequately to fulfil his essential function of intermediary between God and people, and to teach the people the will of God. (" God " and " people " are the dominant words in this part of the narrative.)

That the report is based on a historical fact seems to be certain. There must clearly have been a tradition that in the days of the Desert an attempt was once made, under Kenite influence, to balance the organization of the people from below upwards (as expressed in the units of the " houses of the Fathers ", the clans and the tribes, as well as in the representative body of the elders) by an organization from above downwards. This organization was constituted not in organic units but in mathematical units of decades, and its authorities consisted of representatives selected and appointed by the charismatic leader.

The tradition appears credible. The amorphous system of division by decades will never agree with the genuine forms of life of a people settled on the soil ; it derives from the utilitarian necessities of military expeditions and large caravans. Midian, which seems to have been a loose association of tribes with varying origins, was apparently familiar with both far-ranging razzias and extensive trade journeys into foreign parts. Of the latter something is told in the story of Joseph [a] ; of the former we hear in the days of the Judges.[b] As an attempt to surmount the anarchy of the wandering Israelites this system may have appeared suitable to Moses together

[a] Gen. xxxvii, 28.   [b] Jud. vi, 3 ; vii, 12.

with a careful selection of authorities, since the institution of the elders was obviously inadequate. With the exception of the military field, however, it did not survive the period of the wandering.[93] The description of the daily toil of Moses given by the narrator may appear naïve, yet here as well an appreciable element of reality can be recognized. If we remember what the Biblical narrative has to tell of the in part stubborn, in part jealous particularism of the clans and tribes, a phenomenon which is also to be found in the manner of life of other Semitic peoples, it is possible to understand why Moses set out to graft into the resistant cellular structure of the community a mechanical one that was more easy to handle. The leader summoned by the spirit, who finds that the " burden " of the people which he has to bear [a] is too heavy, and who, in order to do his duty, has to borrow a " soulless " [94] structure from the Midianites, familiar as they were with organization, appears to me a genuine historical phenomenon.

[a] Num. xi, 11.

"UPON EAGLES' WINGS"
(THE EAGLE SPEECH)

THE hour has come. The sign promised to Moses by the voice which spoke from the burning bush is now about to be fulfilled. " At this mountain " Israel is to enter the service of the God. What had come into being yonder only as word must now take on flesh. It is the hour : not of revelation, which had begun with that call " Moses ! " ; it is the hour of the " Covenant ". The man flaming with the urgent truth of his mission has fulfilled the first charge laid upon him ; he has brought the people to the Mountain of God. " In the third month after the departure of the Children of Israel from Egypt, to the very day, they come to the Wilderness of Sinai. . . . And Israel camped there, facing the mountain." And now, as Moses, unsummoned, like a messenger who is come to report to his lord the execution of a mission, ascends the mountain " to the God ", which assuredly means to the place of that earlier revelation, the voice comes, as it were, to meet him ; and YHVH entrusts him with the mission unto the house of Jacob.

This message is a rhythmic utterance, in which once again almost every word stands in the place fixed for it by sound and sense. Only one sentence, " when ye hearken, hearken unto my voice and keep my Covenant ", does not appear to be in place within the firm rhythm here, but would seem to indicate either a reworking or an interpolation. Enigmatically singular and independent, the passage as a whole has sometimes been attributed to later literary strata, with which it actually has certain concepts and turns of phrase in common. In our days, however, the view is increasingly being held [95] that here we have an old, genuinely traditional fragment which goes back to Moses himself ; if. not verbally, then at all events in basic content. Indeed, I know no other text which expresses so clearly and effectively as this what I would like to call the theo-political idea of Moses ; namely, his conception of the relation between YHVH and Israel, which could not be other than political in its realistic character, yet which starts from the God and not from the nation in the political indication of goal and way. In order to see this clearly we must certainly treat the speech as early ; that is, we must understand the weightiest words in it not in the sacral meaning with which they have been vested in the course of time, but in their aboriginal sense.

"You yourselves have seen what I did in Egypt. I bore you upon eagles' wings and brought you unto me." The first part of this verse summarizes the negative aspect of a decisive point of view. In order that Israel might come here to the God it was necessary for that to befall the Egyptians which had befallen them ; and it also had to befall them in such a fashion that Israel itself should see that which befell. Only as those who saw, and seeing "confided", could they be brought to YHVH, to the meeting with Him. And so they were brought to him "upon eagles' wings". Those who consider such an image as this to be no more than a happy metaphor miss the intent of the whole passage. The basis of comparison here is not the speed of the eagles or their strength, which would be an introduction scarcely suited to a first divine manifesto to the assembled people ; at that moment something fundamentally important regarding the historical relationship between YHVH and Israel has to find its expression through the figure of speech used. This is achieved in an image which is admittedly too meagre to be fully comprehended by us : but the early listener or reader certainly grasped the sense. Later it may nevertheless have proved desirable to elucidate it by means of expansion, and a poetic commentary which we have reason to assume reflects the traditional view has been preserved in the late "Song of Moses". [a]

Here YHVH is likened in His historical relationship with Israel to the eagle, who stirs up his nest and hovers hither and thither above it in order to teach his young how to fly. That the latter are taken to mean the peoples cannot be doubted, as in the Song, shortly before,[b] the Highest had allotted their territories to the nations and had fixed their boundaries. The great eagle spreads out his wings over the nestlings ; he takes up one of them, a shy or weary one, and bears it upon his pinions ; until it can at length dare the flight itself and follows the father in his mounting gyrations. Here we have election, deliverance and education ; all in one.

The verse following likewise certainly dealt in its original form with the *berith*, the "Covenant", which called for mention at this spot. Yet it must be assumed that no demand, after the fashion of a prerequisite condition for everything that was to follow, was

[a] Deut. xxxii, 11.   [b] *Ibid.*, 8.

made in it for a docile observance of the sections of the Covenant by Israel ; but that the verse contained the up-to-this-point-unconveyed notification that Yhvh wished to make a *berith* with Israel. The original meaning of *berith* is not " contract " or " agreement " ; that is, no conditions were originally stipulated therein, nor did any require to be stipulated.

In order to gain an idea of what is really comprehended in this concept we can best start with the story of David, which consists of chroniclers' tales that were certainly recorded for the most part soon after the events with which they deal. Here we find two kinds of *berith*, which are not conceptually differentiated from each other. One is the alliance between two people who stand to some degree on the same level, like that concluded by David and Jonathan.[a] This we may describe on the basis of Arab and other analogies as a covenant of brotherhood. That this leads to a mutual undertaking of unconditional support, a faithfulness even unto death, is not stated, and does not have to be stated ; for it stands to reason. The two covenanters have just become brethren, which is quite enough in a social form where the clan is still the central reality of communal life. Any detailed agreement is superfluous.

The other kind of *berith* is found most clearly in the covenant which David, now King of Judah, concludes with the Elders of the Northern tribes.[b] Here there is no common level ; the person at the higher level of power concludes a covenant, not " with " the submitting ones but " for them ". Here, too, no special agreement is necessary, and indeed there is no room for any such thing. The relation of overlordship and service, into which the two partners enter, is the decisive factor. Engagements, concessions, constitutional limitations of power may be added, yet the covenant is founded not on them but on the basic fact of rule and service. According to its principal form, I classify this kind of *berith* as the Royal Covenant.[96] It is this kind which Yhvh makes with Israel.

The argument cannot be offered against this view that in the Genesis narrative there is another kind of Covenant, which the God makes either with living creatures in general,[c] or with a chosen family.[d] This, too, is not a contract, but an assumption into a life-relationship, a relationship comprehending the entire life of the men involved ; according to the situation, however,

[a] 1 Sam. xviii, 3 ; xxiii, 18.   [b] 11 Sam. v, 3.   [c] Gen. ix, 9 ff.
[d] Gen. vi, 18 ; xvii, 2 ff.

not into a relationship which has a political, theo-political character. Only here, only in the Sinai covenant and its later renewals, is it a *berith* between YHVH and the people, between Him and Israel ; no longer Israel as the " seed of Abraham ", out of which a people has to grow, but as the people which has grown out of that seed. And in accordance with this the concept of Royal Dominion is also expressly introduced here.[a]   This life-relationship between the King and his people is the important thing.   In the narrative of the conclusion of the Covenant itself " a Book of the Covenant " is certainly read out by Moses,[b] and the Covenant is considered to be concluded " upon all these words ".   This book, however, has the character not of an agreement but of a royal proclamation The laws contained therein are registered accordingly in the record of the making of the Covenant as those proclaimed in that hour.[c] But these laws cannot claim any priority over those which may be proclaimed later on, and when the people declare after the reading that they wish " to do and to hear ", they clearly signify that they bind themselves not in respect of specific ordinances as such, but in respect of the will of their Lord, who issues His commands in the present and will issue them in the future ; in the respect of the life-relationship of service to Him.

Those who maintain the Kenite hypothesis argue [97] : " If YHVH had been the God of Israel even before Moses, a Covenant would have been superfluous ; for it would have stood to reason that YHVH was the god of Israel and Israel the people of YHVH. Contracts are only made where the demands of the contracting parties differ and may under certain circumstances become opposed to one another.   For this reason it follows of necessity from the idea of Covenant that Israel and YHVH had hitherto been strangers to one another."   But *berith* is not the same as agreement or contract.   YHVH and Israel enter into a new relation to one another by making the Covenant, a relation which had not previously been in existence ; and further could not have been in existence because Israel as a nation, as a nation which was able to elect itself a King and submit to his service, had been constituted only in that hour.   YHVH, speaking from the flame, had anticipated this hour with that *ammi* of His.   He now proclaims that the hour has come, and utters the words about His Kingdom.   In its present form the narrative has the people begin with the Proclamation of the King in the final verse of the Song of the Sea.

[a] Gen. xvii, 6.   [b] Ex. xxiv, 7 f.   [c] Ex. xxxiv, 27.

The older tradition, however, was obviously that according to which the first and decisive word was uttered from above.

The Proclamation of the Covenant is immediately followed by YHVH's assurance that Israel will be for him " a peculiar treasure among all the nations ". *Segulah*, the Hebrew word translated in the Authorized Version as " peculiar treasure ", means a possession which is withdrawn from the general family property because one individual has a special relation to it and a special claim upon it. The meaning of the word as employed in connection with the relation between YHVH and Israel is immediately explained here by the words " for the whole earth is mine ". It is impossible to express more clearly and unequivocally that the liberation from Egypt does not secure the people of Israel any monopoly over their God. From this phrase there is a direct line leading to the warning of the prophet [a] which also refers to the Exodus, the warning which glorifies this God as the one who has also guided other nations on their wanderings, aye even the neighbouring nations which are foes of Israel ; and which glorifies this God as the liberator of the nations. The expression " peculiar treasure " is directly imperilled by an atmosphere of restriction and self-assurance, unless it is accompanied by such an explanation. This we can see in three cases,[b] where the word is used in the Book of Deuteronomy (a work which may well have developed from a collection of traditional sayings of Moses in a number of variant forms, rather like the Hadith of Mohammed in Islamic tradition). All these three passages are associated with the concept of the Holy People, which is also derived from the Eagle Speech. The danger of particularist misunderstanding is so obvious that in the first passage a warning is issued against ascribing the choice made by God to their own importance. The Eagle Speech itself opposes the haughty stressing of the choice by the subsequent message that the choice means a charge imposed on them and nothing more ; and that therefore the choice, so to say, exists only negatively unless the charge is also fulfilled.

This message became obscured for later generations by the fact that, as already mentioned, its great concepts no longer retained their original concreteness, but were understood in accordance with a technical waning-away of meaning. When one reads " you shall become unto me a kingdom of priests and a holy people", it at first strikes us almost irresistibly as though it is not the

[a] Amos ix. 7.   [b] Deut. vii, 16 ; xiv, 2 ; xxvi, 18.

theo-political idea of a factual divine domination which finds
expression here, but a cult conception which aims at being all-
embracing. But that is not so. The period whose loftiest thought
was given shape by the Eagle Speech was concerned not with
" religion ", but with God and people ; that is, with God's people
on a basis of political and social realism ; with what might almost
be called a pre-state divine state. The word *mamlakah*, which is
translated by " kingdom ", means king's rule and likewise, area
of the king's rule ; and the word *kohanim*, which usually means
priests, is synonymous, where it describes a secular court office,
with " the first at the hand of the king ",[a] or with companion,
adjutant.[b] The *mamlakah* comprises those particular servants of the
king who attend immediately upon him. *Mamleketh kohanim* therefore means the direct sphere of rule of the lord, composed of those
of his companions who are at his immediate disposal, his immediate
retinue. All of them, all the children of Israel, stand in the identical
direct and immediate relationship of retainers to Him.

To this corresponds the second member of the sentence, " a
holy people ". And this balancing phrase, as is so frequent in
parallelisms of the kind, is simultaneously a completion, and indeed
a clarifying completion, of the sense. As the elemental meaning
of the Biblical concept of holiness we have to assume a power
drawn and concentrated within itself, which, however, radiates
forth and is capable of exerting both a destructive and a " hallowing"
effect. In relation to YHVH holiness is regarded as His direct
power, dispensing both good and ill ; and thence as the derived
quality of those things and beings which are separated from out
of the unspecified common realm, the " profane ", and have been
dedicated to or dedicate themselves to YHVH ; and which, since
they are dedicate to Him and as long as they are so dedicate to Him,
are hallowed by His holy force.

Therefore *goy qadosh*, as complement of that *mamleketh kohanim*
which means the charging and appointment by God, thus requires
and implies a spontaneous and ever-renewed act on the part of the
people. They have to dedicate themselves to YHVH and remain
dedicate to him, and further they must do this as *goy*, that is, with
their corporeal national existence. Hence the intention is not
the behaviour of the members of the people, as it is later,[c] of
all members of the people as individuals ; as, for example, that

---

[a] *Cf.* I Sam. viii, 18 with I Chron. xviii, 17.
[b] I Kin. iv, 5 ; *cf.* II Sam. xx, 26 and I Chron. xxvii, 33.   [c] Ex. xxii, 30.

they shall refrain from unclean, polluting foods ; but the point at
issue is the behaviour of the national body as such. Only when the
nation with all its substance and all its functions, with legal forms
and institutions, with the whole organization of its internal and
external relationships, dedicates itself to YHVH as its Lord, as its
melek, does it become His holy people ; only then is it a holy
people.

And specifically as that, and as that alone, can it render its
divine leader the services for which He has selected it : as " the
first to his hand " of the " whole earth ", which is " His " ; in
order to transmit His will, which it fulfils by means of its own life.
It is laid upon Israel to factualize, by way of this office and this
dedication, YHVH's choice of them as a peculiar treasure among
all peoples ; this is the *berith* he wishes to conclude with them.

The Biblical narrative makes Moses " offer " his theo-political
message to the elders, and " the whole people " answer through the
latter that they will do what YHVH has said ; that is, that they
would enter the *melek* Covenant, which He wishes to conclude
with them. That what took place at Sinai was understood even
in early tradition as such a Covenant, as a royal pronouncement
from above and as an acclamation of royalty from below, is indicated by the hymn which is placed as the frame of the so-called
" Blessing of Moses ".[a] Even radical critics [98] conclude from
the resemblance between this Psalm and the Song of Deborah
" that in itself it may be old and indeed very old ". But
since Israel is twice referred to in it under the name " Yeshurun ",
which is otherwise found only in two late passages, it is assumed
that the language of the text before us is not so much archaic as
archaicizing. In both those other passages, however, this name
which would appear to derive from the old folk-singers (compare
the title of an old collection of songs, *Sepher Hayashar* or Book of
the Upright) has been taken over with a conscious purpose. Following a few difficult, and in part incomprehensible verses, the hymn
reads with absolute clarity [b] : " And there came about in Yeshurun
a king, when the heads of the people foregathered, together the
tribes of Israel ". No interpretation other than a reference to
what happened at Sinai, which is mentioned at the commencement
of the hymn, serves to do justice to this important passage. The
great *melek* message appears to be the one which is lauded in the
preceding verse to this as " the teaching which Moses ordered us ".[99]

[a] Deut. xxxiii, 1-7, 26-29.　　　　　　[b] *Ibid.*, 5.

Historically considered, the idea finding expression in the Eagle Speech and associated texts is the challenge offered by the Hebrew tribes, departing from Egypt into freedom, to Pharaonism. The freedom is understood by their leader as God's freedom ; and that means as God's rule. Historically considered, this means the rule of the spirit through the persons charismatically induced and authorized as the situation warrants ; its rule on the basis of the just laws issued in the name of the spirit. The entire conception of this royal Covenant, which aims at being all-embracing, is only possible when and because the God who enters into the Covenant is just and wishes to introduce a just order in the human world. Justice as an attribute is in some degree implicit in the old Semitic conception of the tribal gods as judges of the tribes.[100] It achieved completion in the God conception of Israel. The just law of the just *Melek* is there in order to banish the danger of " Bedouin " anarchy, which threatens all freedom with God. The unrestrained instinct of independence of the Semitic nomads, who do not wish to permit anybody to rise above them and to impose his will upon them,[101] finds its satisfaction in the thought that all the Children of Israel are required to stand in the same direct relation to YHVH ; but it achieves restraint through the fact that YHVH himself is the promulgator and guardian of the law. Both together, the kingship of God as the power of His law over human beings and as the joy of the free in His rule, achieve expression in the ideal image of Israel which is found in an old lyric utterance [102] attributed to the heathen prophet Balaam [a] : " One beholds no trouble in Jacob and one sees no toilsomeness in Israel, YHVH his God is with him and *melek* jubilation is in him ". YHVH the " Present One ", is really present among his people, who therefore proclaim him as their *Melek*.

During the period following the conquest of Palestine the *melek* title was rarely employed for YHVH, obviously in order to differentiate Him from the " religious and political Canaanite world with its divine kings and its monarchistic state forms ",[103] and particularly because these *Melek* or "*Moloch* " gods demanded children as sacrifices.[104] But the idea of divine rule remained in existence, as can be seen from the narratives of Gideon and Samuel.[105] During the early period of David's rule it once again, as I would suppose, received magnificent poetic formulation in the four verses now placed at the end of Psalm XXIV, praising YHVH the " hero

[a] Num. xxiii, 21.

of war ", and " the King of Glory ", who enters Jerusalem invisibly enthroned on the Ark of the Covenant. But the factual meaning had already begun to undergo its transformation into the symbolic. Under the influence of the dynasty, which consistently opposed all attempts of the spirit to influence public life, the conception of divine rule soon became quite pallid. Only Isaiah, in the notes of his annunciatory vision,[a] dared to contrast YHVH as " the ", that is, as the true, *Melek* with King Uzziah, whom He had smitten with leprosy. In all later Psalms which sing of YHVH's ascent to the throne, He is only the Cosmocrator ; which means far more in appearance but far less in reality. For the true kingship does not exist without a people who recognize the King. When the whole world appears in those Psalms as such a people, the action is thereby shifted to an eschatological level, to a future becoming-perfect of the Creation. Unlimited recognition of the factual and contemporary kingship of God over the whole national existence, however, is what was required of Israel, in the midst of the historical reality, by the message which found its form in the Eagle Speech.

[a] Is. vi, 5.

THE COVENANT

WHEN those who have grown up in the atmosphere of the Bible think of the "Revelation upon Sinai", they immediately see once again that image which overwhelmed and delighted them in their childhood : " the mountain burning with fire up to the heart of the heavens, darkness, cloud and lowering mist ".[a] And down from above, down upon the quaking mountain, that smokes like a furnace, descends another fire, flashing fire from heaven ; while through the thunder that accompanies the flashing lightning or, it may be, from out of that self-same thunder, comes the blast of a ram's horn.[b] Various attempts have been made to refer this image back to some natural event, either a tremendous thunderstorm or the eruption of a volcano ; but the singular wealth of phenomena, which is inseparable from the description, runs counter to such an explanation. What takes place here is a meeting between two fires, the earthly and the heavenly ; and if either of them is struck out, there is an immediate lacuna in the picture which has so enraptured the generations of the People of Israel and the generations of the Christian peoples. To-day, however, something else is more important than all of this. The spirit of our own times, which has grown mature and more reserved, takes objection to the venerable image. Yonder Moses who ascends the smoking mountain before the eyes of the assembled people, who speaks to the Height and receives from the thunder and trumpet-blasts a response which he brings to his people in the form of commandments and laws,—yonder Moses is not merely a stranger to us, which the real Moses also threatens to become at times when we sense him most ; he is unreal. It is precisely when we make the most earnest efforts to establish a reality, a reality consisting of actual facts, that we are possessed by the feeling that " the words of the Covenant, the Ten Words "[c] could surely not have entered the world thus, in such optical and acoustical pomp and circumstance ; and where the narrative reports them as having been written on Tablets of Stone, things happen quite differently, in silence and solitude. We the late-born, oppressed as we are by the

<hr>

[a] Deut. iv, 11.   [b] Ex. xix, 16, 18 f.   [c] Ex. xxxiv, 28.

merciless problem of Truth, feel in our own minds a singular
belated echoing of the protest which found its expression in the
story of the Revelation to Elijah at Sinai.ᵃ The voice comes not
out of the storm, not out of the fury and the fire, but in " a small
whisper ".

. In any case every attempt to penetrate to some factual process
which is concealed behind the awe-inspiring picture is quite in
vain. We are no longer in a position to replace that immense
image by actual data. It may be that one of those formidable
thunderstorms, by which the Bedouins of this district are still struck
with wonder from time to time as by a heavenly catastrophe, may
have given the wandering people to know the primal force of the
God who had been theirs from the times of the Fathers, yet whom
they now first " came to know " in a nexus of actual events.
Even if that is so, however, we can no longer substitute this for
the traditional picture.

The situation is different in respect of the making of the Covenant and the covenantal meal.ᵇ Critical scholars have justly
remarked on the high antiquity of one or the other of the components ; [106] but the fact of the association of those components,
questionable as it appears in their present literary structure, indicates two stages of a coherent process, since the common meal
belongs to the conclusion of the Covenant ; save that here, according to the sense, it is shown as divided into the two separate actions
of making the offering (verse 5) and eating (verse 11).[107] No
matter how we may check and test the account, no basis will be
found for doubting the essential historicity of what is described as
having happened.[108]

To be more precise, there are not two but seven stages, or rather
seven actions.

First, and clearly before the dawn, Moses builds an altar at the
foot of the mountain and erects, clearly in a circle round about
himself, twelve standing stones—stones which, according to the
ancient conception, could see, hear and testify—" for the twelve
tribes of Israel ". Something analogous is reported in the story
of Elijah ᶜ who, in order to " heal " the broken YHVH altar on
Mount Carmel, employs twelve stones " according to the number
of the sons of Jacob ". The word " Jacob " is followed by the
noteworthy relative clause, " unto whom came the word of YHVH
saying, Thy name shall be Israel ". When Elijah prays to God at

<hr>

ᵃ 1 Kin. xix, 11 ff.   ᵇ Ex. xxiv, 4b-11.   ᶜ 1 Kin. xviii, 30 ff.

the altar [a] the name Israel is again repeated twice, obviously of set purpose, in the fashion of a refrain ; the first time in a passage where, on the one and only occasion in the Bible apart from certain very late texts, the names of Abraham and Isaac are followed not by Jacob but by " Israel ".

The implication cannot be misunderstood. Just as the one single altar was reconstituted with the twelve stones, so has the one Israel been constituted anew now that the people have united afresh around their God. What appears in the narrative of Elijah as a symbol of the restoration is an act of foundation in the narrative of the Covenant made by Moses. In the report of this Covenant, written with reluctance and reserve, the meaning of things that cannot properly speaking be reported is more deeply concealed ; but it finds direct expression when the God whom the representatives of the people " see " [b] is called " the God of Israel ". The Covenant entered into between the tribes and YHVH contains in its very core the Covenant entered into between the tribes themselves ; they became Israel only when they became partners in the Covenant of the God.

We have good reason to assume that here we stand on historical ground. In our own days it has been convincingly demonstrated [109] that the system of twelve tribes in Israel, like so many other " amphictyonies ", is not to be accounted for on the basis of natural growth, but is due to a regulation and division deriving from a specific historical situation. It must be added, however, that a regulation and division of this kind cannot be merely artificial, but presupposes the existence of an organic development. Among all the possibilities available, that specific grouping is selected which has as its basis the number twelve, a number which is sacred to tribal associations ; that is, small units are either allocated to larger ones or else left in their independence as may best suit the circumstances ; but no unit is arbitrarily split. Hence there is to be found here a singular co-functioning of development and decision.

Nowadays, however, there is a widely held view [110] that no twelve tribes of Israel were ever in Egypt, that those who were in that country were the " tribes of Joseph " and their followers ; and that in Canaan these united for the first time into a complete twelve-tribe association with the tribes which had remained there and which had previously constituted a " six-tribe amphictyony ".

[a] I Kin. xviii, 36.   [b] Ex. xxiv, 10.

The presumed union is supposed to have taken place under Joshua's leadership at the " Assembly in Shechem " [a] and only there is the recognition of YHVH by the " autochthonous " tribes assumed to have taken place.

But as a precise exegesis of the important passage goes to show, [111] the arguments adduced are a long way from conclusive. We do not know, to be sure, whether parts of the " Israelite " tribes had not actually remained in Canaan, nor whether and with what measure of success other parts of those tribes had attempted to return to Canaan even before Moses. There are obscure passages in the Bible which can be read as indications in one or the other direction. That only a few tribes, however, undertook the Exodus under Moses' leadership, or that any considerable association existed in Canaan to whom YHVH was alien or who had merely heard talk of Him, is an inadequately-grounded hypothesis. Joshua did not establish a new covenant but renewed the one which was in existence between Israel and YHVH, just as it was repeatedly renewed during the ensuing period after having been seriously broken, in accordance with the practice of the Ancient Orient, where a covenant entered into with a God always admitted of renewal. Joshua did this by re-establishing the Covenant, in accordance with the original intention of the founder, on the basis of an exclusive relationship with YHVH and the elimination of all particularist idols. The *berith*, together with the system of the twelve tribes, was founded by Moses, and the evidence of the report before us does not need to be impugned. We do not know, to be sure, the names of the tribes referred to here, nor can we judge which of them were and which were not identical with those whose names have been preserved by tradition. We do not know which septs or clans were united by Moses as one tribe, nor to which clans grown large he gave the character of tribes. But we may rest reasonably well assured that he, and none other than he, to whom we may well attribute a knowledge of the inner organization of the peoples, educed the tribal system of Israel from out of the natural structure of the national material ; and that by completing the appropriate parts he made it possible to weld them together.

The tribes which have united in the Covenant with YHVH are termed Israel as a collective unit. It might be going too far to assume [112] that the name was " a religious one, a profession of faith, and that it came into being with the foundation by Moses " ; but

[a] Jos. xxiv.

we may consider ourselves quite justified in assuming that, whatever association it may previously have designated, it was seized
upon by the new fellowship ; to which end the interpretation of
the name as " God rules " [113] appears to have been an important
factor. The basic content of the message epitomized in the Eagle
Speech was the rule of God over the " people ". Now, following
on this, the people, *am*, the community, constitutes itself as the
unity of those subject to His rule. " God rules " is the proper
name for the Holy Covenanters, which is what the tribes have
become united for under Moses. [114]

The name may first have been used by Moses as a call or a
watchword, which passed from rank to rank in the still nascent
association, and which sounded like something obvious and self-
explanatory by the time it had reached those who stood hindmost.

This first action, the erection of the altar and the twelve standing
stones, is followed by the second ; Moses sends the " youths of
the Children of Israel " to fetch the offering. In this, the oldest
stratum of tradition known to us, there is obviously as yet no
Levitical priesthood at all, no actual official class engaged in the
offering-up of sacrifices. The assistants of Moses in sacred affairs
are the youths, who are apparently selected without preference
being given to any specific clans. That they are youths is obviously
connected with the fact that, in early stages of religion, the natural
state of chastity is preferred to the acquired one, which we find
elsewhere in Biblical texts [a] as a condition of access to the Holy.
It is reasonable to assume that those referred to are the first-born
who in the early period were apparently devoted to YHVH for
the term of their youth as a substitute for the common Semitic
sacrifice of the first-born ; and who were afterwards [b] redeemed
by the Levites. [115] Yet the term " youth " in the sense of " sacred
servant " irrespective of age was also beginning to come into use. [c]

And now Moses, not as priest for he is none, but as the intermediary between community and Godhead, himself accomplishes
the decisive act of establishing the Covenant ; which in turn
consists of three actions. The blood of the animals offered is
divided into two halves. He scatters the blood from the one half
on the altar and thereby devotes it to YHVH. He binds the people
to the Covenant. (Originally, as it seems to me, the reference
here was not to the reading of a " book ", of a document, but to
the proclamation of the message.) And he scatters the remainder

[a] 1 Sam. xxi, 5.   [b] Num. iii, 12.   [c] Ex. xxxiii, 11.

of the blood, which had been kept in basins, over the people, while repeating the sacramental formula, " this is the blood of the Covenant which YHVH establishes with you ". (In the text this is followed by " upon all these words ", which is presumably a supplement dating from the period in which the proclamation was replaced by a reading.)

What Moses does by this rite, which, though reminiscent of the Semitic custom of Blood Covenant, is nevertheless unique in character,[116] is no pure cult act but a cultic " pre-state " state act.[117] Agreements between God and people are known to us from various places in the Ancient Orient; in Babylon, for instance, as early as the first half of the third millenium B.C., and in Southern Arabia as late as the commencement of the seventh century B.C. But that which took place at Sinai involved more than a contract, more than a fixed, limited agreement. YHVH unites himself with Israel into a political, theo-political unity, " within which the two partners bear the relations towards each other of a primitive wandering community and its *melek* ".[118]

Now Moses, together with Aaron and seventy of the elders, begin to climb up the mountain. On its summit they have to accomplish the final action, the holy meal of the Covenant, and to consume, as guests of YHVH, that portion of the flesh of the offering which has not ascended to heaven in smoke. Here, however, something unheard-of occurs, at the telling of which the narrator breaks into rhythmic words, as though he were quoting verses from a time-old song : " They saw the God of Israel, at his feet as the work of a sapphire pavement, as the very heavens for purity ". After the word " Israel " the word " and " occurs in the text, but as in so many other places, it has the value only of the word " namely ", or of a colon. It is usually assumed either that the reluctance of the narrator prevented him from undertaking a description of the divine manifestation itself, or else that a later abbreviated version replaced an earlier description which had become objectionable. Both views miss what is actually to be found in the verse. If it really told of the seeing of a divine form, it would mean that the redactor had not noticed the vast contradiction to be found between this passage and that other one [a] in which YHVH soon afterwards warns Moses, who wishes to look upon Him, that " Man " cannot see him and remain alive. Would the redactor not have dared to take the steps necessary in order to

[a] Ex. xxxiii, 20.

remove this contradiction, on so delicate a point ? It is true that we repeatedly read of the *kabod*, the radiation of the divine " mass ", which showed itself to the whole people ; but there is obviously a qualitative difference between such a temporary manifestation of light and what would have been the case here. There the redactor would not need to concern himself with any harmonization, but here he would have to undertake one. We cannot come closer to understanding the enigmatic verses unless we are prepared to ask at this point, too, what the reality was that lay at the basis of the report.

Isaiah writes in the note regarding that Vision of Annunciation,[a] in which he was appointed a prophet, that he had seen the Lord " sitting on a high and exalted throne, and his trains filled the temple-hall ". We clearly have to suppose the prophet to be standing in the entry-hall of the Temple at Jerusalem. " He gazes into the depths of the Temple as far as the gloom of the Holy of Holies, where stands the Ark, the Throne and Shrine of YHVH. And then the darkness becomes light, the limited space expands into a vastness, the roof is borne away, in place of the Ark there rises a throne that reaches to heaven ; so vast that the train of the garment worn by the One seated upon it fills the Temple." [119] Visions are subject to optical laws of their own ; yet it is obvious that when the train of light filled the Temple in front of Isaiah, he could not have seen the form on the Throne at all. None the less, this is what he calls seeing the Lord, and of this he says [b] : " The King YHVH of Hosts have mine eyes seen ". He senses his seeing in the radiance as being a seeing of the Radiant. The impact of the sitting on the Throne as such replaces, for him, the form of the One seated on the Throne. This is not later prophetic develop-ment ; it is the aboriginal experience, without an appreciation of which the innermost relation of the Biblical man to his God is not to be understood.

If we disregard the multitude of those who are not interested at all in theophanies related in the " Old Testament ", the present-day world of men may be divided into those who view the theophanies in question as supernatural miracles in respect of which the quest for any reality comparable to that of our own experience is illicit ; and those for whom they are impressive fantasies or fictions which, from a certain aspect, are worthy of consideration. But when we are told in Biblical accounts of early experiences of God that He

[a] Is. vi, 1.   [b] *Ibid.*, 6.

let Himself " be seen " by His believers (the real sense of the verbal form which is customarily translated as " appeared "), we feel ourselves bound to ask what it means ; and this implies, since the word undeniably refers us to a specific kind of practical experience, that we must ask what, more or less, can have been the nature of those experiences. A God who " gives." His worshipper " to see " the land to which He leads him,[a] but who does not as yet permit Himself to be seen, reserving this " being seen " for a specific and particularly important station of the wandering through that land,[b] can in Himself only be an invisible God who, however, becomes visible at will. How, as what, wherein does he become visible ? No prophet had anything to tell of a figure resembling the human until Ezekiel,[c] who was affected by theological speculations and leads us on to the apocalyptical sphere. Nothing is revealed regarding the One on the Throne, even in a popular legend of vision like that of Micah ben Yimla.[d]

The saga of the Fathers, to be sure, particularly in the eighteenth chapter of Genesis with its fondness for narrative, has something to tell of human figures, in which YHVH lets himself be seen. But there is nothing supernatural about them, and they are not present otherwise than any other section of Nature in which the God manifests himself. What is actually meant by this letting-Himself-be-seen on the part of YHVH has been shown in the story of the Burning Bush ; in the fiery flame, not as a form to be separated from it, but in it and through it, is " the messenger of YHVH ", that is, YHVH as the Power that intervenes in earthly affairs, given to be seen by Moses.

And it is in precisely such a fashion, as far as I can ascertain from the text, that the representatives of Israel come to see Him on the heights of Sinai. They have presumably wandered through clinging, hanging mist before dawn ; and at the very moment they reach their goal, the swaying darkness tears asunder (as I myself happened to witness once) and dissolves except for one cloud already transparent with the hue of the still unrisen sun. The sapphire proximity of the heavens overwhelms the aged shepherds of the Delta, who have never before tasted, who have never been given the slightest idea, of what is shown in the play of early light over the summits of the mountains. And this precisely is perceived by the representatives of the liberated tribes as that which lies under the feet of their enthroned *Melek*.

[a] Gen. xii, I.   [b] *Ibid.*, 7.   [c] Ezek. I, 26.   [d] I Kin. xxii, 19.

And in seeing that which radiates from Him, they see Him. He has led them by His great might through the sea and through the wilderness. He has brought them "upon eagles' wings" to this mountain of His revelation. Here He has entered into the Blood Covenant, the King's Covenant, with them. He has invited them to eat here before Him ; and now that they have reached unto Him, He allows them to see Him in the glory of His light, becoming manifest yet remaining invisible.

Even such a "seeing" of the Godhead is dangerous ; for where YHVH is, there the whole of divine demonism can be found as well. But He bestows mercy on whomsoever He wishes to bestow it. The host does not reach out His hand against the "corner-pillars" or "joints" of the people (the basic meaning of the Hebrew word generally used for "nobles" is one or the other). Of set intention the story ends with that phrase which at first sight seems almost queer to us : "They saw the Godhead and ate and drank". The bodily function of eating the covenantal meal must link itself with the continuous consciousness of the Divine Presence. But this consciousness itself has now become less bodily than it was. The verb *hazah*, used in the prophetic field of experience for "seeing", bears less relation to an objective exterior, is more interior, than *raah*, to see. It should be understood as more or less "the inner appropriation of that which is seen".[120]

As the sun rises higher the primal blue grows paler ; but the heart of the hallowed eaters of the hallowed food remains full of the primal blue, such as it had been.

THE WORDS ON THE TABLETS

CERTAIN excerpts from a " Theosophia ", presumably written by an Alexandrian of the fifth century c.e.,[121] have come down to us. In these we are told, among many other memorabilia, that Moses had actually written two Decalogues. The first and hence older of them, reads, " For their altars ye shall smash, their pillars ye shall break, their sacred poles ye shall cut down ", and so on. This refers, of course, to Exodus xxxiv, 13-26, out of which it would be possible to construct ten commandments, though with a certain amount of difficulty. The second is the Decalogue of tradition, Exodus xx, 2-17. To give this view expression in modern scientific terminology, it means that Moses preceded his " ethical " decalogue with an earlier, " cultic " one, which starts polemically and then goes on to various prescriptions. That the commencement proposed by the author, which begins with " his " and refers to the peoples already mentioned, cannot be any real commencement, was apparently not noticed by him.

In a dissertation on the Tablets of Moses, prepared with " indescribable toil ", which the University of Strassbourg rejected, Goethe undertook to prove " that the Ten Commandments were not actually the covenantal laws of the Israelites ". A year and a half later he returned to this thesis in a little paper entitled " Two important and hitherto unclarified Biblical Questions thoroughly dealt with for the first time by a country priest in Swabia ". In this paper he has his country priest offer a view largely identical with that finding expression in the " Theosophia ", which was unknown to Goethe. He begins, however, with the sentence " Thou shalt worship no other God ", which might indeed be the starting-point for a decalogue. Goethe sets out to overcome the " troublesome old error " that the Covenant " by which God pledged himself to Israel " could " be based on universal obligations ". What is regarded by us as the Decalogue is only " the introduction to the legislation " which, in the view of the Swabian village pastor, contains doctrines " that God presupposed in his people as human beings and Israelites." Behind this, however, lies Goethe's actual idea, though not without some contradiction of what has been said : that the history and doctrine of the People of Israel had a particularist and not a universal character until the

time when Christianity was grafted on to its stem. Some decades
later, in his Notes and Studies to the " West-Oestlicher Divan ",
Goethe declared that he had endeavoured to separate " what
would be fitting to all lands, to all moral people " from that " which
especially concerns and is binding on the People of Israel." He
did not specify this separation in any greater detail ; in any case,
however, his views as they find expression in his early work remain
a pace behind those of his masters Hamann and Herder, who
recognized in that particularism the earthly vehicle without which
nothing universal can achieve earthly life.

A century after the " Two Questions " Wellhausen, who was
long followed and in wide circles still is followed without restriction
by critical Bible study, undertook to prove the priority of the
" Goethean Law of the Two Tablets " by means of a comprehensive
critical analysis of sources. Exodus xx and Exodus xxxiv, he
held, are diametrically opposed. " There the commandments are
almost only moral, here they are exclusively ritual." [122] And
obviously, in accordance with a view still prevalent in our own
days, the ritual one must be older and in fact original. The
Decalogue of Exodus xx accordingly appears to be influenced by
the prophetic protest against ritualism, whereas that of Exodus
xxxiv would mirror the primitive pan-sacralism of the Moses
epoch, though after a fashion conditioned by the setting actually
found in Canaan.

If we consider this so-called " cultic " decalogue without
prejudice, we find that it is not a complete whole in itself like the
" ethical " one, but consists of a compilation of appendixes and
complements ; chiefly, further, such as would comprehensibly
derive from a transition to regular agriculture and the civilization
associated therewith. Most of them, supplements almost exclusively, are also to be found in the same or an analogous form in the
so-called " Book of the Covenant ".[a] The complements, on the
other hand, in no case refer to the laws of this book, but only to
those which are found either in the " Ethical Decalogue " itself or
else in prescriptions to be found earlier in the text. Thus the
provisions for the sacrifice or redemption of the animal first-born [b]
are extended to horned cattle.[c] Two characteristic complements to Exodus xx are provided : the prohibition of images,
which in that context has as its subject only such as are hewn and
carved (this still remains to be shown), is extended there to graven

[a] Ex. xx, 22-xxiii, 19.   [b] Ex. xiii, 11 ff.   [c] Cf. Ex. xxii, 29.

images,[a] while the commandment of Sabbath rest is rendered more stringent by being made applicable even to the seasons of ploughing and harvesting, the times of most pressing work in the fields. From all this it may reasonably be concluded that this compilation was younger than the Decalogue in its original form.   It has therefore been justly described more recently as a " secondary mixed form " ;[123] save that it may certainly be considered as older than the redaction of the " Book of the Covenant " in our possession, since it assuredly did not borrow the doublets from the latter.   Still, the selection was clearly made in accordance with a specific attitude, so that we may well assume to have before us the " House-book of a Palestinian Sanctuary ",[124] prepared from old material.

Critical research of the Wellhausen school has for the greater part not, or only inadequately, recognised the real character of this composition.   In general it has not ceased to stress its " great age " and the " influence of the foundation of the religion of Moses "[125] that finds expression in it ; as against which the date of the Decalogue was shifted into ever later times, until the assumption was made that it could belong only to the exilic or post-exilic age ;[126] and must in fact constitute the catechism of the religious and moral duties of Israel in Exile ;[127] and that as such it must be " a product of the religious needs of Israel in Exile ".[128]   Supporters of a more moderate point of view still found it necessary to explain that the Ten Commandments were " both impossible and superfluous for archaic Israel ".[129]

As against this negative self-certainty, the past three decades have seen the emergence of the feeling that it is necessary to examine the situation once again, and irrespective of all preconceptions and theories.

For the greater part the argument had been conducted on the basis of single commandments, which were held to be incompatible with the social and cultural, moral and literary conditions of the early period ; to which the protagonists of the Mosaic origin of the Decalogue had replied by characterizing the passages which were questionable in respect of content and language as later supplements, and in turn laid bare an incontestably original Decalogue. Now, however, the stress is being shifted to an increasing degree from the parts to the whole.

[a] Cf. Ex. xx, 23.

The thesis of the impossibility of such high ethical standards in those days lost its force when the publication and translation of Egyptian and Babylonian texts led to the dissemination of information regarding, and appreciation of, a reality in the history of the human mind which has received the name of the Ancient Oriental Moral Code, but which might rather be regarded as the ancient Oriental tendency to commingle cultic prohibitions and postulates with those of a moral kind.   In those texts which have become best known and are also most characteristic, a confession of the dead before the Judges of the Dead found in the Egyptian " Book of the Dead " (deriving from the period in which the Exodus from Egypt took place), and a " catalogue of sins " from the Babylonian conjuration tablets, the moral part is the greater by far ; [130] and this fact is quite sufficient in itself to break down the general assumption that cult necessarily preceded ethics.   But even if we turn our attention to the so-called primitive races and read, say, the tribal lore of an East African tribe,[131] which the elders pass on to adolescents about to be admitted into the community, we observe that their real concern is with the correct relations between the members of a family, the members of a clan ; and furthermore the important fact of the repeated stressing that this is the will of the god, of the " Heaven Man ". The most thorough-going opponents of a Mosaic origin for the Decalogue therefore no longer reject the possibility that Moses may have proclaimed moral commandments such as those to be found in the Decalogue.   " The moral commandments of the Decalogue ", says one of these opponents,[132] " belong to those basic laws with which even the most primitive of societies cannot dispense."

So the question at issue is now held to be whether Moses could have regarded the moral commandments " as the totality of the basic prescriptions of religion ", and whether he really presented " the *collection* of these commandments as the religious and moral norm par excellence " ; which, however, " would appear improbable and unthinkable in the highest degree, according to the evidence of the sources ".   " The question ", says another critic,[133] " is not whether Moses could have established certain individual religious and moral demands with this content, but whether Moses, taking into consideration all that we otherwise know of his religious attitude, can be believed to have been capable of compressing the basic demands of religiousness and morality in this Decalogue, while excluding from it all the other motives which at the time were of importance in religious and moral life ; whether he can be supposed to have done this with a genius which would find its parallel only in Jesus and which, indeed, would needs have been far greater in the case of Moses, who stands at the beginning of religious development, than in that of Jesus."

What is meant by the words " all that we otherwise know of his religious attitude " in this context is explained as follows : from the material of the most ancient sagas we received quite a different picture of the personality of Moses than that which we must assume in order to comprehend the Decalogue as having been his work. " Moses the sorcerer, the healer, the dispenser of oracles, the Faustian magician is a different figure from the man who summarized the essence of piety and morality in the few lapidary sentences of the Decalogue." But quite irrespective of the basic problem, regarding which it is possible to hold very different views, as to which, namely, are the oldest sagas, and even assuming that in these Moses appears as a thaumaturgist and the like,—what conclusions could be drawn from this ? On the same page of a book, to which the scholar just quoted refers, we first read [134] : " Moses the Faustian magician is an entirely believable figure of the steppes ", and thereafter, " the deeds of the ancient heroes were already felt by their contemporary world as wonders and enchantments, and those heroes themselves may likewise easily have regarded them in the same way." That Moses himself experienced and understood many of his own actual deeds, particularly the decisive ones, as " wonders ", or more correctly as deeds of his God performed through him, is obvious ; which, however, does not transform him into a " Faustian magician ", but if anything into the contrary ; while the idea that he himself regarded anything he did as " sorcery " seems to me to lie beyond all proof. In legend, to be sure, and to some degree even in the legend which blossomed in the minds and memories of those who were present, something of the kind may have taken place—clearly under the influence of Egyptian conceptions [135] ; those people, thirsting for miracle, whose remoulding memory allowed them to remember events as they did not occur and could not have occurred, were prepared to transform God Himself into a sorcerer, and with Him His messenger. The same process was doubtless at work, and very early at that, in the legend of Jesus. It was not enough to glorify his healings ; the legend set him also walking on the sea, giving his commands to the winds and turning water into

wine. Great is the work of the Saga, and as ever it still thrills
our heart [136] ; that, however, should not prevent us from penetrating wherever possible beyond the veil of legend and, as far as
we can, viewing the pure form which it conceals.

In this nothing helps us so much, with Moses as with Jesus and
others, as those utterances which, by use of criteria other than a
general judgment derived from the saga material about the " religious attitude " of a person, may properly be attributed to that
specific man with whom we deal. There is certainly no doubt that
Moses took over archaic rites that were charged with magical
meaning. Yet, as we have seen in the case of the Passover, the
Sabbath and the Blood Covenant, he brought about a fundamental
transformation of meaning in them without in this way depriving
them of any of their vitality ; but rather while rejuvenating this very
vitality by transmuting it from a nature vitality to a historical one.
The change in meaning which he introduced was drawn by him
from the same ground of faith, the same kind and power of faith,
which was given imperishable form in the first three of the Ten
Commandments. It is not hard to understand, when one has at
length touched this ground of faith, that Moses worded these and
specifically these basic demands ; no less but likewise no more ;
and fashioned them into a unity.

An attempt must be made, however, to render the situation
even more clear in its details.

What the critics have been arguing more recently against the
Mosaic origin of the Decalogue refers, as has been said, not to the
content of the individual commandments but to their elevation to
the level of fundamentals of religion ; or, I would prefer to say,
to fundamentals of community life under the rule of God. This
has been demonstrated with particular impressiveness in connection
with the prohibition of statues and images ; nor can we choose
any better example in order to elucidate the actual facts.

One of the most radical of critics has admitted [137] that the
iconoclastic movement in later Israel may with some justification
have referred itself to Moses. As among the ancient Arabs and
in the early days of the Semitic cultures in general, Art does not
appear to have been put to use in the cult practices. We know
that the pre-Islamic Arabs [138] were beginning to convert stones to
images of gods by bringing out a natural resemblance, say to a
human head, with the aid of art. Between this primitive cultural
situation and the later tendencies directed against images of the

god, there lay the essential difference that the primitive Semites regarded their imageless cult as a natural usage, whereas it constituted a programme of reform for the later ones. What is natural would not require to be fixed by any separate or especial commandment. The cult in which absence of images is a principle could therefore, it is claimed, not derive from the days of Moses.

Edvard Lehmann has justly pointed out [139] that it is often difficult to decide whether a cult is imageless because it does not yet require images or because it no longer requires them. But there are historically important constellations in which the appearance of a great personality during the pre-image period anticipates the highest teachings of the post-image period in a simple form that cannot be improved upon.

We must first realize that matters are by no means simple as regards the pre-image stage in Mosaic Israel, if we assume that the latter was under Egyptian influence ; not as regards the belief in some gods or other, but in respect of the custom of making images of the gods believed in. If this was indeed the case, a conflict must necessarily have come about between those who could not or did not wish to break down this influence, and those who wished to eradicate it. If, however, we assume that the unabbreviated wording of the " prohibition of images " is of early date (I mean that, although only verse 4a belongs to the original text, the rest of the verse has been added very early) the prospects continue to expand before us, seeing that in that case we have before us more than a prohibition of images. For that prohibition is followed by a prohibition of the worship of any of the figures that could be perceived in the heavens, on the earth or in the water (" And every figure that . . . and that . . . . and that . . . , bow not down before them and serve them not "). In Egypt the great national gods appeared in the forms of beasts and other natural beings. Hence, once the " other gods " have been excluded in verse 3, there is an implicit prohibition of worshipping YHVH himself in an image or in one of the natural forms.

We penetrate even deeper when we base our viewpoint on what we know of the God of Israel.

Originally He was what has been called a " god of way ",[140] but He differed in character from all the other gods of way. The function of a god of way, who accompanies and protects the wandering nomads and the caravans through the wilderness, was exercised in Mesopotamia by the moon, the god " who opens the way ", and his assistants. In Syria it was the evening star who served this purpose. (Characteristically enough such a god of way of the Nabataeans, whose name meant roughly " He who accompanies the tribe ", was apparently considered by Epiphanius to be the deified Moses.[141]) It is assuredly something more than a mere coincidence that the name of the city of Harran, which together with Ur was the chief city of the moon cult and in which Abraham separated from his clan, meant way or caravan, and would appear to have designated the spot " where the caravans met and from which they started out ".[142] The God by whom Abraham, after " straying away " from Harran, is led in his wanderings, differs from all solar, lunar and stellar divinities, apart from the fact that He guides only Abraham and His own group,[143] by the further fact that He is not regularly visible in the heavens, but only occasionally permits Himself to be seen by His chosen ; whenever and wherever it is His will to do so. This necessarily implies that various natural things and processes are on occasion regarded as manifestations of the God, and that it is impossible to know for certain where or wherein He will next appear.

It may be supposed and is readily understood that among the Hebrew tribes resident in Egypt the guiding function of the ancient clan God had been forgotten. But this clearly is what revives within the spirit of Moses in Midian when he meditates upon the possibility of bringing forth the tribes. The God who meets him wishes to resume His guiding function, but for " His people " now. With His words, " I shall be present howsoever I shall be present ", He describes Himself as the one who is not restricted to any specific manner of manifestation, but permits Himself to be seen from time to time by those He leads and, in order to lead them, to be seen by them after the fashion which He prefers at the given moment.[144]

Thus it can be understood that clouds, and smoke, and fire, and all kinds of visual phenomena are interpreted by Moses as manifestations from which he has to decide as to the further course through the wilderness ; as to the whither and the how. But always, and that is the fundamental characteristic, YHVH remains the invisible One, who only permits Himself to be seen in the flame, in " the very heavens ", in the flash of the lightning. Admittedly anthropomorphic manifestations also alternate with these ; but none of them shows an unequivocally clear-cut figure with which YHVH might be identified.

For this reason He should not be imaged, that is, limited to any one definite form ; nor should He be equated to one or other of the " figures " in Nature, that is, restricted to any one definite manifestation. He is the history God, which He is, only when He is not localized in Nature ; and precisely because He makes use of everything potentially visible in Nature, every kind of natural existence, for His manifestation. The prohibition of " images " and " figures " was absolutely necessary for the establishment of His rule, for the investiture of His absoluteness before all current " other gods ".

No later hour in history required this with such force ; every later period which combated images could do nothing more than renew the ancient demand. What was immediately opposed to the founder-will of Moses makes no difference : whether the memories of the great Egyptian sculptures or the clumsy attempts of the people themselves to create, by means of some slight working of wood or stone, a reliable form in which the Divinity could be taken with them. Moses certainly saw himself as facing a contrary tendency, namely that natural and powerful tendency which can be found in all religions, from the most crude to the most sublime, to reduce the Divinity to a form available for and identifiable by the senses. The fight against this is not a fight against art, which would certainly contrast with the report of Moses' initiative in carving the images of the cherubim ; it is a fight to subdue the revolt of fantasy against faith. This conflict is to be found again, in more or less clear-cut fashion, at the decisive early hours, the plastic hours, of every " founded " religion ; that is, of every religion born from the meeting of a human person and the mystery. Moses more than anybody who followed him in Israel must have established the principle of the " imageless cult ", or more correctly of the imageless presence of the invisible, who permits Himself to be seen.[145]

Thus in the case of the sentence whose antiquity has been the most strongly disputed, we have shown that the roots of these commandments and prohibitions derive from a specific time and situation. However, this leaves open the decisive question as to whether the whole Decalogue as such, as collection and composition, can be explained in terms of this specific time and situation ; whether it can be assumed that Moses separated and unified precisely these phrases as an absolute norm, out of the wealth of existent or nascent sentences regarding the right and the unright, regarding what should be and what should not be ; while excluding all cultic elements.

First we once again meet the argument of " primitivity ", although in attenuated form. It is claimed [146] that at the Mosaic epoch the religion of Israel could not have possessed tendencies such as would have permitted the manifestation of a " catechism ", in which the cult is consciously thrust into the background and the main content of the religion is reduced to purely ethical sentences. An assumption that this could have occurred is said to be based on " a lack of understanding of both the mentality and the civilization of the Mosaic epoch ".[147] The " prelogical " thinking of those times is supposed to have included the primacy of the " sacral system " ; for " in his religion and the practice of his cult primitive man has the means of producing everything that he needs badly ".[148] And in this sense even " the loftiest efflorescence of Egyptian culture " is regarded as primitive.

The use of such a concept of primitivity leads to a questionable simplification of religious history. Religions as complexes of popular practices and traditions are more or less " primitive " at all times and among all peoples. The inner conflict for faith, for the personally experienced reality, is non-primitive in all religions. A religious change, an interior transformation which also alters the structure, never takes place, however, without an internal conflict. Particularly as far as the religion of Israel is concerned, we cannot comprehend its ways and changes at all unless we pay attention to the inner dialectic, to the at various stages and in various forms ever-recurrent struggle for the truth of belief, for revelation.

That this conflict began at the times of Moses, and indeed that he waged the primal fight from which everything subsequent, including the great protests of the prophets against a cult emptied of intention, can find only its starting-point, is proved, even though generally in legendary form, by the great and small stories which tell of the " murmuring ", the rebellion, the insurrection ; and in most of which we recognize or sense the presence of a religious problem in the background. The people wish for a tangible security, they wish to " have " the God, they wish to have Him at their disposal through a sacral system ; and it is this security which Moses cannot and must not grant them.

This, however, should not in any way be taken to mean that Moses had " founded a clear and conscious anti-cultic religion " [149] ; that is, a religion directed against the cult. Nothing is so likely to interfere with a historical cognition, which is one not of categories but of facts, as the introduction of alternatives formulated in so extreme a fashion. There can be no talk here of simple rejection of the cult. It is quite enough to bear in mind, to begin with, that a semi-nomadic life does not encourage a high degree of cult practices and institutions, here in particular there is clearly a very ancient tendency " to place morality above the cult ".[150] Further, it should also be remembered that all those elements which were liable to militate against the exclusive service of YHVH have been eliminated. For what remained there was need of a change not of form, but only of sense and content, in order to satisfy the purpose of Moses. The sacral principle remained ; but the sacral assurance, the sacral power of utilizing the God, was uprooted ; as was demanded by His character and essence. This sacral power was replaced by the consecration of men and things, of times and places, to the One who vouchsafes His presence amid His chosen people, if only the latter persevere in the Royal Covenant.

And why are there no cultic ordinances in the Decalogue ? Why is it that in the domain of cult nothing more is done than the prohibition of the false, not the prescription of the correct deeds ? Why is the prescription of circumcision not to be found ? Why is Sabbath observance required, but not that of the New Moon festival ? Why the Sabbath but not the Passover ? Does not this, for instance, indicate a late origin, seeing that in Exile, far from the Temple, the Sabbath came to be the centre of religious life ?

All these and similar questions taken together mean : why does the Decalogue contain these precise commandments, these and none other, no more and no less ? Why have these been joined together as the norm, and where in those early days could the principle be found in accordance with which the association took place ? Naturally this question also comprehends the analogous questions which arise within the ethical field, such as : Is it possible to suppose that in the time of Moses there could have been a prohibition of " coveting ", which, in contrast to all the other prohibitions, was aimed not at action but at a state of mind ? Or on the other hand, why is there no prohibition of lying ? [151]

It is desirable to offer a single and comprehensive answer to all these questions ; and necessarily that answer will have to deal with both selection and composition. Hence the literary category as such must be a subject of interest. Why should there be a decalogue or anything resembling a decalogue ? Why these ten

commandments and no others ? Why, which in turn means : to
what end ? To what end, and that in turn means : when ?

In order to find an answer we must first disabuse ourselves of
the widely-held view that the Decalogue is a " catechism " which
supplies the essence of the Israelite religion in summary fashion, in
articles of faith that can be counted on the ten fingers, and are
specially " prepared for learning by heart ".[152] If we have to
think of ten fingers, then rather those of the law-giver himself,
who was first a law-finder and who, so to say, sees in his two
hands an image of the completeness requisite ere he raises those
two hands towards the multitude. We miss the essential point if
we understand the Decalogue to be " the catechism of the Hebrews
in the Mosaic period ".[153] A catechism means an instruction for
the person who has to be in a position to demonstrate his full
membership of a religious community on the basis of general
sentences which he recites either in complete or in abbreviated
form. Such a catechism is correspondingly prepared partly in the
third person as a series of statements, and partly in the first as a
series of articles of personal faith.

The soul of the Decalogue, however, is to be found in the word
" Thou ". Here nothing is either stated or confessed ; but orders
are given to the one addressed, to the listener. In distinction to all
catechisms and compositions resembling catechisms, everything
here has reference to that specific hour in which the words were
spoken and heard. It is possible that only the man who wrote
down the words had once had the experience of feeling himself
addressed ; possibly he transmitted that which he heard to his
people not orally, taking the " I " of the god in his own mouth as
though it were his own, but only in written form, preserving the
necessary distance. At all times, in any case, only those persons
really grasped the Decalogue who literally felt it as having been
addressed to them themselves ; only those, that is, who experienced
that first one's state of being addressed as though they themselves
were being addressed. Thanks to its " thou ", the Decalogue
means the preservation of the Divine Voice.

And if we now not any longer formulate the question from the
point of view of literary criticism but in accordance with strictly
historical categories, the Decalogue again shows its difference
in kind, its antithesis in fact to all catechisms. It is both legislation
and promulgation, in the precise historical sense. What this
means is that the intention to be recognized in it refers neither to

articles of faith nor to rules of behaviour, but to the constituting of a community by means of common regulation. This state of affairs has been obscured through the fact that the contents of the single commandments are partly " religious " and partly " ethical ", and that if the single commandments are considered on their own they seem, even in their totality, to be directed towards the religious and ethical life of the individual, and appear to be capable of realization there. Only when the whole Ten Commandments are considered as a whole can it be recognized that no matter how repeatedly the individual alone is addressed, it is nevertheless not the isolated individual who is meant. If the " religious " commandments are taken by themselves and the " ethical " by themselves, it is almost possible to gain the impression that they derived from a culture in which religion and morality have already become separate spheres, each with a special system and a special form of speech. If they are regarded in their connection, it will be observed that there are no such separate fields at all here, but only one as yet undifferentiated common life, which requires a constitution containing " religious " and " ethical " elements in order to achieve a uniform growth.

Here the unifying force has to start from the conception of a divine lord. The disparate material out of which the people develop shapes itself into a closed national form as a result of their common relation to Him. Only as the people of YHVH can Israel come into being and remain in being. The constitution appears not as something objective, to be taken at its own intrinsic value, but as an allocution by Him, a thing which can be actualized only in and through a living relationship with Him. It therefore begins by His designation of Himself as the One who brought forth and liberated Israel addressed ; including each and every person addressed in Israel. God does not wish to speak as the Lord of the world that He is,[a] but as the One who has led them forth from Egypt. He wishes to find recognition in the concrete reality of that historic hour ; it is from that starting-point that the people have to accept His rule.

This calls for and conditions a threefold commandment through a threefold prohibition. First : a commandment of an exclusive relationship of worship by means of the prohibition of other gods " in my face ". Secondly : a commandment of self-dedication to His invisible but nevertheless manifesting presence, by means of a prohibition of all sensory representations. Thirdly : a commandment of faith to His name as the truly " Present One " through

[a] Ex. xix, 5b.

the prohibition of carrying that name over to any kind of
" illusion ",[154] and thus of admitting that any kind whatsoever
of illusive thing can participate in the presence of the Present One.
This, to be sure, prohibits idol-worship, image-worship and magic-
worship. But the essential reason for which they have been
prohibited is the exclusive recognition of the exclusive rule of the
divine lord, the exclusive leadership of the divine leader ; and to
this end it is necessary to recognize Him as He is, and not in the
shape with which people would like to endow Him.

This first part of the Decalogue, which bases the life of the
community on the rule of the Lord, is built up in five phrases,
all beginning " Thou shalt not " (the two phrases, beginning with
"for", appear to be later supplements). If the final verse of the third
section is restored to an original shorter version, it can be seen to
consist likewise of five phrases beginning " Thou shalt not ".
(We therefore, to be precise, have a group of twelve commandments before us.) Between these two groups comes a central
section containing the commandment of the Sabbath and the
commandment to honour parents (in shorter versions), both
commencing with a positive injunction. The first, a " religious "
one, refers back to what went before : the second as " ethical "
refers ahead to those that follow.

Between the two of them, however, there is a connection
other than the purely formal one. The two of them, and only
these two among all of the Ten Commandments, deal with *time*,
articulated time ; the first with the closed succession of weeks in
the year, the second with the open succession of generations in
national duration. Time itself is introduced into the constitutional
foundation of national life by being partly articulated in the lesser
rhythm of the weeks, and partly realized in its given articulation
through the greater rhythm of the generations. The former
requirement is provided for through the repeated " remembering "
of the Sabbath day as that which has been consecrated to YHVH ;
and the latter by the " honouring " of the parents. Both of them
together ensure the continuity of national time ; the never-to-be-
interrupted consecution of consecration, the never-to-be-broken
consecution of tradition.

There is no room here for the mention of special individual
festivals alongside the Sabbath. The Sabbath represents the equal
measure, the regular articulation of the year ; and further, one
which is not simply taken over from Nature, which is not strictly

lunar, but is based on the concept of the regular consecration of every seventh day. It is not the exceptional, not that which has to be done only at certain times and on certain occasions, but that which is of all time, that which is valid at all times, for which alone place must be found in the basic constitution. The cult is not in any way excluded ; but only its general prerequisite postulates, as they are expressed in the first part of the Decalogue, and not its details, have found acceptance here in accordance with the main purpose.

If the first part deals with the *God* of the Community and the second with the *time*, the one-after-the-other of the Community, the third is devoted to the *space*, the with-one-another of the Community in so far as it establishes a norm for the mutual relations between its members. There are four things above all which have to be protected, in order that the Community may stand firm in itself. They are life, marriage, property and social honour. And so the damaging of these four basic goods and basic rights of personal existence is forbidden in the most simple and pregnant of formulas. In the case of the first three the verb does not even possess any object ; as a result of which the impression is given of a comprehensive and absolute prescription.

But these four commandments in themselves are not enough to protect the Community from disorganization, on account of all the kinds of inner conflicts which might break out. They apply only to actions, to the active outcome of passions or feelings of ill-will directed against the personal sphere of other people ; they do not involve attitudes which have not passed into action.

There is one attitude, however, which destroys the inner connection of the Community even when it does not transform itself into actual action ; and which indeed, precisely on account of its passive or semi-passive persistence, may become a consuming disease of a special kind in the body politic. This is the attitude of envy. The prohibition of " covetousness ", no matter whether it was without any object in its original form [155] or read, " do not covet the house—i.e., the content of the personal life in general, household, property, and prestige [a]—of your fellow-man ", is to be understood as a prohibition of envy. The point here is not merely a feeling of the heart but an attitude of one man to another which leads to a decomposition of the very tissues of Society. The third part of the Decalogue can be summarized in its basic

[a] *Cf.* Ex. i, 21.

tendency as : Do not spoil the communal life of Israel at the point upon which you are placed.

Since, as we have seen, it is the will towards inner stability of the Community which determined the selection of commandments and prohibitions, we must, if the Decalogue is ascribed to a later period, necessarily note the absence of some phrase reading more or less as follows : " Do not oppress thy fellow-man ". In a community which was being broken up from within, as we know was the case during the period of the Kings in Israel, by a vast increase of social inequality, by the misuse of the power of property in order to gain possession of smaller properties, by the exploitation of the strength of the economically weaker and dependent ; in a community wherein, generation after generation, rang the great protest of the prophets, no central and authoritative collection of the laws indispensable for the inner strengthening of the community could have been thinkable which did not expressly combat social injustice. It is appropriate to a period in which, to be sure, inequality of property is already to be found ; but in which, taking the whole situation into account, that inequality does not yet lead to any fateful misuses, so that the immediately obvious danger deriving from it is envy and not oppression.

But we can fix the period in question even more precisely. Within the individual clan and even the individual tribe there had always been, as we are also aware from other Semitic peoples, a solidarity which interdicted and directly punished every transgression of a member against the personal sphere of life of another. What was lacking in wandering Israel, fused together of related and unrelated elements, which was joined on its wanderings by other elements, was a sense of solidarity as between the tribes. What Israel needed was the extension of its tribal solidarity to the nation. The members of each separate tribe knew " thou shalt not kill ", " thou shalt not commit adultery ", " thou shalt not steal ", they had them deeply engraved in their consciousness in respect of other members of their own tribe ; an analogous " Israelite " consciousness, however, had hardly begun to come into being. The constituting of a people out of clans and tribes, which Moses undertook, made the expansion of the specific tribal prohibitions to the relations between the components of the people as a whole an unconditional necessity. At no later period was the need so urgent as at this plastic and fateful hour, in which it was necessary to build the " House of Israel " out of unequally suited, unequally cut stones. A wandering into the unknown had begun under the most difficult external circumstances. Before that wandering could be given a destination it was necessary to shape, no matter in how raw and clumsy a fashion, a folk-character which would have the capacity, as a homogeneous being, to follow a road to a destination. This, in turn, indispensably required the proclamation of a basic constitution founded on the principles of unlimited rule of the one God, equable duration of Israel throughout the changes of years and generations, and the inner cohesion of those members of Israel living as contemporaries at any one period.

The situation of Moses has been compared, not unjustly,[156] with that of Hammurabi, who made his code in order to establish a strong unity among all the city communities of his kingdom, despite their many and varied customs and laws. But Hammurabi was the victorious ruler of a firmly established kingdom ; Moses was the leader of an inchoate, stubborn horde during the transition of that horde from a lack of freedom into a problematic freedom.

Admittedly we must not imagine Moses as a planning, selecting and composing legislator directed by certain motives of "biological social necessity" ; for his consciousness as for that of his successors in the work of codification, admittedly, " only the demand of the law was decisive, in order to manifest divine commands that are of absolute authority ".[157] But here we are not justified in attempting to discriminate too precisely between conscious and unconscious processes. Moses can only be understood as deriving from the terrain of an elemental unity between religion and society. He undertook the paradoxical task of leading forth the Hebrew tribes only because he had been possessed, in his direct experience, by the certainty that this was the will of the God who called those tribes His People. He aims at nothing else than to prepare the Community for this God, who has declared that He is ready to be their covenantal Lord ; but, and for that very reason, he must provide Israel with a basic constitution, in order to make Israel united and firm in itself. For him God's dominion over the people and the inner cohesion of the people are only two aspects of the same reality. From out of those words, " I, YHVH, am thy God who brought thee out of the land of Egypt" which flood into his expectant spirit, gush forth all the remaining ones in a stream that is not to be stayed ; and as they gush they gain their strict order and form. To be sure, he is not concerned with the soul of man, he is concerned with Israel ; but he is concerned with Israel for the sake of Yhvh. For this reason all those who came after him in Israel, and were concerned with the soul of man, had to start from his law.

Thus, in so far as any historical conclusions are at all permissible from texts such as those before us, we have to recognize in the Decalogue " the Constitution by which the host of Moses became united with their God and likewise among themselves " [158] ; save that this host should not, as sometimes happens, be understood to be a " religious " union, a " Yahveh League ",[159] a cult association,[160] a " congregation " [161] ; for, despite their deliquescent state, reminiscent as it is of a saturated solution before crystallization, they are a complete society, a people that is coming into being. It is a " unique event in human history " [162] that the decisive process of crystallization in the development of a people should have come about on a religious basis. Irrespective of the importance of the typological view of phenomena in the history of the spirit, the latter, just because it is history, also contains the atypical, the unique in the most precise sense. This is true particularly of the religious document of that crystalloid unification : of the " Decalogue ".

It has been supposed [163] that, in spite of the fact that the original short form to be laid bare within it " contains nothing which speaks against its composition at the time of Moses ", nevertheless " it is impossible to trace it back to Moses himself, because in its literary style every Decalogue is impersonal ". But do we really know so much of " Decalogues " in general that we have to subject this one to a typological view in order to discover what is possible and what is impossible in respect of it ? All other sections of the Pentateuch and other books of the Bible, which it has been the practice to describe as Decalogues, are either loose and, as it were, accidental or else are of indubitably literary origin ; this one alone is fully self-consistent in its nucleus and aims at the mark like a perfect instrument, each word charged with the dynamism of a historical situation. We cannot under any condition regard something of this kind as an " impersonal " piece of writing but, if at all, only as the work of that particular man upon whom it was incumbent to master the situation. May this be a hypothesis, it is undoubtedly the only one which affords us what is requisite : namely, to insert a combination of words found in literature into a sequence of events such as would be possible within history.

A demand is voiced, and quite properly, to ascertain what " position in life " such a text may have had ; which means, more or less, at which celebration it was likely to have been regularly read aloud. Even more important, however, than the question of that which is regularly recurrent, namely, of the reality of the calendar, is that of the first time, that of the reality of innovation. This too can be answered only by hypothesis and assumption ; but it can be answered.

If we attempt to gain the view of a sequence of events from the texts which we have sifted, it is first necessary, despite everything which may appear to speak in its favour, to reject the theory that " the Decalogue was the document on the basis of which the Covenant was made ".[164] The concept of the document in the making of the Covenant appears to me to be secondary, and to have derived from the fact that the Covenant was misunderstood at a later period as the conclusion of a contract. In any case, however, the Decalogue has the Covenant not as its subject, but as a prerequisite condition.

In a message which must underlie our Eagle Speech, but which cannot be reconstructed from it, Moses brings to his rank and file, as he had already brought to the elders, YHVH's offer to establish the *berith*, which would unite both of them, the God and the human host, into a living community ; in which YHVH would be the *melek* and Israel His *mamlakah*, His regal retinue, YHVH would be the owner and Israel the especial personal property chosen by Him, YHVH would be the hallowing leader and Israel the *goy* hallowed by Him, the national body made holy through Him. These are concepts which I take out of the version before us, but which must already have been either contained or latent in an undifferentiated form in the original source, if the latter was to fulfil its function.

The host accepts the offer ; and in the blood rite which had already begun earlier, and wherein the two partners share in the identical living substance, the Covenant by which YHVH becomes " *melek* in Yeshurun " [a] is concluded. The process is completed in the contemplation of the heavens and the holy meal. This might be the proper place for a report of the representative to those represented, in which the motto " Israel " was given out and taken up ; a report that has not come down to us. What now has to follow sooner or later is the proclamation of the *melek* YHVH. It is this which seems to me to be preserved in the " Decalogue " as restored

[a] Deut. xxxiii, 5.

to its original nucleus. Here YHVH tells the tribes united in
" Israel " what has to be done and what left undone by them as
Israel, and by each individual person in Israel (an induction into
such a new and exclusive relationship will consist, naturally, for
the greater part, in a prohibition of that which must henceforward
be left undone) ; in order that a people, the people of YHVH
which has to come into being, should come into being. In order
that it should really become His people it must really become a
people ; and vice versa. The instruction to this is the Ten Commandments.

Whether this proclamation was made immediately after the
conclusion of the Covenant or only in the course of the " many
days " [a] of the sojourning at the oasis of Kadesh is a question that
may be left open. It seems to me, on the other hand, as already
said, more likely both from the introduction to the passage
commencing " I ", as well as from the prose-like structure of the
sentences, that the manifestation took place in written form. That
it was written down on two tables is a tradition which is worthy
of belief. Tables or stelæ with laws ascribed to the divinity, are
known to us both from Babylon and from early Greece ; as against
which there is not a single historical analogy,[165] to the best of my
knowledge, for the frequently-assumed imaginary transformation
of stone fetishes, thought to have been kept in the Ark, into tablets
of the law. It may well be conceived that the tablets on which
Moses wrote in truly " lapidary " sentences the basic constitution
given by YHVH to His people " in order to instruct them " [166] were
erected and again and again inspected and read out ; until the
departure from that spot made it necessary to place them in the
Ark.

The story of the tables as told in the book of Exodus consists of
a series of tremendous scenes, which have always aroused the fervent
emotions of believing hearts. Moses summoned to the summit of
the mountain in order to receive the tables which YHVH Himself
has written for the instruction of the children of Israel [b] ; Moses
ascending into God's cloud and remaining there for forty days
and forty nights [c] ; Moses receiving from God the " Tablets of
the Testimony " written by His finger [d] ; Moses on the way down
from the mountain becoming aware of the " unbridled " people,
and in flaming fury flinging the tables away from his hands, so
that they smash below on the mountain-side [e] ; Moses, at the

---

[a] Deut. i, 46. [b] Ex. xxiv, 12. [c] *Ibid.*, 18. [d] Ex. xxxi, 18. [e] Ex. xxxii, 19.

command of YHVH, hewing two fresh tables from the stone
"like the first", in order that God may write upon them again
and again ascending the mountain with them [a] ; Moses with the
tables in his hand receiving from the mouth of the God who
"passes him by" the revelation of God's qualities [b] ; Moses again
standing forty days and forty nights on the mountain without
food and drink and writing on the tables "the words of the
covenant, the ten words" ; he and not YHVH, although YHVH
had promised him to do this Himself, and hence, from the viewpoint and for the purpose of the redactor, who considered that the
two passages were mutually reconcilable, functioning as the
writing finger of YHVH [c] ; and Moses going down with the new
tables, the skin of his face radiant from his contact with God, and
he himself unaware of it.[d]

If we wish to keep before us a sequence of events possible in
our human world, we must renounce all such tremendous scenes.
Nothing remains for us except the image, capable of being seen
only in the barest outline and shading, of the man who withdraws
to the loneliness of God's mountain in order, far from the people
and overshadowed by God's cloud, to write God's law for the
people. To this end he has hewn stelæ out of the stone for himself.
It must be stone and not papyrus. For the hard stone is called to
testify, to serve as a witness. It sees what there is to see, it hears
what there is to hear ; and it testifies thereto, makes present and
contemporary for all coming generations that which it has to see
and hear ; the stone outlasts the decaying eyes and ears, and goes
on speaking. In the same way Moses, before the Covenant was
made, had erected twelve memorial stones—such as men making
covenants were accustomed to erect [e]—for the twelve tribes which
were to become Israel at that hour.

Now, however, he goes further. After all, there is one means
of placing a more comprehensive, clearer, verbally dependable
witness upon the stone. That is the wondrous means of writing,
which for early Israel was still surrounded by the mystery of its
origin, by the breath of God, who makes a gift of it to men. By
means of it one can embody in the stone what has been revealed
to one ; so that it is no longer simply an event, the making of the
Covenant, but also, word by word, it continues to serve as evidence
of a revelation, of the law of the King. What Moses says may be

[a] Ex. xxxiv, 1, 4.   [b] Ibid., 5-7.   [c] Ibid., 28.
[d] Ibid., 29.   [e] Gen. xxxi, 45 ff.

clumsy, but not what he writes ; that is suitable for his time and for the later times in which the stone will testify.

And so he writes on the tables what has been introduced to his senses, in order that Israel may come about ; and he writes it fittingly, as a finger of God. And the tables remain as " tables of testimony " or " tables of making present ",[a] [167] whose function it is to make present unto the generations of Israel forever what had once become word ; that is, to set it before them as something spoken to them in this very hour. It may well be assumed, although there is no tradition extant to this effect, that in the days before Samuel the tables were taken out of the Ark at extraordinary moments and elevated before the people, as had once been done in the wilderness, in order to restore them to the situation in which they had been at Sinai. Reports about this may have been destroyed after the Tables were placed in the Holy of Holies of Solomon's Temple together with the Ark, which was now deprived of its mobile character [b] ; obviously in order that they might become immovable themselves, and no longer serve as the occasionally reviving original witnesses, but should remain nothing more than relics of dead stone.

And at an unknown hour they pass out of our ken. The Word alone endures.

[a] Ex. xxxii, 15.   [b] 1 Kin. viii, 9.

THE ZEALOUS GOD

FOR reasons both of style and of content I have accepted the view that the original Decalogue was not so long as that which we now possess, and that it was largely constructed in succinct imperative sentences ; which, however, does not in any way mean that an origin in the days of Moses must be denied to all elements which can be separated out after this fashion. This applies in particular to the sentence, so generally discussed at all times, of the " Jealous God ".[a]   With the possible exception of the last two words (" and who keep my commandments "), which tend to disturb the parallelism of the structure, this has so archaic a stamp that certain of the protagonists of the " Original Decalogue " [169] have held that it ought to be transposed to the commencement of the Decalogue in place of the present introductory verse.   Yet the introductory verse, the nuclear passage of the Revelation is so " unmistakably ancient " [170] that it will not do merely to remove it from the place which alone is suitable to it.

The situation is different as regards the verse of the Jealous God. This likewise obviously fits into an early connection but not necessarily here, in a passage which, in its nature as proclamation of the God as God of the Covenant, with whom the people have just entered into a community of life, does not require any threat of punishment at this particular point.   On the other hand, it seems to me that there is an inner association between this and certain other laws, which also point more or less to the period of Moses but are not included in the Decalogue.

" I YHVH thy God am a jealous God, ordaining the iniquity of the fathers upon the sons unto the third and fourth generation of those that hate me, but doing mercy to the thousandth generation of those that love me."   Two of the elements of the sentence, the characterization of the God as a jealous one and the differentiation between those that hate him and those that love him, are again to be found in similar form in passages which should be regarded as effects and applications of this.   A distinction between the foes of YHVH, who are marked for downfall, and those that love him, who ascend in their course like the rising sun, is drawn with the

[a] Ex. xx, 5b-6.

141

strongest urge of fighting faith at the close of the Song of Deborah.[a]
" Foes " in this Song clearly means not merely the foes of Israel,
who are for that reason the foes of Israel's divine leader and commander, but also those within the people itself who at the hour of
battle refrained from coming to the aid of Yhvh, and who are
therefore provided with a curse [b] ; " lovers " are those who
unconditionally adhere to Yhvh and follow him, those devoting
themselves to Him of their own free will.[c] It is of great importance
that this expression of personal feeling is chosen as the designation
of the following of the God ; and this applies equally to the
Decalogue sentence by which, it seems to me, the song has been
influenced.[171] The guilty ones have to bear the burden of their
guilt as a load extending beyond their own person if they are
haters of God ; they are faced by the lovers, over whom the flood
of mercy pours forth, reaching far beyond them in distant waves.

But what kind of guilt is it that is spoken of here ? According
to the context of the Decalogue idolatry and the like are meant ;
and this view seems to be confirmed by the introduction to Goethe's
" Cultic Decalogue ",[d] where the jealousy of Yhvh stands in relation to the worship of another god. But the same association is
also found in the report of the historic assembly at Shechem,
in a verse [e] which there is no adequate reason for regarding as
later than its context. It is clear that in these two passages the
thing about which God is jealous is exclusive devotion to Him,
the rejection of the demands of all other gods. This, however,
does not in any way mean of necessity that the sentence in the
Decalogue, considered on its own intrinsic merits, bears the identical
meaning. We must therefore now consult it by itself.

Our question must naturally refer to the precise sense of those
much discussed words : " Ordaining the sins of the fathers upon
the children unto the third and fourth generation ". The verb
paqad, which I render by " ordaining " or " co-ordinating ",
originally means " to arrange ", then " to set in order ", " to fix
an order ", " to restore order ". The order between heaven and
earth, disturbed by guilt, is restored by the punishment. That
this should take place " unto the third and fourth generation ",
can only mean, since there is no reason to assume any arbitrary
introduction of the figures, the precise number of generations or
direct lineal successors which a man living to a ripe old age is likely
to see gathered round him. This in turn can be understood in

[a] Jud. v, 31.　[b] Ibid., 23.　[c] Ibid., 2.　[d] Ex. xxxiv, 14.　[e] Josh. xxiv, 19.

two different ways : either that the guilty one sees how the consequences of his guilt work themselves out on his grand-children or
great-grand-children, or else that his punishment comes to affect
those of his descendants who are then alive.   The passage in the
Decalogue itself does not tell us which of the two possible interpretations is correct ; and so we must extend our inquiry to other
passages, which may stand in some inner connection with it.

When we consider the undoubtedly early laws of the Pentateuch,
with the exception of the Decalogue, which deal with the punishment of transgression, we find that there are very few, only two
to be precise, in which the divine speaker does not rest satisfied
with prescribing for the tribunals a punishment fitting the guilt,
but offers a prospect of His own vengeful intervention.   Both of
them [a] refer to transgressions of a " social " nature, to an injustice
committed against one's fellow-man and which is of such a kind
that it is not amenable to human justice.   Both divide themselves
sharply from their contexts by the force of language and rhythm,
which does not recur in any other of the single laws to be found in
the so-called " Book of the Covenant ".   Further, none of the
collections of Ancient Oriental laws with which those of the Bible
have been compared offer any kind of analogy to this singularly
exalted tone, nor to this kind of divine warning of an expiation of
guilt brought about from on high.   Most of the modern commentators think of re-working and interpolation when trying to
account for this.   To me, however, it seems, despite a certain
syntactical clumsiness, that the two laws are both cast in the same
mould ; and it correspondingly seems to me that the small group
to which they both belong is part of the oldest stratum of Mosaic
legislation, i.e. " Words of YHVH ",[172] sayings " which appeal
to the conscience and the sense of responsibility before the com-
pelling God ".

The first of the two laws forbids the oppression of any widow
or orphan : " For if he cries, cries unto me, I shall hear, hear his
cry, and my wrath will flame, and I shall slay you with the sword,
and your wives shall be widows and your children orphans ".
The unjust Community, the Community containing both those
who behave thus and those who tolerate such behaviour, is visited
by war ; and the offspring living at the time will be affected by
the death of the fathers.   The second law holds out the prospect
of the same divine hearing of the outcry of the oppressed, if the

[a] Ex. xxii, 21-22, 25-26.

right of pledging is subjected to abuse ; and behind it as well a judging intervention of the God is to be understood. Both laws have a character which can be described, alike in content and tone, as none other than proto-prophetic. The small group of four laws to which they belong leaves me with the impression that they must be the sole remaining vestige of a longer series, in which more succinct commandments, such as verses 20 and 24, may have alternated with expanded ones such as the two under consideration here. And I could well imagine that the series was introduced by the Decalogue sentence of the "jealous" God, and that it possibly ended with the phrase which now serves as the close of the small group : " For I am a gracious one ".

It may admittedly be argued that the adjective here can mean only "jealous" in the usual sense, as is shown by the usage of the verb deriving from the same root. But the pertinent noun is not infrequently used to characterize the zeal of the fighter ; and that is what is meant here. YHVH zealously fights His "haters" ; and these are not only the people who have other gods "in His face ", but also those who break up the society founded and led by Him, through their injustice to their fellow-men. The "religious" and the "social", the exclusive service of YHVH and the just faith between men, without which Israel cannot become Israel, cannot become the people of YHVH, are closely connected.

I have indicated that social inequality in the midst of the people of Israel at the time of Moses had not extended so far that such a commandment as "Thou shalt not oppress thy fellow-man" required to be inserted in the basic constitution. At the same time there certainly must already have been such a quantity of oppression in the wandering host that the dangers involved therein had to be counteracted by single specific laws, which surrounded and completed that central massif. Such single laws were not written on tables, but possibly on a scroll ; and presumably not on one single occasion, but, in the course of time, in connection with particular happenings, which called for the promulgation of new laws of this kind in order to combat the evil. All this is no more than conjecture, and will probably never become more than conjecture. Yet, in our vision, we see this man Moses at times, following some new and wearing experience with his people, entering the leader's tent, sitting down on the ground and for a long time weighing in his soul whatever may have befallen ; until at length the new comprehension rises to the surface and the new word oppresses his throat; till it finally darts across into the muscles of his hand, permitting a new utterance of the Zealous God to come into being on the scroll.

The effect of the association of this jealousy or zealousness until late times with the " social " laws can be seen from the example of a commandment at the beginning of the " Book of the Covenant "ᵃ, the commandment to liberate the " Hebrew " slave in the seventh year.   This law, it is known, shows some resemblance to one in the Code of Hammurabi, which specifies liberation as early as the fourth year ; though only of those enslaved for debt. The important difference between the two codes lies in the fact that in Israelite law the decision is left to the will of the slave, who, if he refuses to be liberated, has the lobe of his ear pierced as a sign of life-long slavery. (This procedure cannot but remind one of another law in the Hammurabi Code, according to which that particular slave who denies his owner with the words " You are not my lord " has an ear cut off, whereas, in Israel, the slave is marked with the degrading sign because of his having renounced liberty.)

Here the differentiating characteristic is not the practical mildness but the basic recognition of personal freedom of choice.   In Babylonian law the slave, foreign as well as indigenous, is a " chattel " [173] ; the Hebrew slave, in Israelite law, is a person. There the relationship is unilateral, while here it is mutual.

The Hethite slave law also shows a noteworthy humanity. What distinguishes the law of Israel in essence from it is the close relationship between the religious and the social element.   Since Israel is the " peculiar property " of Yʜvʜ, no person in Israel can be, properly speaking, the slave of any other person in Israel.[174] All belong to the God, and are therefore free to make their own decisions.

This basic feeling, to which " it is impossible to find a parallel within the old Oriental circle ",[175] is spirit of Moses's spirit, no matter when the presumably archaic law may have found its actual formulation.   And we are also presumably justified in ascribing to the man by whom the Sabbath was inaugurated the initiative for extending the Sabbatical manner of thought into the cycle of the years ; in which, as in the days, six units of work and dependence have to be followed by one unit of liberation.   Once

ᵃ Ex. xxi, 2 ff.

in history, shortly before the fall of the Kingdom,[a] the king and
the princes in Judah understood a military disaster as being due to
the non-fulfilment of a particular commandment.   It was not a
cult law, but that commanding the liberation of the slaves, which
they recognized as having been the cause of YHVH's zeal against
the beleaguered Jerusalem.

[a] Jer. xxxiv, 8 ff.

THE BULL AND THE ARK

THE Biblical narrative relates that while Moses remained on the mountain to hear the injunction of God and to receive the Tablets from Him, the people, despairing of his return, demanded that Aaron should fashion them gods (*elohim*) to go before them. They greet the image of a young bull made by Aaron with the cry : " These are thy gods, O Israel, who brought thee out of the Land of Egypt ". They offer up sacrifices and celebrate a festival, apparently orgiastic in character. Coming down the mountain, Moses sees the bull and the dances ; and in an upsurge of fury he flings from his hands the tables written by God, so that they shatter. Reaching the camp, he summons to him all those who have remained true to YHVH ; and these, who belong chiefly to his own tribe of Levi, go forth with the sword at his behest " from gate to gate ", and reduce all resistance.

In the Book of Kings it is told [a] that after the division of the Kingdom, Jeroboam, the elected king of the northern tribes, established a separate cult in order that the people should no longer make pilgrimages to Jerusalem at the annual festival. He resolves to erect young bulls of gold at the ancient cult centres of Bethel and Dan, and shows them to the people with the words : " These are thy Elohim, O Israel, who brought thee out of the Land of Egypt " ; and as priests for them he appoints outsiders, " who were not of the Levites ".

The conform wording of the two tales, and particularly of the two sacral proclamations, is striking ; and it is impossible to avoid the question of the relation between them. It is generally assumed that the tale of the backsliding of Jeroboam is the older, and that the story of the " Golden Calf " came into existence under its influence. But a comparison of the two contexts and of the situation implicit in them would rather appear to show the opposite. The sacral cry rings strangely in the mouth of Jeroboam. He wishes to establish a rival to the Jerusalem Ark ; but since the latter has been withdrawn into the Temple it is regarded no longer as the symbol of the wandering and leading God, but of the One who protects the holy city by His presence ; whereas on Sinai, naturally enough, all the thoughts of the people revolved round

[a] I Kin. xii, 26 ff.

their previous and future guidance through the desert.   And while
the plural " thy *elohim* " is surprising in Jeroboam's mouth,[176] its
use as an utterance of the people in connection with their heathenish
demand reminds us of the way in which Abraham speaks of his
God to the prince of the Philistines,[a] as well as the way in which
the Philistines speak of the Ark of this God.[b]   It fits with greater
ease into the early period.

In addition, the fact that motifs so unpleasant for the hierarchy
of the Jerusalem Temple as Aaron's share in the responsibility and
the breaking of the first Tablets were accepted by the redactors
speaks for their antiquity and traditional character.[177].   Hence it is
most probable that the undoubtedly tendentious description of the
" sin of Jeroboam " was influenced by the generally familiar tale
of the " Calf " ; or more correctly the former description put to
use what was already to be found in the latter.   The author has
Jeroboam making defiant use of the words which, according to
the tradition, the people cried out in their hour of greatest wrong-
doing.

In the historical reality Jeroboam would certainly not have
thought of setting himself against the divine law which had been
handed down.   When he made his young bulls of gold he did not
think of representations of YHVH, and assuredly did not have
images of any other God in mind.   His " golden calves " were
intended to be an improvement on the brazen oxen which carried
the basin in Solomon's Temple, and simultaneously to fulfil the
function of the Ark and serve as a throne for the invisible YHVH.
Underlying these as much as the Ark, although in a grosser form,[178]
is the idea, which is quite familiar in the history of religion, " that
a divine or demonic guest is given an occasion to be corporeally
present through the allocation of an empty seat ".[179]   The bull is
chosen as bearer of the God because popular Semitic phantasy has
been deeply impressed by him through stone images of the fourth
millennium [180] (from the district round that Harran out of which
Abraham journeyed to Canaan) and then particularly through
Hittite art,[181] he being the holy animal on whose back the Weather
God stood.   So it can be understood that Elijah did not speak
against the " Calves ", nor did Jehu do away with them[c] ; and
what Hosea alleges against them in supercilious and mocking
fashion is clearly due to the fact that the common people, as may
easily be conceived, did not know how to differentiate for any

[a] Gen. xx, 13.   [b] I Sam. iv, 8.   [c] II Kin. x, 29.

length of time between a god-bearer and a representation of the God Himself, and kissed the pedestal [a] " as though it were the God himself ".[182] The narrative of the Book of Kings transfers this attitude to the intention of Jeroboam, which is sometimes [b] treated as idolatry. The spiritual leaders, however, were awake to this danger even earlier. It has justly been observed [183] that the Prophets, who so gladly compare YHVH with the lion, very carefully avoid any use of the bull as a metaphor for this purpose. The reason for this can be found not in the images at Bethel and Dan, but in the fashion after which the people tended to comprehend them. Similar tendencies, finding expression in more elementary forms, can be assumed to have been already present in the early days.

Nothing of the Court literature of Jeroboam and his dynasty has come down to us. " Together with the calves of Dan and Bethel, what was sung about them has sunk out of knowledge, expunged from the collections of the holy songs of old." [184] But it may well be assumed that in the Northern Kingdom the tradition of the image of the bull on Sinai assumed a form which justified the animal carrier instead of the Ark, and also permitted a stand to be taken against the " people-slaying " Levites, without in any way affecting the reverence requisite towards Moses. All that was necessary was to relate, on the one hand, that part of the people had gone beyond the original intention, and on the other, that the Levites abused the orders which they had received.

But what is the position as regards the nucleus of fact that lies behind the tradition ? Is it possible to find any traces of such a nucleus at all here, in this passage which is apparently the most difficult in the Pentateuch when regarded from the textual and literary viewpoint ? The basic question with which we must start is that of the period at which the " Ark of the Covenant " came into being, and the reasons for bringing it into being.

The view that the Ark is of Mosaic origin is once again being accepted. Between Moses and Samuel, in whose early days we already find the Ark in the full light of history despite the fact that the narrative of its capture [c] contains legendary elements, no other period can be thought of in which this, the greatest symbol in the Israelite faith, can have been introduced. It is " a genuine migrating sanctuary ".[185] Archæological and ethnological findings have confirmed its period.[186] That it was not entirely analogous to those related utensils which have been discovered may possibly be explained on the assumption [187] " that the technically un-educated wanderers imitated such vessels without equipping them in accordance with their basic principles, as required by arch-æology ". Here too, I personally prefer to leave room for the initiative of the man who can be believed to have had the ability to change both the form and the sense of a symbol already to be found in the world of the Ancient Orient.

The much discussed alternative of an empty throne of God, as we repeatedly find it in the history of religion,[188] or a box, is not a proper one, as thrones of God in box form are not uncommon.[189] Nor do we need to question the authenticity of the tradition regarding the contents,[a] as there is no lack of reports describing the placing of documents that are holy, or to be hallowed, at the feet of the divinity. What is important is the synthetic function by which these elements are brought together and join in a unity with which another was combined, namely, the Palladium which can be carried like a litter, just as we know it from the war expeditions of Bedouin tribes.[190] It is precisely this synthetic function which, in a very specific fashion, induces us to look around for a person who would have been capable of exercising it, and also for a situation of such a kind as would lead the person in question to do so—that would, indeed, awaken the specific synthetic function within him. The elements out of which such a synthesis can come into being are always present in the history of religion ; in order that it should come into being, however, a person must be postulated who, by virtue of his knowledge and thinking, is capable of seeing the elements together ; and a moment has to be postulated which compels him, because of its peremptory needs, to associate those elements in a fresh organic form. We now find that we can formulate the question as follows : was there a moment in the life of Moses which drove him overpoweringly to unite and mould the elements familiar to him from extended observation and knowledge of tradition, and to make some new formation out of them ?

For the host, which has to advance without any knowledge of the way into the " great and fearful wilderness ", [b] the problem of guidance occupies the centre of the relations to the God, which have been renewed for them through the extraordinary man who has taken them in his charge. He has brought them an assurance

[a] 1 Kin. viii, 9.   [b] Deut. i, 19.

from this God, namely, that He wishes to lead and protect them ; indeed, he has taught them that such constant assistance, such a capacity for remaining present with those chosen by Him, is an attribute of this Being and is indicated in His name. But the constant and uniformly functioning oracle to which they had looked forward has not been provided for them. At their stations on the way the extraordinary man used to wait for some kind of sign or other, coming out of the mist or from somewhere else, before he ordered them to commence their journey afresh. They never knew what might happen at the next moment ; they could never depend on being able to rest next day in a pleasant oasis in order to recover from the hardships of the journey. He said, to be sure, did that man, that God goes before them and that He makes His presence known by one or another sign ; but the sole firm and unshakable fact was, in the last resort, that the God could not be seen ; and all said and done you cannot actually follow something which you cannot see. All said and done, it is only the man who is followed, and they can all see how often he is uncertain, when he withdraws himself into his tent and broods for hours and days on end, until he finally comes forth and says that what has to be done shall be done in this and this way.

What kind of guidance is this, after all ? And does it not mean that there must be something not quite in order between him and the God, if he cannot produce the God ? He says, to be sure, that the God is not to be seen ; that in spite of His being present it is impossible to get a sight of Him—but what can that mean ? If you have a God, then to be sure you can naturally see Him as well ; you have an image and His strength is in that image. To be sure, it is whispered (the Decalogue, it has to be remembered, has not yet been proclaimed) that the man declares no image should be made of the God ; but that is just sheer nonsense, after all. As long as you have no proper image you will have no proper guidance. And now, to cap it all, the man has vanished completely. He said that he is going aloft to the God up there, when we need the God down here just where we are ; but he has not come back, and it must be supposed that that God of his has made away with him, since something or other between them was clearly not as it should have been. What are we to do now ? We have to take matters into our own hands. An image has to be made, and then the power of the God will enter the image and there will be proper guidance.

That was the way talk must have gone in the camp. People growl, they dispute, they vociferate. The representatives appointed by Moses intervene. Action is taken against them. In vain does Aaron seek to act as go-between. A riot begins.

For riot it must have been. If it then reached the point of making the " calf" we cannot ascertain from the report, which is vague and improbable in its technical details. It is possible that motifs have been transferred here from what Hosea castigates as the first great national sin, the goings-on at Baal Peor,[a] when the people, already within the magic circle of Canaanite culture and sexual rites, engaged in holy promiscuity with the Moabite women. Nevertheless the sacral proclamation, " these are thy *Elohim*, O Israel, who brought thee out of the land of Egypt ", which apparently derives from an early tradition, would seem to indicate that the situation arose at Sinai itself. It is therefore permissible to assume the erection of a clumsy image of a bull under Aaron's mediation and assistance ; admittedly without being in a position to say by which of the ancient Oriental religions it is likely to have been influenced. For this, naturally, a more primitive religious stage than that of the bull of Jeroboam must be assumed ; a stage at which it was believed that the power of the God took up its abode in the mighty creature and worked through it. The wording of the sacral proclamation is in accord with this.

However that may be, there must certainly have been a riot. There is no other way by which it is possible to understand that the effect on the inimical Bedouin tribes of the district was described as a derisive whispering [b] ; bull worship and orgies were not very likely to have made such an impression on them. An indication of this also seems to have been retained in the ancient verses, reminiscent as they are of vestiges of a primitive ballad, which Moses and Joshua exchange when they hear the noise made by the people.[c] Joshua says : " Noise of war is in the camp." Moses replies first : " No noise of voices (*anoth*) of victory, no noise of voices (*anoth*) of defeat " ; and then adds a phrase out of which the art of Hebrew punctuation (which turned " *anoth*" into " *annoth*") has brought forth the following meaning : I hear the sound of singing alternatively, which would indicate the mirth of feasting. An uninitiated reader of the unpunctuated text, however, would have to understand : " the sound of voices I hear ", and would, necessarily and with obvious justice, assume that a word has been

[a] Num. xxv.   [b] Ex. xxxii, 25.   [c] *Ibid.* 17 f.

omitted. Here the context indicates a word with the meaning of riot.[191]

The behaviour of Moses in the camp, underlying which there seems to be a historical nucleus, points in the same direction. He places himself in the gateway of the camp and calls : " Whoever belongs to YHVH come to me ! ", thus showing his conviction that what happened was directed against YHVH; which would not be quite suitable to the erection of an animal image to represent YHVH, particularly prior to the proclamation of the Decalogue. Then the revolt is suppressed by force of arms at the order of Moses, in a bloody battle regarding which the important fact is that the split clearly runs right across the tribe of Levi ; since Moses praises those Levites who remain faithful [a] because they did not spare either sons or brothers.[192] The riot seems to have developed into an internal fight between the Levites, which now reaches its decisive stage.

Once the catastrophe is at an end, however, what had befallen overwhelms Moses, as we may well suppose, even more than at the moment of the first upgush of fury. Since it may be assumed that the archaic passage on the tent,[b] which stands here by itself, chronologically belongs to this particular point, it shows us a scene of melancholy clarity. Moses takes " the tent ", his leader tent,[c] [193] which has hitherto stood in the midst of the camp, and sets it " for himself" outside the camp, where it always has to be set thereafter at the stations of the way ; but no longer as a human leader's tent. He calls it the " tent of meeting " or " tent of coming together " ; and that is what it has to be, no longer devoted to anything other than the audiences granted him by his Lord. Henceforward he can no longer enter the tent in the midst of the camp, as he had presumably been accustomed to do ; he can no longer seat himself upon the ground and wait for that which we call inspiration—an abstract word, which has become almost too familiar, yet from which the original vivid sense of a wafting-in of the divine breath has not yet passed away.

As before, Moses' own place remains in the camp of " Israel " ; there he belongs now as previously ; but he can no longer expect his God to come and visit him in a place that has been polluted. If he wishes to question YHVH thereafter, he must leave the camp, he must go out to the tent that is guarded by Joshua the most faithful one ; and the people, shaken and changed by that which

[a] Ex. xxxii, 29.   [b] Ex. xxxiii, 7-11.   [c] Cf. Ex. xviii, 7.

has befallen them, reverently watch him from time to time, each man standing at the entry to his own tent. He does not prohibit any of the people who wish to do so from coming to God about any matter ; they may approach the holy tent as they were wont to do, in order that counsel, instruction, decision might come to them from thence. But these are individuals ; YHVH no longer has any contact with the people as such.

That is the basic feeling of Moses after the catastrophe. But his feeling does not remain like that. It is rectified for him by a new experience of God.

Behind the ingeniously constructed [194] conversations with God, which have had so great an effect on the view taken by later generations of Moses' relations with God, we feel a reality that has been lived through. We have to regard it as a reality that Moses, after having been zealous for his zealous God, entreats Him not to forsake the people whom He has brought hither " upon eagles' wings ", now that they have been unfaithful to the newly-concluded Covenant ; but that He should go on leading them. And further it is an unmistakably genuine biographical characteristic that while Moses is in " the cleft of the rock ",[a] which the narrator assumes to be a familiar spot (presumably because [b] it is near the place of the revelation at the Burning Bush), he, Moses, begs for the grace of the One who once addressed him from the flame, and is overwhelmed by a new experience of God. Its central content appears to be found in the words of YHVH [195] which in the text, admittedly, precede the entry of Moses into the cleft, and which combine with and complete the previous " I shall be present howsoever I shall be present " : " I shall be gracious unto whom I shall be gracious and I shall be compassionate unto whom I shall be compassionate ".[c]

Here it should be observed that whereas the first of the two verbs, indeed, gives expression to the superior favour of the Lord, the root used in the second has, in its noun form, the meaning of " mother's womb ", thus pointing at the intimate nearness of the God. Moses had once learned two things in one at this spot : that YHVH is present with His own, yet cannot be bound to any one fashion of manifestation. And likewise he now learns two things in one : of the graciousness and mercifulness of YHVH, which are named [d] as His essential attributes, and of His liberty to show those attributes of His to whomsoever He wishes to show them. ·This word of God, however, is preceded [a] (although in a section possibly independent of this one) by one which sounds as though it were an immediate application of the other to the situation : " So my face is to go with ?   Shall I then cause you to rest ? " And only following that comes Moses' urgent, " If·thy face does not go with, do not bring us up from here ! " [b], and then [c] the divine consent to the request.

It is important, in the sequence of texts which we find before us, that YHVH first has compassion and thereafter says that He is the compassionate One.   The authenticity of this sequence, its conformity, that is, to experience, is incomparably more important than all the literary and critical issues which have been raised in connection with it.   Whoever it was that wrote the one passage down, and whoever it was who wrote the other, they both together, if there were two of them, have with the aid of the redactor brought something to biographically consistent record which could only be experienced and not contrived.   We know of no one in the history of Israel other than Moses to whom this basic experience can be attributed ; and in his life we know of no other moment for it than that of this crisis.

But the narrative reports that after Moses received the consent he turned to YHVH with a fresh request [d] : " May my Lord go in our midst " !   It is clearly not sufficient for him that God's " face " goes with.   How should this be understood ? [196] That God's " face " goes with means, since Moses has just been told that whoever sees it must die,[e] that YHVH goes ahead of the people in order to overthrow foes who meet them on the way [f] ; for which reason Moses also talks in this connection [g] of the impression on the world.   And this meaning still echoes in the Deuteronomic review,[h] where it is stated that YHVH had led the people out of Egypt " with His face ".   It should also be borne in mind how He had looked upon the Egyptian camp at the Red Sea, and *through that looking* had prepared its downfall.[i] At the tent YHVH *talks* to Moses " face to face " [k] ; but when His face moves with the tent which has been removed and set before the camp, and the deadly gaze meets the approaching foe, absolute protection has been provided for the people.

[a] Ex. xxxiii, 14.   [b] *Ibid.*, 15.   [c] *Ibid.*, 17.   [d] Ex. xxxiv, 9.
[e] Ex. xxxiii, 20, 23.   [f] *Cf.* Num. x, 35.   [g] Ex. xxiii, 16.
[h] Deut. iv, 37.   [i] Ex. xiv, 24.   [k] Ex. xxxiii, 11.

Moses permits himself to go even further. His last request is
that YHVH should not grant Israel merely His external protection
but fuller forgiveness, that He should also grant them His accompanying presence within the camp [a] ; that He should not merely
guide them through the wilderness but should also secure them
inner guidance to support and safety. By this he aims at something
greater than the mere restoration of the relationship which had
existed before the straying. He does not merely wish to be permitted to bring the tent back into the camp ; he requests a journey-
ing in the midst of the people, a closeness manifested in all ways
and in all needs ; yet which nevertheless should not have any
destructive effect.[b] YHVH's answer to the request is missing in
our text, for the verse following cannot be understood as a response.
Yet even from this fragmentary text it is possible for us to re-
construct a biographical reality ; and one which at the same time
constitutes a reality in the realm of the history of faith. For at
precisely this point comes the establishment of the " Ark of the
Covenant ", which is capable of providing the exact earthly basis
of realization for which Moses had asked. If this establishment was
preceded by a great praying experience, as the narrator sets out to
describe it, then it must have included the granting of the final
request.

The establishment by Moses of the Ark of YHVH is not described.
The late literary information about its erection [e] at the beginning
of the divine instructions for the building of the " Tabernacle "
i.e., the other, unhistorical tent, naturally cannot fill this gap ;
although the description of this " idealized model of a tent sanctuary
which actually once existed " [197] certainly includes some old
tradition within it. The conversations with God supply us with
part of what has been left out, insofar as they mirror afresh those
inner conditions which had been prerequisite. No matter how
much the generation passing on the tradition, and the authors who
wrote it down, may have reshaped the reality that once was lived
through, we are nevertheless given another glimpse into that
moment in the life of Moses which overwhelmingly drove him to
unite and mould the elements available to him from extended
observation and knowledge into a new formation ; empty God-
throne, shrine for documents, and portable Palladium. It was
necessary to give the people legitimately, that is, in a fashion
corresponding to the character of YHVH, that which they had

[a] Ex. xxxiv, 9.   [b] Cf. Ex. xxxiii, 3.   [e] Ex. xxv, 10 ff.

wished to fashion illegitimately ; that is, after a fashion running counter to the character of YHVH. They had to be given the utensil which would represent and warrant the presence of their invisible leader.   The Royal Covenant is followed by the building of the Throne.

We have no reliable reports as to the original appearance of the Ark.   If, as it seems to me may be assumed, the cherubim were already part of it, then we have to distinguish between them as the actual seat of the throne and the shrine as the foot-stool of the throne ; as was expressly done later for the Ark introduced into the temple of Solomon.[a]   The heavenly beings have flown down, so to say, in order to prepare for YHVH the seat of the throne on which He descends when He desires ; for this, the fact that He sometimes descends thereon, is what is meant by the descriptive term " Who is seated upon the cherubim ",[198] the original presence of which in the old narrative text where it is found [b] we have no adequate grounds for doubting.[199]

The King does not always sit on the throne ; He seats Himself upon it when He wishes His function as ruler to become manifest to the senses.   Then he places His feet upon the shrine in which His proclamation to Israel is preserved in stony witness.   The objectified word of the constitution is repeatedly overshadowed afresh by the invisible presence of its first speaker ; and as at the time of the Psalmist [c] so in the days of Moses, the people may well have prostrated themselves at the " stool of His feet ".[200]

That " certain technical skill " necessary for the preparation of such a sacral object can be assumed " more easily among the Canaanites than among the Hebrew tribes in the wilderness " [201] is indisputable.   The question, however, should not be so framed as to ask where the making of the Ark is " more probable ",[202] but whether its coming about in the wilderness is historically possible. In an undoubtedly early text we read [d] : " And when the Ark began moving Moses said : ' Arise O YHVH and scatter Thy foes, so that Thy haters may flee before Thy face ! ' " Here it is our scientific duty to ascertain whether the purport of this text can historically be reliable ; for wherever this prerequisite is satisfied, a text has the right to be regarded until further notice as historical compared with a hypothesis which does not find support in any text whatsoever.   If an authentic literary document like this points to

[a] Ezek. xliii, 7.   [b] 1 Sam. iv, 4 ; 11 Sam. vi, 2.   [c] Ps. xcix, 5 ; cxxxii, 7.
[d] Num. x, 35.

a specific historical situation as that in which a sacral institution of such power was born, it is a basic law of methodology not to permit the " firm letter " to be broken down by any general hypothesis based on the comparative history of culture ; as long as what is said in that text is historically possible.   That it is possible, however, is no longer a matter of doubt, now that the concept of the absolute "primitivity" of wandering Israel has been outgrown.[203]

The Royal Covenant is followed by the building of the throne. Moses and the representatives of Israel saw the footstool of the One who sat invisibly enthroned over the mountain, and it was " a work of sapphire tiles " ; now, out of the simple material available to him, he prepares a simply-joined Ark for YHVH to rest His feet upon when He visits the people chosen by Him in order to lead them in their wanderings and in battle.   Over it, and possibly fashioned in the shape of yonder cloud-forms made radiant by the rising sun, rise the cherubim, in order that their Lord should take His place to ride upon their horizontally-extended wings, which touch one another.[204]

This should, of course, not be understood to mean that the Ark is " a representation of the heavens as the cosmic throne " of YHVH,[205] which in turn would mean that Babylon is the country in which the cherubim originate.[206]   The name certainly points to Babylon, and naturally, notwithstanding the spontaneity of intention, similar forms from ancient Oriental plastic art, Egyptian to be sure rather than Babylonian as far as can be judged on the basis of the material known to us, may have been the subject of imitation. But although, as I suppose, the Ark has borrowed one or another motif from the heavenly vision of the elders, it does not in any way pretend to be a representation of the heavenly Throne.   In its purpose it is a meagre and necessarily dissimilar earthly substitute for it.   And YHVH who, when visiting His people, takes His seat upon it does so not as Cosmic King but as the *Melek* of Israel.   The Babylonian divine thrones are nature symbols, that of Israel is a history symbol ; and the tablets with the " I " of the God who has led the people out of Egypt are an inseparable part of it.   Only in the period of the State, when the theo-political realism succumbed to the influence of the dynastic principle and the Kingdom of YHVH was transfigured and subtilized into a cosmic one lacking all direct binding force, did the nature symbolism prevail ; since the aim then was to abstract living history from the domain of the Kingdom of God.

We do not know why the designation "throne" for the Ark was avoided.[207] But we are entitled to assume that it was felt necessary to maintain the association of the tablets of the constitution as the basis of the Covenant, the expression and sign of which is the Divine Presence. For this reason it was necessary to keep the shrine character of the utensil clearly in consciousness. The throne was the inspiring and the shrine the obligating part. Without the constant counter-balance of the shrine the throne might easily have given the people a false security ; as we repeatedly hear in later times out of the mouths of the prophets.

We have seen that the Biblical sequence of time is the correct one for the three decisive moments of the removal of the tent from the camp, the great praying experience and the conception of the Ark. When did Moses place the Ark in the tent ? When he brought the tent back into the camp. And when did he bring it back ? When the Ark was there.[208] For the Ark is the assenting response of God to the person praying.

If we wish to allocate a category from the history of religion to the resting tent in which the Ark stands—each of them separately and both of them jointly an "expression of God's local unboundedness "[209]—we have to think of those tents of divinities travelling with the armies which we know within the Semitic civilization in the cases of the Assyrians, the Carthaginians and the Arabs. That the God does not reside within the sanctuary, but manifests himself in it or on it, reminds us of the difference [210] between residential and manifestation temples in Babylon. Despite all this the unjustly questioned early association of the tent and the Ark finds its singularity in the fact that what appears above or in the sanctuary is not a cult image but the Invisible One.

In Babylon the god dwelt invisibly in his chamber, provided with bed and table, within the residential temple, and was visible in the manifestation temple in the form of an image. In Israel he had nothing more than a manifestation temple and no image and, without any image, His presence was directly and immediately experienced.

The foundation of this great Sacrum, like the foundation of all great symbols and sacraments in the history of religion, came about as the realization of a paradox : an invisible God is sensed by the fact that He comes and goes, descends and rises. The view that YHVH was imagined as residing above the Ark or actually in it misses the sense of this singular reality of faith. The effect of the

Ark symbol was clearly so great that the movement of the God was virtually sensed as a corporeal thing ; so that the invisible God was Himself apprehended. This is more than a continuous abiding ; it is an ever-renewed coming, appearing, being present and accompanying. For the promise once developed from the name of the God that he would " be there " from time to time, and always at the moment when His presence was necessary, there is no more adequate material substratum to be thought of than this. What the old wandering God of the Mesopotamian steppe means when He says to David *a* [211] that He has gone about until this day " in tent and dwelling-chamber " and that He does not demand anything else, is not merely a simple state of being carried about ; it is this coming and accompanying and disappearing and returning.

The belief in the concentration from time to time of the Divine Presence must, to be sure, have been transferred in the popular mind to the Ark and the tent themselves ; yet every such " coarsening of concept " [212] can lead, through the counter-movement of the spirit which it calls forth, to a new deepening of the conception ; a deepening which admittedly also contains within itself the danger of abstraction ; that is, of a reduction in the awareness of vivid reality. The hour of establishing a great symbol is apparently the only one in which spirit and sensuous presentation maintain their balance. Nevertheless, when Jeremiah or one of his disciples *b*,[213] shortly after the Burning of the Temple, prophesies a time at which the Ark of the Covenant will no longer be remembered, since then the whole of Jerusalem will be called the Throne of YHVH, we should recognize this as being a development of the original intention of the foundation ; for if the whole human world has become the Kingdom of God, then Jerusalem as its midst should be His Throne ; as once the Ark was Israel's wandering centre when YHVH became King of the people.

In Canaan the tent and the Ark appear to have been long separated from one another, not only during the exile of the Ark but also after its restoration through David *c* ; until, as reported *d*, they were both brought to the Temple under Solomon, but were obviously not united. The Ark is placed within the Holy of Holies ; of the tent we hear nothing more. However, we should not, with our historical comprehension of faith, regard as separated what was associated in the hour of foundation. The Ark, bearing the invisible and silent but effective Divine Presence,[214] went

a II Sam. vii, 6.   *b* Jer. iii, 16 f.   *c* II Chron. i, 3 f.   *d* I Kin. viii, 4.

ahead in the wanderings and campaigns ; to the tent sheltering it at quiet times within the camp came the Presence, invisible as the voice which talks to Moses—in early texts out of the dark of the " Pillar of Cloud ", [a] and in later texts " from between the two *cherubim* " [b]—yet visible to the people (this is told, to be sure, only in narratives that are of late literary origin) as the radiation of the Divine substance, as the *kabod* ; whether it be in the cloud lit up by the red of morning [215] or in the sheet-lightning [216] flashing incessantly near or far across the night sky ; but always visibly directed towards or pointing to the tent.

It came to show and to warn, to arbitrate and to judge. Both of them, Ark and tent, belong to each other as the symbol of the double function of the *Melek* : that of leading His people through and defending them in an inimical world, and that of directing them through all the inner obstacles towards " holiness ".

[a] Ex. xxxiii, 9.   [b] Num. vii, 89.

THE SPIRIT

WHILE the narrative portion of the Book of Exodus is constructed in two large epic sequences, the story of the Exodus and the story of the Revelation, the narrative section of the Book of Numbers consists of single incidents loosely grouped round a doubtful itinerary. Two kinds of story appear to have been selected and redacted out of what seems to have been no more than fragmentary material : those which were necessary in order to record the important stages of the further wanderings, and those which seemed suitable for bringing out the character of Moses and the relation between him and his environment. The latter include the stories of the descent of the Spirit upon the elders, and of the revolt of Aaron and Miriam.

Since it is held that prophecy, with the spirit of which these narratives are imbued, did not develop prior to the days of Samuel or even later under the influence of Canaanite ecstaticism, the summary view [217] that those strata of the Moses Saga in which we meet the prophetic element must all be secondary can well be understood. This approach to the development of prophecy in Israel, however, is contradicted by the fact that of the two elements of " possession by Spirit " and " seeing hidden things " which have fused together therein, the former is in no way limited to the Syro-Phœnician cultural world. Indeed, it is also met with among the Arabs, whose ancient poets spoke " words of daemonic possession " [218] ; whose ascetics used to fling their clothes off their body in their ecstasy like Saul [219] ; among whom even to-day the " knowing ones " of the genuine Bedouin tribes have themselves inspired by music like Elisha,[220] while the simpletons, who are regarded as " temporary residences " of the good spirits, run through the streets of the villages vaticinating like the *nebiim*.[221]

The second element is already quite familiar to us in the early Arabic culture. I mean those " seers ", called " masters of the mysteries " by certain modern Bedouin tribes,[222] who in the hour of vision cover their faces and speak of themselves not as I but as Thou, " because they speak not in their own name but in the name of the spirits which address them ".[223] In which connection it should, however, be noted that they also prefer to describe such " hearing " as " seeing ".[224]

The first of these two elements exerted a decisive influence in Israel on the development of the ecstatic bands of *nebiim*, as we know them in particular from times of crisis such as that of Samuel ; and it influenced individual prophecy in Israel thereafter with a varying degree of force. The second, an element found fairly equally in the Old Arab and early Israelite cultures, seems to derive from a common root, out of which it developed in differing fashions.[225]

The historical Moses should be considered against the background of such early developments. It may be asked with which of these two elements he should be associated, how far his personal character can be understood on this basis, and how far that character stands out from it. These questions refer to two comparisons ; one with Israelite ecstasy and the other with Israelite seership.

The two comparisons already seem to have been of importance for the authors and redactors of the book out of which evolved the Book of Numbers. This interest showed itself most strongly in the shaping of the story of the descent of the Spirit on the elders (comparison with collective ecstasy) and the story of the revolt of Aaron and Miriam (comparison with seership). An associated interest, that of comparison with extra-Israelite seership, was satisfied by the inclusion in the Book of Numbers of the folk-book of Balaam ; apparently, however, without having led to any reworking of the latter in the sense of comparison.

Hence it is incumbent upon us to test these stories in order not only to see how the conceptions of later prophetic circles regarding the person and personality of Moses find expression here, but also how far these conceptions correspond with the historical image of Moses which we are able to win ; that is, whether they merely constitute attempts to provide " a nebiist touching-up of the Moses image ",[226] or whether we ought rather to consider them as revealing some vestiges of the oldest conception of the workings of Spirit and of Vision of God in Israel.[227]

The story of the descent of the Spirit upon the Elders [a] lies before us in a singular fusion with the story of the gift of the quails. It has not merely been grafted on to this tale, which was clearly originally connected with that of the manna,[228] but has actually grown into union with it ; in such a way, however, that the separate branchings of both can still be distinguished.

[a] Num. xi.

On the way from the Wilderness of Sinai to the Wilderness of Paran the people are infected by the desire of the " rabble " who had joined them at the Exodus, and " weep " again because they remember the good food which was so plentiful in Egypt that it was given to be eaten " for nothing ".

Moses complains to YHVH that he cannot give the people the meat which they demand ; and with this he connects the general complaint that the burden of " this people " is too heavy for him. In His reply God tells Moses to bring together seventy men of the elders at the Tent of Meeting, that He, God, would " set apart " of the *ruah* that is upon Moses, and would lay it upon them, in order that they may help him in bearing the burden of the people. And again He links this with the promise to the people that they would receive meat to eat until they were sick of it. Now both things are fulfilled. The *ruah* descends upon the elders and compels them to ecstatic cries and movements ; but the uniqueness of the occasion is stressed, for " they did not do it anymore ".[a] And after this there again comes a *ruah*, a wind that is, from YHVH, which drives quails in from the sea.

To begin with, it is the antithesis of flesh and spirit which had led to the interweaving of the two successions of events. The twofold process takes place on the two levels of being. The antithesis current among the prophets between the earthly " flesh " and the heavenly " spirit "[b] is intended to find its expression in this. It is supplemented by the double meaning of the word *ruah*,[229] which, just like *pneuma* and *spiritus*, originally meant the afflation, the wafting, the wafting from heaven, the wafting of wind and the wafting of spirit ; which are associated for primitive man because he feels and comprehends the enthusiasm which overwhelms him, the overpowering working within him of the spirit, as the stormy breath of a superhuman power which has penetrated into him ; and as with himself, so with others. The Biblical authors draw from this double sense all that it can offer ; from the lofty pathos of the beginning of the story of the Creation, where the *ruah* of God, wafting of the wind and wafting of the Spirit that are still together in their pristine unity, hovers above the first waters ; until the bitter mockery of the prophet[c] who speaks of the *ruah*, that is the spirit of the wind which enters into the mouths of the " false prophets " talking to the kings, and which turns them into so many windbags. In thus fusing the

[a] Num. xi, 25.   [b] Is. xxxi, 3.   [c] 1 Kin. xxii, 21 ff.

stories of the quails and the elders the purpose was to make the reader feel that both, the working in Nature and the working in the soul of human beings, are the one work from on high ; and are indeed, in the last resort, the identical work from on high.

At the same time, however, a clear distinction is drawn in respect of the gifts of the spirit. The *ruah* " is " over Moses ; on the " Seventy " [a] it comes to rest, leads to extraordinary but temporary behaviour on their part ; and the fact that they have once experienced this condition, this stirring up and perception of all the forces, thereafter enables them to help Moses in " bearing " the people. Moses himself does not require to undergo any such process ; he to whom the Voice has spoken, as one person to another, has become the carrier of the Spirit, of a resting and constant spirit without any violent effects ; a spirit which is nothing other than an assumption into a dialogic relationship with the Divinity, into the colloquy. As against this, the *ruah* which takes possession of the elders is an impersonal, wordless force, and if they do " speak " under its influence, what can be grasped from them [230] is certainly not the group of words that transmits a meaning, a message or a command.

The spiritual experience of the elders corresponds in every way to the workings of the *ruah* of which we learn in the period following the Conquest of Palestine, from the first great " Judges " until the commencement of the Kingdom [231] ; and which is found with most clarity in the case of Saul. On one single occasion the spirit descends upon the charismatic one and turns him into " another man ", endowing him with special powers for his office.

It is not a subsequent interpretation of history which finds expression here. It is the character of the historical period itself, of the particular one which begins with Moses. Moses, of course, appears as raised above the " Judges " and their spiritual experience ; and that also should be understood as a recognition of a historical truth seen from the perspective of faith. For Mission is greater than induction into office, even that of commander in a war of liberation, as in the cases of the Judges and of Saul. The Mission takes place above the sphere of the impersonal *ruah* ; it takes place in the sphere of the Word.[232]

It has justly been remarked that the pre-exilic prophets whose writings have reached us do not treat the ecstatic experience, with which they were quite familiar, as of the same rank as the Word ; [233]

[a] The selection already to be found in Ex. xxiv, 1, 9.

that they mostly refer to it only in passing or not at all ; in fact, they prefer to avoid the concept of *ruah* and almost always characterize the word entering into them as the source of their speech. However, it should likewise not be left without remark [234] that the Divine Word itself needs to be understood as having the character of a power which works in and through the people to whom it turns. This second sort of effect, it is true, appears to be broken and restricted through the human substance ; a fact which finds strong expression in the complaint of Moses. At Sinai, when God had forgiven the people at Moses' urgent entreaty, He had said to the latter [a] that he, Moses, had found favour in His, God's, eyes. Now [b] Moses reminds God of this [c] in an unusual, indirect fashion, by speaking as though God had not said anything of the kind to him at all, while at the same time making use of the same words : " Why have I not found favour in your eyes, that you put the burden of all these people upon me " ! He is unable to bear it " on his bosom " ; it is too heavy for him.

These are words which, in their relevancy to a precise situation, may really be thought of as constituting part of an actual prayer by Moses. The truth is that they continue the personal objections which he had offered when his mission was announced to him at the Burning Bush. When he had then asked " Who am I " ? YHVH had answered : " Indeed I shall be present with thee " ; and after that He had been present with him in the struggle against Pharaoh. Now, however, when it is necessary to " carry " this " heavy " people, God leaves it to him alone ! In reply God shows him that He is " present " internally as well.

As the emissary of YHVH Moses is contrasted with, and elevated above, the elders who have been possessed by the *ruah* of YHVH. But the narrator does not wish this superiority to be understood as something desired by Moses himself, who was " very humble ", [d] but as the fate with which he has been charged by God and which oppresses him. He tells an episode [e] regarding two men who remained amid the tents of the camp instead of " going forth " to the Tent of Meeting, which stood in the midst of the circle ; and who were possessed by the Spirit where they stood. Joshua, now mentioned for the first time since the conversation at the descent from Sinai as conversing with Moses,

---

[a] Ex. xxxiii, 18.

[b] This part of Numbers xi may well be derived from the same author or else has been influenced by him.

[c] Num. xi, 11.   [d] Num. xii, 3.   [e] Num. xi, 26 ff.

wishes the latter to "withhold" the presumptuous fellows. Moses, however, disapproves of his "zeal" on his behalf; if only, says he, the whole people were nebiim! It is worthy of remark that he does not make use of the verb employed in the previous account, and stating that those possessed by the Spirit "behaved themselves like prophets", that is, expressed themselves in ecstatic fashion like the bands of nebiim : but instead he employs the substantive itself. Hence what he means is not a transitory state but the summons in virtue of which a man has immediate contact with Godhead and receives its behest directly.

By saying this, Moses only reiterates in another basic fashion and as a wish what YHVH had commanded to Israel in the Eagle speech : that they should become a royal retinue of kohanim, of direct and immediate bondsmen of their Melek. This is not the speech of a period " in which the institution of nabi was already in a state of deliquescence " [235] ; but rather " the hope that at some time the Spirit might be shared by all was already in existence at an early day ".[236] This hope, which is reminiscent to us of " eschatological thought ", is admittedly not Mosaic in the strict sense ; but it may be ascribed to the after-effects of Moses' spirit. The narrator extracts these words from the situation with great art and wisdom. For when the whole people have become nebiim, in direct contact with God, it would no longer be necessary for somebody to be charged by God with the function of bearing them on his bosom like an infant.

Moses is subjected to comparison with the seers of Israel in the following section, reworked but old at core, which tells how Miriam and Aaron " talk against Moses ", and are summoned by YHVH to the tent, where they are reproached by Him. Miriam, who obviously took the leading part in the revolt (it seems to me that this particular point does not belong to the reworking) is also punished by a skin eruption, which is later healed at Moses' entreaty ; whereas Aaron, the forefather of the priesthood, departs without punishment here as in the story of the " Golden Calf ". The reason for the " talk against Moses " is his wife, who is described here for some reason not clear to us [237] as a Kushite, which in general would mean Ethiopian woman. That Miriam and Aaron now begin to worry about her is presumably to be explained [238] by the fact that in the original sequence this passage may have been directly preceded by the visit of Jethro, who brought back the wife and children of Moses.

That Miriam takes the lead would seem to indicate that this is a family affair. The Biblical statement that Aaron and Miriam were Moses' brother and sister (or possibly half-brother and half-sister by another mother) may well be correct, despite the various doubts which have been expressed. It has been assumed with probable justice [239] that Moses derived from an old Hebrew family of "seers"; we know analogous facts from other cultures, particularly from that of the Arabs.[240] What the brother and sister reproach Moses with is doubtless conditioned not by a general tendency to keep the blood pure, but by the concept that continuation of the gift of seership in the clan would be unfavourably affected by the alien element; a concept which would permit certain motifs in the stories of the patriarchs to become clear, if the persons of the "fathers" are regarded as historical, and as recipients of revelation and heads of religious communities.[241]

Only through this can it be understood that when YHVH speaks to the two rebels he talks not of Zipporah but only of Moses. The purpose is to elevate Moses above all seership. With his gifts and works he is not a member of a clan possessed of a hereditary *charisma*, but remains entirely a person; the person sent by God, the personal bearer of a personal, one-time office. He is YHVH's servant or bondsman, who is "entrusted with His whole house"; and so he has to administer Israel as God's people and kingdom, as His "peculiar possession".[242]

The rhythmic divine speech is left vague at certain decisive points. If here, as in so many similar cases, there is an ingenious play of words, it should be understood in the sense that God makes Himself known to the prophets "in vision" but to Moses "visually and not in riddles". They have visions which must first be interpreted; but he is shown God's purpose in the visible reality itself. To them God speaks "in dream", but to Moses "from mouth to mouth"; by which, apparently, relationship is expressed [243] still more intimate than that conveyed by the phrase "face to face" [a]; the word is blown into the man as from a breath, it "inspires" itself into him.

Most difficult is the description of the exceptional position of Moses in the final statement that he looks on "the appearance of YHVH". Here it seems to me that the stress should be laid upon the word translated "look on", which is never used of prophetic vision. Only of Moses had it already been told [b] that he did not

[a] Ex. xxxiii, 11.   [b] Ex. iii, 6.

dare " to look towards God ". Moses does not see or look at a divine form, but he looks on the appearance of Yhvh—in every thing in which it can possibly be looked on ; and that is what we repeatedly meet with regarding him in the story of the revelations, from the appearance which addressed him out of the flame but which was no semblance separated or separable from that flame, till the seeing of the " back " of God, which was a seeing of the *kabod*, of the radiation of Yhvh " in the cloud ".[a]

If commentators on God's speech to Aaron and Miriam are of the opinion [244] that even strictly historical consideration would have to deal with a primacy on the part of Moses, " admittedly while rejecting any arrogation to him of an entirely different kind of revelation", this can be assented to for the time being. Nevertheless we should not regard the speech of God as though it were a free composition aiming at the glorification of Moses. Behind this speech, it seems to me, is concealed some reminiscence, albeit a faded one, of the man who recognized his God, the God who is present at every time in the way in which He is present—who recognized Him in his natural appearances " visually ", and who experienced His word as breathed into his innermost self. That is classically Israelite in character, but is none the less unique in its purity and strength. And even if we were not to read anything about it, we would still have to postulate an experience of the kind as underlying such words and such a deed.

The folk-book of the Aramaic soothsayer Balaam, whose native country was presumably the Aramaic Hauran,[245] appears to be fused together from ancient and more recent songs and narratives, the oldest of which seem to date from the time of the Judges and the latest from the time of the great Israelite kingdom. Its fixed nucleus would originally appear to have been only the two first verse utterances, which used to be included by the popular bard in a prose version freely constructed by him [246] ; the rest was a gradual accretion. The basic attitude is expressed in the first two utterances and the older part of the second utterance [b] [247] ; " For there is no augury in Jacob and no divination in Israel : in time it is said to Jacob and Israel what work God has in hand ". He who utters this as high praise sets out himself to practise augury [c] and receives his fee as a divinator.[d] [248]

[a] Ex. xxxiii, 18, 23 ; xxxiv, 5. [b] Num. xxiii, 23.

[c] Num. xxiv, 1. [d] Num. xxii, 7.

There is an obvious tendency in this contrasting of the concepts that have passed from the verses into the narrative. At first Balaam is the image of a genuine *nabi*. The spirit of God comes upon him, Yнvн " meets him " and " places utterance in his mouth.[249] But he engages in divination and augury, and Yнvн has him say that in Israel, in God's people, neither is to be found ; neither is needed there, because God, at the right moment, informs His people through the man whom He sends them, of the meaning of the given situation, of that work which He, God, now has in hand, and what He demands thenceforward from Israel ; and that is precisely what Israel needs to know, no less and no more.

Balaam is not sent ; God makes use of him, but does not commission him. Balaam is an individual who has the gift of an Art, but who has not been summoned to a Work. He is not the leader of a people ; he has no people to whom he is required to state the meaning of any given situations. For that reason he engages in divination and augury ; and so a rift comes about in his *nabi* function, and deprives the latter of its essence. The true *nabi* scarcely ever presages a fixed, unchangeable future ; he announces a present that requires human choice and decision, as a present in which the future is being prepared. Balaam is far from the sphere of human decisions, which means that he is far from the sphere of divine commandment. Yнvн puts the utterance into him, but has no personal contact with him and does not reveal His commanding will to him, except in so far as He instructs him as to what he should say and what he should not say.

In his words [a] Balaam praises Israel because Yнvн their God is with them ; and by this the poet once again takes up the old motif of the Annunciation to Moses, the motif of the meaning of God's name. But he, Balaam, does not know this kind of presence on the part of God. He continues : " and the shout of acclaim for the *melek* is within him " ; by which the poet means the event which always recurs in the camp of Israel, even in his own time ; the jubilation of the people round the tent of their divine leader. Yet Balaam can know even this, the kingship of God, only from without. To be sure, he expresses the personal wish at the end of his first utterance [b] to die the death of these " upright " or " straight " ones. Yet the life of the people who " dwells alone " must remain alien to him in its essence. Close as he may come to

[a] Num. xxiii, 21.　　　　　　[b] Ibid., 10.

Israel in his utterances, it is inaccessible to his divinatory and augurial character.

What Israel is it that the poet has in mind? From whence does he derive his acquaintance with an Israel which knows no trouble and no misery,^a and which does not want to have anything to do with magic and divination? His purpose is not adequately grasped by a reference to " idealization ". He doubtless aims at a tradition. What he has in mind cannot be anything other than Moses' idea of Israel. Moses had wished for such an Israel, he had desired life, marriage and property to be secure, and envy to be eradicated among the people; and he had directed his sense of mission and his utterance of the will of God against magic and mantic practices.

Moses is not named or mentioned in the folk-book of Balaam. But he, who feels himself called to tell Israel in time what work God has in hand, is the unseen opponent of the soothsayer and interpreter of omens. True, the Balaam story, as we have it, " reaches its peak in the meaningful blessings predicting and indeed effecting the happy future of Israel, and which therefore must have been genuine; that is to say, effected, from the Israelite standpoint, by YHVH ".[250] But in addition to this the narrator is certainly very much concerned to show that, by these blessings from the mouth of the heathen, the unsouled *nabi*, YHVH confirms what has been founded by His true emissary. Here, too, in the enthusiasm for the jubilation of the King in the camp of Israel, which is placed in the mouth of the stranger, the purpose which has set its stamp on the Eagle Speech is still effective.

^a Num. xxiii, 21.

THE LAND

ACCORDING to the account in the Book of Numbers [a] and the parallel narrative in the Book of Deuteronomy,[b] Moses sends spies from Kadesh to Canaan. They bring back good and bad tidings. Shaken by the unfavourable part of the reports, the people lament, speak of appointing themselves a new head and returning to Egypt; those who offer them opposition are in danger of being stoned. At this point YHVH intervenes; He wishes to destroy the people, and to let the offspring of Moses serve for the making of a fresh one. Moses intercedes and wins forgiveness for them, but the sinful generation is condemned to perish in the wilderness; "forty years" must pass ere Israel enters Canaan.

Now the people suddenly resolve to depart for Canaan at once. Against the will of Moses and without the Ark of the Covenant, they make a sortie against the Amalekites and Canaanites living in the mountains, and are defeated.

It is scarcely possible to win any historical core of fact out of the narrative; save that the Amalekites, who had been compelled to relinquish Kadesh to the incursors, had united themselves with the neighbouring tribes and prevented further advances, for an entire generation as it would seem. Yet the story seems to hold an implication that Kadesh, where Israel obviously stayed for a long time, was the station at which the people became directly aware of Canaan as the goal of their wanderings.

Here Kadesh should not be understood as meaning a single spot, but the entire group of level valleys lying south of Palestine on the way between Akaba and Beersheba, which link up with the place of that name; valleys surrounded by hills, where springs gush forth, so that sometimes the water bursts from the clefts and crannies of the rocks. The land is rich in water and fruitful for the greater part; here and there, indeed, of a "paradisical fruitfulness".[251] To this day the soil, which is several feet deep, still provides the Arabs who till it with rich harvests of grain when there has been a good rainy season.[252] The district has noteworthy remains of Syro-Canaanite culture, dating from the second half of the second millenium B.C., including a fortress which is supposed [253]

[a] Num. xiii, xiv.   [b] Deut. i, 22-46.

to have been already standing when Moses and his hosts came there ; and the presence of which makes it possible to explain the Biblical description of Kadesh as a " town " or fortified place.[a]

The people may have fixed on this spot, which was so suitable for the purpose, as the centre of their movements ; where, presumably on the Midianite model,[254] Moses remained with the Ark and the armed Levite guard, while the tribes swarmed forth. The fruitful soil was tilled, as had already been done by the " Fathers ",[b] with primitive but productive methods ; and the herds were driven to pasture in the neighbourhood.[255] The Hebrews had returned not only " to the place of the Fathers "[256] but also to their form of life.

But is the urge to Canaan to be attributed, as some think, to the fact that the rapid increase of the people made it necessary to find more room ? Or was Kadesh regarded from the very beginning as no more than a station, the prolonged sojourning in which was an outcome of the historical circumstances ? Is the promise to Moses of a " good broad land "[c] to be explained as due to a later shaping of the Exodus tradition, or ought we to understand it as an essential motive in Moses' own actions ? When Moses departed from Egypt, did he wish only to liberate the tribes ? Or did he wish to lead them to settle as well ? Was the memory of the Canaan of the Fathers at work in him as a hope and aspiration ? In the religious field he had sought and found, in a passionately remembered past, the basis of the future which he wished to build. Was this equally true in the field of actual history ?

In our own times critical investigation is once again beginning to recognize [257] that " the element of the promising of the land in the legends of the Fathers is not in itself a free creation of the Yahvist, a predating, perchance, of the needs of the tradition of the Occupation of the Land, but belongs to old and indeed to the oldest traditions ". In other words : it will not do to view the stories of the Fathers as no more than a pseudo-historical justification of the claim to Canaan.[258] It has been emphatically pointed out [259] that the Fathers owed their position in the Israelite traditional sagas primarily to their function as recipients of revelation, and at the same time to the relations of the divinities revealing themselves to them " to genealogically confirmed associations, to clans and tribes "[260] ; as well as to the fact that this type of religion contained within itself " a tendency to the social and the historical ",

[a] Num. xx, 16.   [b] Gen. xxvi, 12.   [c] Ex. iii, 8.

which "corresponds to the conditions of life in nomadic tribes ".[261]

But from the fact that each of the Fathers has a separate designation for the God who revealed Himself to him—Shield of Abraham, Fear of Isaac, Paladin of Jacob—it would be quite wrong to conclude that three different gods are meant. He who receives a tradition from the father or the inaugurator regarding the latter's God will certainly identify the God who appears to himself with the God of that tradition ; yet at the same time he will give expression to the fact of his own immediate and personal relationship, which is so basically important for him and his circle, by employing some fresh appellative. " Isaac recognizes the God of Abraham, who, however, was also his, Isaac's, own God, in a peculiar fashion deriving from his own personal biography ; and so forth."[262]

If that is so, we must ascertain in how far it is still possible for us to examine the texts available to us with regard to a common concrete content of that revelation ; and further, a content which contains an implicit trend towards the social and historical. We are entitled to regard the promising of the Land as such a content. These men announce that a God has led them hither in order that they, like some herald in the name of the king, may proclaim His name over the holy cities of this land, as a sign that He is about to come in order to claim them as having been his own from the beginning, and to take possession of them.[a] [263] That God promises them in specific connection with this that he wishes to " give " it to their offspring as the community of those who confess Him and serve Him. This is actually, as far as I can see, something so pregnant as to be without parallel in the history of religion ; yet there is a primal lushness and freshness about it, such as cannot be synthesized in the laboratories of tendentious literature.

And it is very understandable historically that such a revelation continues to exert an effect. As we saw in considering the duologue at the Burning Bush, no distinction can be drawn between the " God of the Fathers " and the One who revealed Himself to Moses. Aye, the identity of the two, and with that identity the fulfilment of the ancient promise, cannot be imagined or supposed save together with the tremendous meaning of this revelation for Moses, which sets his personal activity into motion. Moses discovers himself as the agent and carrier of this fulfilment. It is of necessity part of the message which he brings to the people.

[a] Gen. xii, 8 ; xiii, 4 ; xxi, 33 ; xxvi, 25.

I tend to doubt whether the settlement of the people, with all its full concrete implications, can have become clear to him until this point. As far as can be judged, the tribes in Egypt were in all likelihood restricted to cattle-raising in the main, and the period of forced labour is scarcely likely to have served them as a preparation for agriculture ; neither in Midian nor afterwards in Egypt could Moses ever have come to realize all the external and internal transformations that were bound to be involved in a transfer to a predominantly agrarian form of life. I tend to suppose that this can have begun to become clear to him only at Kadesh, with the beginning of the people's experience in some measure of tilling the soil.

As the thought of the land became more concrete, however, Moses would also have begun to consider the necessity of legal provisions such as might serve to regulate the new form of life in a fashion that could secure the conditions of a just social life, which he may well have known from nomadic tribal traditions and his own experience with the people, against grave disturbance. And here as well he would have had to start out from his basic idea, that of the real and direct rule of God ; which would necessarily have led to the postulate that God owns all land.

The name Kadesh means " sanctuary " [264] ; since ancient times [a] it had been called " Fountain of Judgment " ; it was a holy well. When I sat under the ancient oak in the grove above one of the sources of the Jordan in the extreme north of Palestine, at that unmistakable place of judgment which the Arabs still call " The Hill of the Judge " near Dan (which itself is also a name meaning " Judge "), I began to comprehend what Kadesh must have been in the far south of the country, and what had happened there. Moses, as had been the custom of the Fathers, had laid claim in the name of YHVH to the time-old hallowed place — we do not know anything about the god or spirit to which it had been dedicated. There he must not merely have pronounced judgment but must also have " set up law and judgment " [b] ; that is clearly the duty and function of every leader of a people in such a situation, where he cannot draw on a fixed legal tradition adapted to the given conditions of life. Yet far beyond all the requirements of the moment, his mind may well have meditated on what must become precept in order that the at that time as yet unrealized people of God might become a reality under more favourable conditions.

[a] Gen. xiv, 7.   [b] Ex. xv, 25.

Research in principle treats Israelite land law as predominantly post-Mosaic, because Moses in the wilderness cannot very well be supposed to have concerned himself with the entirely different type of organization to be found in the life of a settled people. Historically, however, it is quite thinkable that a legislator, who has in mind a fundamental transformation of the economic structure of a people, should also draft a legal system corresponding to that change ; even though along very general lines only. To which it should be added that even the very modest agricultural attempts at Kadesh might already be sufficient to make the promulgation of certain provisions appear necessary to the leader, who is intent on the inner cohesion of the community.

In addition, it must be remembered that no innovations were involved as far as the world of the Ancient Orient was concerned. We know, for example, that in the old Arabian civilization " God, King and People was the juridical formula for the State " (in which formula the king functions as representative of the god, and as intermediary) ; and that in connection with this the soil was considered to be the property of the god.[265] Though the documents which have become known to us have to be dated many hundreds of years after Moses, it is scarcely possible to doubt the high age of the basic idea ; particularly when we meet with cognate concepts at Babylon in the middle of the Third Millenium B.C.

As can so frequently be found in Israel's treatment of ancient Oriental spiritual values, the land law of the Bible transformed what was already existent into a realistic view which does not rest satisfied with any mere symbolism. Yet at the same time it elevated this pre-existent material into a higher sphere of meaning and word ; while basing itself upon the principle expressed in the words of God [a] : " For the earth (the land) is mine ; for you are dwellers and sojourners with me ". To-day this sentence is once again recognized as " very ancient ".[266] It is found in a text which, as a whole, belongs to a late literary period and is composed of various stylistic shreds [267] ; but this certainly does not justify us in refusing to attribute it to Moses. The Israelites must, it would seem, have described their relations to Egypt in such terms ; and the warning, found recurring even in the oldest part of Biblical law,[b] not to oppress the " dweller ", since they themselves had been in his situation when in Egypt, and therefore know his " soul ",

[a] Lev. xxv, 23.   [b] Ex. xxii, 20 ; xxiii, 9.

clearly has very deep roots in the historical memory of the people. Just as the children of Israel have left the service of Egypt for the service of YHVH, so from having been dwellers in Egypt they have become dwellers with YHVH. The introductory words " for the earth is mine " is also reminiscent of the words of the Eagle Speech : " For the whole earth is mine ". On both occasions God lays claim to the earth ; on one occasion, however, namely in the Eagle Speech, in respect of his rule over the peoples of the earth ; and on the other, in the words about sojourners, in respect of possession of the soil, the soil of Canaan.

However, another motif seems to have become associated with the sense of these ancient words, and in it the belief of Moses in the one Lord, an early and powerful belief, is given expression.

In the, at all events, very old legal stratum of the so-called Book of the Covenant the command is found [a] to " let fall " the cultivated land, fields, vineyards and olive-groves, in the seventh year of their cultivation, and to " forsake " their yield so that " the needy ones of your people may eat therefrom " ; what they leave over may be consumed by the " beasts of the field ". The scanty and " somewhat abrupt " [268] formulation seems to be something like a preliminary note calling for later elucidation and precise definition. At the same time it is marked with that vivid force of expression which is so often characteristic of such notes. At the beginning of the section in which the " dwellers " passage is to be found [b] the underlying idea of the law is expressed more precisely, and in three respects : first that the seventh year is a " Sabbath unto YHVH " like the seventh day ; second, that it should be a Sabbath for the soil, in which the latter should lie fallow and thus find rest like Man on the seventh day ; third, that what it yields shall belong to all and sundry in common, freeman and bonds, Israelite and sojourner, man and beast. Here we obviously have the " better and more complete text " [269] ; or more precisely the expansion of that first sketch. The relationship between these two should not be taken as meaning that in the beginning there was a practical economic and social humanitarian provision, which was afterwards expanded and extended into the religious sphere by a later theology. Rather was the seventh year in Israel the period since time immemorial of a " fallow-lying which was sacral in intention, for the duration of which the right of usufruct enjoyed by the Israelite clans in the soil and land which fell to their

[a] Ex. xxiii, 10 f.　　　　　[b] Lev. xxv, 2-7.

lot was invalidated, and the sole and exclusive right of possession of Yahveh once more becomes manifest ".[270] " The idea of the equality of all creatures " [271] is certainly characteristic of the Sabbatical year, as it is of the Sabbath itself; but it is as creatures of the one Creator that they are all equal to one another ; and as on the day dedicated to YHVH, so in the year dedicated to Him, they receive the same rights in one or the other sphere, in one or the other form.   And here the thought is certainly at work " that the soil shall be free for a time, so that it should not be subjected to the will of human beings, but left to its own nature ; in order that it may be no man's land ".[272]   But just because it belongs to God, the soil must be made free again and again.   Here the cosmic, the social and the religious aspects are still in their roots united ; they cannot yet be separated from each other.

The epoch in which such a unity was still possible can be fixed. For this reason it has justly been said [273] that the establishment of the institution of the Sabbatical year " is thinkable only at a time when the Israelite tribes had not yet entirely foreaken the semi-nomadism of their early days and, though they have already begun to engage in agriculture, to be sure, have not yet made it the centre of gravity of their economic life ".   It is true that " for this stage the final period before and the initial period after their occupation of Palestine can equally well be thought of".   But the earlier, Kadesh that is, is indicated by the as yet undiminished concentra-tion of the wandering hosts and the intensity of the initiative of Moses ; and at no later time can anything similar be found that will bear comparison with these two.

The view has been expressed in various quarters [274] " that the abolition of the preceding legal situation in respect of land during the seventh year was originally a complete one ", as complete as in the later law regarding the year of Jubilee (which, incidentally, is not to my mind late in its nucleus, and certainly not merely " theoretical ", but was rather intended to afford an extension of the period of restoration, because the one originally provided for was not observed).   Hence, according to this view, in the Sabbatical year there was a fresh allotment of landed areas to the single families, such as can still be found taking place annually among certain Arab semi-nomads after a fashion reminiscent of the Biblical terminology.[275]

If this assumption is correct, and so it seems to me, then it was the purpose of the Sabbatical year to lead to a renewal of the

organization of the society, in order to start afresh. The renewal
of the land in the fallow period and the renewal of the people in
the restoration of the original equality are associated. "The
unconditional connection of the people was intended to preserve
the consciousness of common ownership. of land and soil." [276]
But this consciousness necessarily had to strike deep roots ; it had
to be nourished in its deeps by a knowledge of the life of the earth,
on which the life of human beings is dependent.

So we are entitled to assume that Moses continued his Sabbatical train of thought and, while making use of the economic
tradition of the semi-nomads, conceived the idea of overcoming
the continually-expanding social harm for ever by ensuring the
restoration, in each ensuing Sabbatical year, " of the normal situation of the national community of Israel after all the deviations and
wrong developments of the preceding six years ".[277]

The " normal situation " in question is that particular one in
which the people found itself when it entered into the *melek*
covenant and was prepared to fulfil it, that is, to bring about a
genuine community ; and it is this particular situation which
Moses wishes to establish afresh again and again in despite of all
" deviations and wrong developments" which might occur.
What an isolated social contemplation might regard as a restoration
of a normal situation, to a view including the religious element it
becomes manifest as a renewal of the Covenant in the seventh year,
the year of " letting fall ", during which the old Mosaic law is read
out aloud at the Feast of Tabernacles before the assembled people
in later days.[a] It becomes manifest as " a reconducting of the
national community to the ideal basis of their existence, a renewed
obligation of all members of the people to the will of Yahve,
without which the union of the tribes into a national entity would
not and could not have come about ".[278]

Various scholarly hypotheses have been spun about Kadesh.
Thus it has been supposed [279] that this had been the district of the
Tribe of Levi since time untold, and that Moses was a priest of
that tribe. " The cultic site at the Burning Bush, which presumably lay in the same valley ", had been " held in high esteem
far beyond the territory of Levi, among all the neighbouring
tribes " ; and at " the great festival of Yahwe" with which
" was associated an annual fair and market standing under the
protection of the truce of God ", the priests of Levi functioned as,

[a] Deut. xxxi, 10 ff.

"intermediaries and arbitrators between the tribes and the individuals".

An attractive picture, but here the historian goes an unwarranted distance from the texts which are available to him. What the latter provide is only that Moses made the fortified spot at the holy well of judgment into a centre of "Israel", at which he gave out the law and instructed the people. As the journey to Canaan became more and more plain as the task impending, first as immediately ahead and then, after the unfortunate issue of fighting, as a task for which they would have to equip themselves a long time in advance, Moses must have seen it as necessary to draft the fundamental principles of the land law on the basis of the experiences gained at Kadesh.

These had to be principles suitable for protecting the settled people from the dangers of settlement, from the inequality of land ownership that threatened the community with decomposition. No institution of the "once-for-all" kind seemed to be capable of prevailing here against the rapacity of those who possessed more. Here Moses, while supporting himself by the customs of the semi-nomads, brought from the deeps of his Sabbatical thought, in which time is rhythmically articulated, the principle of a regular restoration of the initial state of affairs, to be regulated by arranging the years according to the holy number ; just as the days of the week had been arranged according to the holy number. And for Moses any effective arrangement is intimately bound up with consecration to YHVH ; in fact it is the consecration which properly speaking establishes the order.

The Sabbath consecrated to YHVH establishes the unit of the week ; the Sabbatical year consecrated to YHVH establishes the unit of seven years. As the Sabbath unites the busy household community in the common freedom of God, surmounting all the differences of the working days, so the Sabbatical year, surmounting all the differences which have ensued and accrued in the preceding six years, unites the busy national community in the common free-dom of God. There the concrete foundation is the joint resting of human beings who have worked for six days ; here it is the resting of the soil which has been tilled for six years. All the other pro-visions are bound up with this one. Just as those who have become slaves are liberated in the seventh year, which certain scholars [280] even identify with the Sabbatical year, so in the Sabbatical year, if those plausible assumptions were to be correct, the equality of ownership of the impoverished families with that of the enriched ones is re-established ; while the abolishment of, or the respite for, debts ameliorates the situation of the indebted individual, and enables him to fall back once again on his share of the family property. At the same time a great symbol of the common accessibility to all men of the nourishing earth is established by the equal right of all creatures to enjoy the usufruct of the earth in the Sabbatical year.

And above all this there hovers the consecration to YHVH, to whom the earth belongs and who, by means of that earth, nourishes His dwellers and sojourners. They ought not to thrust one another aside, they ought not to impoverish one another permanently or enslave one another ; they must again and ever again become equal to one another in their freedom of person and free relation to the soil ; they must rest together and enjoy the usufruct together ; the times dedicated to God make them free and equal again and again, as they were at the beginning.

The land is given to them in common in order that in it and from it they may become a true national Community, a " Holy People ". Such is the unfolding of the promise of Canaan to the Fathers, which had doubtless lived on in the Egyptian exile, even though almost forgotten. This earth, so YHVH had promised the Fathers, He would give to their " seed " [a] ; in order that they might become a berakah, a blessing power.[b]

[a] Gen. xii, 7.   [b] Ibid., 2.

THE CONTRADICTION

WE read [a] of another revolt ; the one known as the revolt of " Korah and his band ". Its nucleus of fact is barely to be identified under the thick layer of tendentious treatment, the purpose of which was clearly to equip the privileged position of the " Aaronid " priests vis-à-vis the " Levites " with all the sanctions of the Mosaic period. The only thing which can be regarded as certain [281] is that in the original report there was no question of any action of the Levites as Levites.

On the other hand, it would be regarding things from far too narrow a perspective if we were to see here nothing more than a protest on the part of the laity against the appointment of the Levites to the cult service ; a fight against the priestly class in general on the grounds that priests are held to be superfluous. [282]

Nothing is reported in the early stratum of the Pentateuch with regard to the establishment of an actual priestly class. The existence of priests is referred to in passing on one occasion [b] ; but we are told nothing about the functions which were exercised by them. Whatever is found in the so-called Book of the Covenant which implies the exercise of such functions does not offer any adequate grounds for the assumption of an organized priestly class in the days of Moses. Here, in any case, the officiating cult group, if it exists, does not show the quality of pathos proper to the sacral power. The obscure hint of an appointment of the Levites— nothing more than such a hint is to be found in the ambiguous phrasing [283]—following the suppression of the rebellion [c] can scarcely be regarded, if recourse is had exclusively to the old texts, as more than an indication of services of watch and ward, to be rendered thereafter by the Levites at the tent of the leader, now elevated to the status of tent of God, without any actual priestly activities.

This tent is not a tent of offering. In the old textual stratum very little information is given us about sacrifices ; only on very rare and extraordinary occasions are communal and conventional sacrifices made, and then clearly not by any actual priestly caste. With the exception of Moses, nobody engages in the holy action ;

[a] Num. xvi.   [b] Ex. xix, 22.   [c] Ex. xxxii, 29.

182

there is no participation by Levites, and Moses, too, performs his
function not as a professional priest but as the leader of the people ;
as we afterwards also find, for example, in the case of Samuel.
The tent, to be sure, might be described as " an oracle tent ", but
nobody except Moses has anything to do in the tent with that
oracle.

It is true that in a text which probably derives from the time
before the period of the kings but is post-Mosaic,[a] reference is
made to a divine bestowal of the oracular instruments called
Urim and Thummim, to the Levites or to one of them.   But the
narrative texts available to us do not give us any *point d'appui* for
relating this to a particular event ;   and it appears most likely
that the instrument, of which we hear in a dependably early story
only as belonging to the time of Saul, was introduced after the
death of Moses and as his legacy, in order to ensure the continuation
of the oracular function which, however, had been conducted by
him without any instrument.

Possibly the process of back-dating to the Mosaic period came
about by way of the mysterious reference to be found in the
" Blessing of Moses ".   In general it seems to me that the period
of the conquest of the land must have been decisive for the development of a regulated and somewhat centralized cult and a
permanent (in addition to the fluctuating) priestly class ;   this can
be understood from the entire nexus of circumstances.

Be that as it may, all the reports deriving from early days about
the priestly functions of the tribe of Levi are not sufficient, in spite
of the penetrating efforts of scholars,[284] to make any common front
of " laymen against Levites " seem credible as the historical nucleus
of the story of Korah and his band.   This nucleus does not appear
to have been a protest against any " clerical class ", but rather to
have been directed against the special status of Moses in person ;
in which those closest to Moses (though perhaps not Aaron in
particular)[b] may well have been included.

Here, too, we can best start with a passage which appears to
go back to early days, but the wording of which has been so
altered in the course of the priestly treatment of the narrative that
its antiquity has no longer been recognized.   This passage[c] reads
as follows in the form before us : " Enough of you ! For all the
community, all of them, are holy and YHVH is in their midst, so
why do you exalt yourselves over the assembly of YHVH ? "   The

[a] Deut. xxxiii, 8.   [b] As in the present text of Num. xvi, 3.   [c] Num. xvi, 3.

later terms *edah* community, and *qahal* assembly, congregation,[285] have been submitted, it seems to me, for the original words *goy* and *am*. This means that the narrative in its present form has been artistically and of set intent constructed round the word *edah*, which is used in a double sense : community (the whole nation) and band (the separate group rising in revolt), while in addition the root *qahal* is used alternatively in the sense of assembling the people and of banding together.[286]

If we restore the original words, two associations which are worthy of remark become clear. The word *goy*, people, associated with the word *qedoshim*, holy, is reminiscent of the expression *goy qadosh*, holy people, found in the Eagle Speech, a form which is found in the Bible at that one place, and at that one place only ; and *am* YHVH, people of YHVH, is found in early strata of the Pentateuch (Num. xvii, 6 belongs to a very late one) only in the words with which Moses replies to Joshua's misgivings in the story of the Descent of the Spirit [a] : " Who would grant that the whole people of YHVH were prophets, that YHVH grant his spirit over them ! "

The purpose, in suggesting a cross-reference to these two passages, seems to me unmistakable. The protesting party base themselves on the two utterances made by Moses himself, in which he referred to all Israel as holy, as consisting exclusively of direct servants of YHVH, and again to all the individuals in Israel as prophetic carriers of the spirit of God ; one, it is true, in the form of a commandment, and the other in that of a wish. " Korah and his band ", consisting of Levites and laymen who have confederated, say : " The people do not have to become holy first, the people are holy, for YHVH is in their midst ; the whole people is holy, and because it is holy all the individuals in it are holy."

On this they base their attack against Moses and his kinsfolk : " If all are holy you have no priority over the others. If all are holy, there is no need for any mediation. If all are holy there is no need for human beings to exercise any power over other human beings. Everybody is given instruction directly by YHVH as to what he is to do."

This contradiction rising out of the midst of the people, which converts the words of Moses into their opposite, changing as it does request and hope into insolent self-assertion, was conditioned and made possible by one of his great works, the establishment of

[a] Num. xi, 29.

the Ark of the Covenant. The people as people necessarily understood the occasional descent of YHVH in their midst as a residence
of YHVH in their midst, and such a residence as a guarantee of the
holiness of them all ; while their common holiness was bound to
appear to them as an adequate reason for throwing off the yoke of
what should be done and what must not be done, the yoke that this
man Moses imposed upon them, the holy people, hour by hour,
and day by day, in the name of God ; as though God dwelt with
him alone ; as though he alone had access to God.

Moses had endeavoured to preclude this danger by placing the
shrine with the Tables of the Law at the feet of YHVH. But he
himself, after all, had made the Invisible more visible to his people
than the stone upon which His will was written. For the people
as people the Divine Presence meant that they possessed the god ;
or, in other words, that they could transform their own will into
the will of God.

The issue here is at bottom something rather different from the
question of priestly functions, or indeed the question of cult in
general. Though it is directed, to be sure, against Moses, yet no
matter how deeply and strongly religious motives are associated
with the passions at play here, they are not directed really
against Moses as priest. This if only for the reason that though
Moses himself, as said, actually carries out or directs the cult acts
in which the community as such has to be represented, he does not
become a priest as a result ; he carries them out and directs them
as the man who represents the community where the latter has to
act " before God ". And equally the fact that he receives and
transmits the expressions of God's will does not turn him into a
priest ; for the manner of this reception does not admit of inclusion
in any tradition of divinatory methods ; it is unique to him, to
Moses ; it comes into being from his religious experiences and
vanishes with him.

He takes over cult elements and transforms their form and
meaning ; he introduces fresh cult elements ; but he has no cult
office.[287] The priest is the greatest human specialization that we
know. In his mission and his work Moses is unspecialized ; he
is conditioned not by an office but by a situation, a historical
situation.

Moses' character is eminently historical ; that of the priest,
even when he delivers an oracle in given historical situations, is
eminently non-historical. This, however, does not mean that

Moses is " not a priest but a prophet ".[288] It is true that the way in which he receives the revelation is largely prophetical, even though the institution of the tent and all that is associated therewith does make a considerable difference ; but his activity in history, as leader of the people, as legislator, is what separates him in character from all the bearers of prophecy known to us. For this reason Moses likewise cannot be comprehended merely as a combination of priest and prophet ; moreover, he is not to be comprehended at all within any exclusively "religious" categories. What constitutes his idea and his task : the realization of the unity of religious and social life in the community of Israel, the substantiation of a ruling by God that shall not be cultually restricted but shall comprehend the entire existence of the nation, the theo-political principle ; all this has penetrated to the deeps of his personality, it has raised his person above the compartmental system of typology, it has mingled the elements of his soul into a most rare unity.

The historical Moses, as far as we are capable of perceiving him, does not differentiate between the spheres of religion and politics ; and in him they are not separated. When " Korah and his band " revolt against Moses, it is not to be interpreted as meaning that they rise against his cult privileges as such ; for these privileges as such are not stressed and might as well be non-existent.

Rather do they rise at first against the fact that *one* man leads the people in the name of God. But they go beyond this and revolt against the fact that this man decides in the name of God what is right and what is wrong. "The whole people, all of them, are holy ", and therefore nobody can give orders or issue prohibitions to anybody else in respect of what the latter's own holiness suggests to him. Since the people are holy, command-ments from without are no longer necessary.

It should not be supposed that later stages of development are introduced here into the words of Korah. The attitude which finds expression in these words is known to us from far more primitive stages. In many of those tribes which are labelled as primitive, such motives have contributed vastly to the establish-ment of secret societies. A chief or shaman, whose authority is supported by a superhuman power, can be combated in two ways. One is to attempt to overthrow him, particularly by shaking faith in the assurance that he will receive that support, and to take his place, which is precisely what some suppose to have been the nucleus of the story of Korah [289] ; that is, a manifestation of the personal struggle for power known to us from all phases of human history, and one which in general leaves the structure of society unchanged. The second method is to cut off the main roots of the leader's power by establishing, within the tribe but external to the official tribal life, a secret society in which the actual, the true, the "holy" communal life is lived, free from the bonds of the "law"; a life of "leopards" or "werewolves" in which the wildest instincts reach their goal on the basis of mutual aid, but in holy action. Once they have succeeded in abducting the god, all further robbery is no more than taking possession by means of him. From this separate life it is natural that vast and varied social and political effects should afterwards be felt in the life of the tribe, *vis-à-vis* which the secret society regards itself as the "true" tribe, spinal column and driving force of the tribe; as the tribe, so to speak, in so far as it really dares to be its own self.

This phenomenon, which can be observed throughout the inhabited world, is regarded much too superficially if it is considered to be nothing more than a masking of the urge of the libido to become unfettered. The people who set rebellions of this kind under way are not merely endeavouring to find a sanction for the satisfaction of repressed lusts, but are in all seriousness desirous of gaining power over the divine might; or more precisely, of actualizing and giving legitimacy to the god-might which a person has in himself, the "free" one, as against the one which is "bound" by the chief or shaman, with all the taboos used to fetter it. This tendency can admittedly be realized only by placing those who are not members of the secret societies in a state of nonfreedom and exposure, such as is in many cases far worse than any previous abuse ever was; but this is only, as one might say, a secondary effect, which is regarded as being unworthy of any consideration.

It is easy to adduce analogies at higher levels of development, particularly out of the history of antinomist sects and movements. The issue is always that of "divine freedom" against "divine law"; but at these higher levels it becomes even more clear than at the more primitive stages that the isolated divine freedom abolishes itself. Naturally God rules through men who have been gripped and filled by His spirit, and who on occasion carry out His will not merely by means of instantaneous decisions but also through lasting justice and law. If their authority as the chosen ones is disputed and extended to all, then the actual dominion is taken away from God ; for without law, that is, without any clear-cut and transmissible line of demarcation between that which is pleasing to God and that which is displeasing to Him, there can be no historical continuity of divine rule upon earth.

The *true* argument of the rebellion is that in the world of the law what has been inspired always becomes emptied of the spirit, but that in this state it continues to maintain its claim of full inspiration ; or, in other words, that the living element always dies off but that thereafter what is left continues to rule over living men. And the *true* conclusion is that the law must again and again immerse itself in the consuming and purifying fire of the spirit, in order to renew itself and anew refine the genuine substance out of the dross of what has become false. This lies in the continuation of the line of that Mosaic principle of ever-recurrent renewal.

As against this comes the false argument of the rebels that the law as such displaces the spirit and the freedom, and the false conclusion that it ought to be replaced by them. The falsity of this conclusion remains hidden and even ineffective as long as the " eschatological " expectation, the expectation of the coming of the direct and complete rule of God over all creatures, or more correctly of His presence in all creatures that no longer requires law and representation, is maintained unweakened. As soon as it slackens, it follows historically that God's rule is restricted to the " religious " sphere, everything that is left over is rendered unto Caesar ; and the rift which runs through the whole being of the human world receives its sanction.

Indeed, the false would become true as soon as the presence of God comes to be fulfilled in all creatures. It is here that the greatness and the questionability are to be found in every genuine eschatology ; its greatness in belief and its questionability *vis-à-vis* the realities of history. The " Mosaic " attitude facing this is to believe in the future of a " holy people " ; and to prepare for it within history.

These remarks are essentially relevant to our subject, for they help us to understand the tragedy of Moses. Everything subsequent to the antagonism between Moses and Korah appears to us as having been already present in the seed therein, if only we view Korah in large enough terms. Then we recognize that here the eternal word is opposed by eternal contradiction.

But something peculiar must also be added : the waywardness of Bedouin life, which often survives the nomadic stage.[290] This elementary need of people to be independent of other people may develop in two opposite directions, according to the particular personal temperament with which it is associated. It can grow into an unconditional submission to the will of God and His will alone, but it may also become empty stubbornness, which does not wish to bow to any order because order is, after all, nothing but human order. On the one hand we see here the devotion to the Kingdom of God carried out by a person's deepest self, such as can and should be inspired in spontaneous fashion ; and on the other the resistance offered by the deepest self to the coming of the Kingdom ; so that a man submits to his own wilfulness and feels, or endeavours to feel, that very wilfulness as that which is religiously correct, as that which brings salvation, as holy.

This schizoid development from a common root meets us in Israel as well as in the pre-Islamic and Islamic Arab worlds. When Moses bases Israel's becoming a " king's retinue of *qohanim* ", that is, the beginning of the Kingdom of God, on spontaneity, on " doing and hearing " without compulsion, he relies upon that Bedouin waywardness ; trusting and assuming that they, who do not wish to recognize any other master than the Lord of the world alone, will truly recognize Him. Until the present day Israel has really existed in the precise degree in which Moses has proved right. But by doing what he did, Moses also encouraged the contrary development from the identical root. The fact that Korah is able to make use of Moses' own words against him has a tragic purport.

Moses does not wish to use force, he does not wish to impose himself, he wishes to bring the men of his people so far along that they themselves can become *qohanim* and *nebiim*. He is " humble ". But this humility of his, which is one with his fundamental faith in spontaneity and in freedom, is precisely what provokes the " Korahite " reaction among men of the Korah type. Since, however, his whole work, the Covenant between God and people, is threatened, he must now doom the rebels to destruction, just as he once ordered Levites to fight against Levites. There is certainly something sinister underlying the legend of the earth which opened its mouth and swallowed up the rebels.

It was the hour of decision. Both Moses and Korah desired the people to be the people of YHVH, the holy people. But for Moses this was the goal. In order to reach it, generation after generation had to choose again and again between the roads, between the way of God and the wrong paths of their own hearts ;

between "life" and "death".[a] For this God had introduced Good and Evil, in order that men might find their own way to Him.

For Korah the people, as being the people of YHVH, were already holy. They had been chosen by God and He dwelt in their midst, so why should there be further need of ways and choice ? The people was holy just as it was, and all those within it were holy just as they were ; all that needed to be done was to draw the conclusions from this, and everything would be found to be good. It is precisely this which Moses, in a parting speech placed in his mouth and which appears to be a development of one of his traditional utterances, calls Death ; meaning the death of the people, as though they were swallowed up while still alive.

Therefore he was zealous ; he was zealous for his God as the one who sets a goal and shows a path and writes a guide to that path on tablets and orders men to choose again and again, to choose that which is right ; and he was zealous against the great and popular mystical Baal which, instead of demanding that the people should hallow themselves in order to be holy, treats them as already holy.

Korah calls that Baal by the name of YHVH ; but that does not change anything in his essence.

[a] Deut. xxx, 15.

BAAL

THE events which follow on the revolt of Korah in the Biblical narrative are chronologically even more opaque than what precedes them ; but in any case they fall chiefly in the later period of the wanderings through the wilderness. Among them one stands out by reason of the fact that Hosea, one of the first and greatest of the prophets who used the written word as their medium, regarded it as the crisis in the fate of Israel.[a] As when a wanderer through the wilderness unexpectedly finds fresh grapes (here Hosea may be striking a note drawn from a reminiscence of the story of the spies), or when a person who has planted a fig-tree sees the first ripe fruit gleaming before him on the sapling " in its beginning " ; so had it seemed to YHVH when He " found " Israel who came to meet Him ; joyous astonishment at the sight of the people who appeared as though renewed in freedom, joy of the creator of the peoples, who finds here the first ripe fruit on the tree of the human race ; that is what the prophet describes his God as feeling. " Then they came to Baal Peor and dedicated themselves unto the shame-idol and became (the same) beings of abomination as that which they loved."

Hosea does not blame his people for any earlier revolt, but this one he sees as a defection on their part. Just as a man vows and dedicates himself to YHVH as a Nazarite (this is the meaning of the verb), so did they dedicate and submit themselves to the idol of shame, to the Baal ; and this association with the idol transformed them in their innermost selves, so that they became as horrible as he was. Thus Hosea, the tragic lover who was the first in the world to say what the love between a god and a people might be,[291] accuses Israel of unfaithfulness.

After the accounts of Miriam's death and then of that of Aaron, of transit negotiations, of battles and of Balaam's sooth-saying, we are told in the narrative [b] how the Israelites (the early tradition would presumably have reported this of only one part of the people, say of a single tribe), who by that time are camping on the boundaries of Moab, that is, who have already reached sown land, permit themselves to be led astray by the maidens of the country ; they participate in their sacrificial meals and prostrate

[a] Hos. ix, 10.   [b] Num. xxv, 1 ff.

themselves before their tribal god. " And Israel yoked themselves together unto Baal Peor."

This Baal is not identical with Kamosh, the tribal god of the Moabites, but like the Canaanite Baal gods in general is a local god of a special kind and with a special cult. This cult consists chiefly of " cult prostitution " or, more correctly, of fertility rites aiming at an increase through human action of the strength of the divine pairings, the matings of Baal and Baalat, meaning " owner " and " owneress ", who bring about the fruitfulness of the soil. That this is so seems also to be indicated by the queer expression used only here [a] and in a Psalm [b] referring to this passage. The noun tsemed derived from this verbal root tsamad means a brace of animals harnessed together and providing a specific service through the resultant unity. The dative " unto Baal Peor " indicates for whom the service was carried out here.

The Baal who meets the God of Way of the wanderers at the threshold of the agrarian civilization is the divinity who has been worshipped by the Canaanite peoples in the fashion which seemed proper to them as the unconditional prerequisite of fruitful farming.[292] In countless forms at the fruitful places of the country teem the Baalim and the Baalot, and always in pairs ; together they engage in the mystery rites by which the downpour of water always makes the soil of the earth fruitful again. This mysterious phenomenon is again and ever again viewed with astonishment by early man ; that wherever ample moisture is given to the earth, whether out of its own deeps, whether from fountains flowing down out of the mountains or the hills, whether in the form of rain or dew from heaven, the earth multiplies from within itself whatever seed is placed in it. And this is ascribed to the powerful effects of divine matings.

Out of this, and corresponding to the conception of the earthly Baalim, evolves that of the heavenly Baalim ; who concentrate in more differentiated civilizations such as that of the Phœnicians into the mighty rain-god Baal who is also . " the lord of the deep wells " (as he is called in a text from Ras Shamra). And since from the " primitive " point of view the power of all imitative actions of this kind on the part of human beings merges into the actions of the gods—or since, rather, according to this point of view, all similar actions are basically one and the same and, given the proper intention, will exert a uniform effect, particularly when a divine action

---

[a] Num. xxv, 3, 5.   [b] Ps. cvi, 28.

takes the lead,—the magical sexual rites develop into orgiastic cults.

These are not to be regarded as libidinous excesses, although they naturally could not exist without the driving force of the libido. A deep experience of the unity of organic life, such as is proper in particular to the soul-stirring discoveries of the earliest period of tilling the soil, found misled but elemental expression.

What met YHVH on the threshold of the Promised Land is therefore nothing less than the spirit which holds sway at the initiation of settled tilling of the soil. Where a man settles in order to win the blessings of the soil from out of its midst, there he finds moisture, there he finds the domain of Baal; and there it is meet and proper for him, and for the human pair, to imitate the gods and contribute to their holy work.

On this was based the cultivation of the soil in Canaan. "The Baalim are truly the owners of the fields, which are wooed by ploughing, and there is no luck if they are not served as they desire." [293] This is what "the daughters of Moab" taught the sons of Israel when the latter "began to whore unto them". Free sexuality as a sacral labour of uniting men and gods and as the element serving as sacral fundament of the most important human economic activity, was what confronted YHVH on the threshold of Canaan.

Moses' aim, which was clearly growing stronger and stronger, was directed to the settlement of the people. He wished, we may well translate his purpose into our own style of thought, to heal the people of the simultaneously lax and obstinate character it had assumed in Egypt; he wished to heal it by active union with the soil inhabited by and promised to the Fathers, in order that the people might be able to become the "People of YHVH". Now, however, on the very threshold of Canaan he sees, threatening the soul of Israel, the misdemeanour which is held to be the fundament of agriculture, and hence the fundament of settlement. Human sexuality becomes bound up with a divine sexuality; the divinity is drawn down into the duality of corporeal nature; and the relation of man and wife, destined in Israel by YHVH to help make the seed of Abraham "into a great *goy* ",[a] is, when reft away from holy lawfulness, misused for the service of the pair of idols. The "sin of the Amorite", which the story of the Fathers darkly hints at [b] as the reason why the peoples settled in Canaan

<hr />

[a] Gen. xii, 2.   [b] Gen. xv, 16.

would have to be supplanted by Israel,[294] threatens to become the sin of Israel.

· The contradiction from without, which overwhelms Moses here after the contradiction from within, goes to the very deeps of his consciousness of God. The unity of his God, not one that is thought of from the aspect of the general point of view, but one believed in and known as the exclusiveness of relations to him, is dependent on God's being above sex. A sexually determined God is an incomplete one, one who requires completion ; it cannot be the one and only God. Among the motives for the so-called prohibition of images, which we have seen is really far more since it is actually a prohibition of fixing any form for YHVH, this is apparently one of the most important : if the God were to be represented in any specific human or animal form, and if that form were to be recognized as the form of the God, even symbolically, He would of necessity be drawn down into the sphere of sexuality. That is why the symbol of the bull was one of the animal symbols to be most firmly combated. No other animal can serve so intensely as this one for symbolizing the power of procreation ; justly does it bear the rain-pouring god of the weather on its back ; and it corresponds to the nature of the Phœnician Baal that, as we are told in one of the Ras Shamra epics, he pairs in the fields, while in the form of a bull, with his sister in the form of a wild cow ; and he begets a bull-calf.[295]

It is true that anthropomorphism is necessary and legitimate for the style and language of the Bible, and that we owe two great concepts to the metaphorical description of YHVH in human terms : that of His divine love for Israel as developed by Hosea and Jeremiah, and that of His fatherhood, which we first meet in Moses' original words to Pharaoh : "Israel is my first-born son". But the anthropomorphic metaphor must preserve its character, it must not transgress the bounds of spirituality ; it has to give people what they need but must not affect the essence of God. This is what the anthropomorphism of the Old Testament accomplishes ; and it is on account of this that the latter has given the religions what they require to satisfy the demand for proximity to God without making God's unity in any way questionable.

The YHVH religion is doubly threatened by the nature of the Baal : by the elimination of the God from the central position in the new cultural life, and as against this that Baalization which converts the God himself into a Baal. The war against both dangers continues for centuries in the religious history of Israel ; Elijah and Hosea are its protagonists. We are not told what Moses already felt regarding it when he saw his people falling away to Baal Peor. But we may well assume that he, having at last reached the Land of Promise, knew to the very deeps of his heart how much inner struggle would still be required before the promise could find its true fulfilment.

THE END

IT is not one of the functions of this book to examine and elucidate the Biblical reports, which have apparently come down to us as scanty and unconnected remains of a tradition that is lost for the greater part, regarding the unsuccessful negotiations with Edom and the skirting of that country ; regarding the apparently ambiguous relations with Moab ; regarding the victorious wars against Sihon, King of the Amorites and Og, King of the Bashan ; and regarding the settlement of certain Israelite tribes east of the Jordan. The results of investigation may be taken as showing that these for the greater part have a historical nucleus ; that in actual fact certain neighbouring peoples to Israel appeared too strong to be challenged, whereas largely successful campaigns were conducted against others. From time to time the Biblical text reports the share of Moses in these political and military activities ; but even where he is not especially mentioned we have the right to imagine him planning, deciding and directing. Biographically speaking there is far less to go upon in this final stage of his life, in respect of which we are not even given an approximate length of time. We only feel, when looking at the meagre fragments, that the guiding power continues unabated in an unaging soul. That soul itself understands its power as the strength to allow itself to be guided, and we may understand it in the same way with him ; as long as we do not ignore the fact that that really is a strength, and indeed the strength that is above all others.

And now, the Biblical narrative reports,[a] Moses is informed by God that he should prepare himself for death. On account of a " stubbornness " [b] or " unfaithfulness ", [c] the character of which cannot be clearly and unequivocally elucidated, he is forbidden to tread the soil of Canaan. Only from the summit of a mountain may he look upon the land. At his request to appoint his successor to the leadership, in which connection he is visibly thinking first and foremost of leadership in war, Moses is authorized to induct Joshua into the office.[296] What he has to do is to place his hand upon him, with the gesture of identification which we know from the sacrificial cult. Joshua is already possessed of the spirit ; of set purpose the narrative has Moses calling on God as the " God of

[a] Num. xxvii, 12 ff.　　　[b] Num. xxvii, 14.　　　[c] Deut. xxxii, 51.

the spirits in all flesh ", that is, the endower of the individual
spirit. Now he, Moses, has to indue Joshua with something of
his "radiance ", of the *maiestas* [297] which he possesses.

The figure of Joshua is not easy to grasp historically, as the
book that has been given his name is a confluence of traditions
differing very widely in value, while his position during the lifetime of Moses is not made quite clear in the books of the Pentateuch.
There are some [298] who regard him as a tribal chief, resembling
the so-called Great Judges in the Book of Judges, who fought and
won in a single battle, and Joshua may well be regarded as actually
the first of the "Judges "; even though, as it seems to me, in a
far more extensive sense. There is also a view [299] which would
attribute to him the greater part of the work of Moses, particularly in the religious field. And again there is another [300] which
would transfer him into a period earlier than that of Moses ; and
according to which he led the first departure of the Israelites to
Canaan, while Moses led the second.

To me the arguments which have been offered against the
Biblical account of the relation between Moses and Joshua do not
appear strong enough. Despite the scanty material, we can nevertheless fashion ourselves a consistent picture of the functions of
Joshua under the leadership of Moses. Moses entrusted the youth-
ful Joshua at a critical moment with the guarding of his leader
tent, which had become the divine tent. He entrusted it to him,
a man of the tribe of Ephraim, and not to any of the Levites, not
even to his brother or his own son. (It appears that at a later
time this function, which had become a collective one, was entrusted to the group of Levites who had remained faithful.) This
is, on the one hand, in accord with the uncertain character of the
relations between Moses and his clan ; while on the other it fits
in well with the obviously complete absence of any dynastic inten-
tions which we observe in him.

It is entirely in harmony with the nomadic and semi-nomadic
style of life that Moses should by choice educate his spiritual son
and successor. The nature of the particular qualities which led
him to choose the young Joshua is not told us, but in the two
brief conversations between them of which we are told we learn
two things : his " zeal " for Moses and his physical and instinctive
interest in everything connected with fighting. Possibly we ought
to assume, even though the texts are silent about it, that the next
stage was preceded by a decisive participation of Joshua in the

suppression of one of the revolts ; maybe of that particular one the noise of which sounded in his ears like the alarms of war. This would make it immediately understandable that Moses should now transfer to him the leadership of the external battles, in which Joshua passes the test and emerges a victor.

At the same time there is an important difference between the characters and temperaments of the two men. Joshua lacks that which is the constituent element in the attitude and actions of Moses ; he does not receive revelations. " Spirit is in him ", but the spirit of God does not come to him. YHVH has selected him for an office, but He does not deem him worthy of associating with him. Naturally nothing of this needs to be altered because of either the fragmentary account of the manifestation near Jericho,[a] characteristically the apparition of a heavenly commander, operating in its clearly literary style with fixed requisites, or the words of God to Joshua which are occasionally reported. No personal experience to be compared with that of Moses can be glimpsed anywhere.

This absence is clearly decisive for Moses' resolution. There ripens within him a thought which is rich in consequences, the thought of what has to be done : the division of powers. Those functions which were united in him, in Moses, namely the sacral utterance of oracles, the direction of communal offerings and the political organization and leadership of the people's life, must be divided between two men, two kinds of men, two series of men ; the second of such a kind as to be united with the military leadership.

Here what was to develop in coming generations, the duality of " priest " and " judge " in Israel, finds its historical origin. We do not know how this process was carried out in detail. It is possible, in spite of the fact that the reference to Eleazar the Priest in Numbers xxvii, 19 seems quite secondary, that it was not Aaron but his son who was dedicated as priest, and that in this way the *authoritative* priestly class was finally introduced. It is possibly during one of these late hours in the life of Moses that the oracular instruments, the Urim and Thummim, which are of presumably Kenite origin, first make their appearance. These he himself may well have kept but did not use, and clearly did not permit others to use ; now, however, he appears to have handed them over to the priest as indispensable for his sacral successors.

[a] Josh. v, 13 ff.

At all events, what was united in the person of Moses is now reft asunder, and the rift runs right through the organization of the people established by him. For not merely his personal task was based on the same man receiving the will of God and directing its execution ; it is one of the firmest foundations of his *work* that " religion " and " politics " are inseparable. What had become reality in the spirit and character of this unique man, the unity of human leadership of a collective body in the name of God, was what he had introduced despite all obstacles as an objective unity of public order in the social reality. There had been the sacral sphere including that of the cult ; but it was impossible to exempt oneself, by means of cult performances, from the commandment of God regarding the right behaviour towards men (the third part of the Decalogue). There was the sphere of public life, comprehending that of politics ; but it was impossible to make political decisions which would contradict the command of God to serve Him exclusively (the first part of the Decalogue).

Now the division of powers, which Moses found imposed upon him by the needs of a personal succession due to the situation in which a newly-summoned leader might be required almost at a moment's notice, inevitably induced the first urge towards a separation of the two spheres. No matter how faithfully the Judge and the Priest co-operated in administering their holy heritage, the separate legislation of the two spheres deriving from the division would of necessity have its effect in splitting what was marked for unity, in the order of the people and, together with that, in every individual soul as well. Moses does something, for the sake of maintaining the work, as a consequence of which a central part of the foundation of his work is broken down. The final scene in the tragedy of Moses, like those which had preceded it, derives from the resistance of the human material. Moses wished for an entire, undivided human life, as the right answer to the Divine revelation. But splitting up is the historical way of mankind, and the unsplit persons cannot do anything more than raise man to a higher level on which he may thereafter follow his course, as long as he is bound by the law of his history.

The Book of Deuteronomy, which presumably evolved over a period of several centuries out of ever-renewed oratorical elaboration by preachers and legislators of certain traditional sayings of Moses, aims at transmitting to us the parting address of Moses, which he delivered to the people " in the fortieth year ". No

matter whether it really was precisely forty years or, as may be
presumed, a considerably shorter period (in any case it was far
more than the four years which Goethe assumes) : we can still
feel in the polished rhetoric of the book something of the closing
period of the wanderings, of the hour of leave-taking after a long
journey together.   Among the sayings which, whenever they may
have received their form known to us, show signs of an early spiritual
origin, one of the most important is that promise of God [a] that at
times He would send the people a prophet like to Moses, in whose
mouth He would place His words like Moses, and to whom they
would have to hearken.

This, going far beyond the problem associated with the succession, is an admission of a higher continuity resulting from the ever-
repeated renewal out of the spirit.   We are entitled to regard
this as containing, at its core, a genuine hope on the part of Moses.
He regards himself not as a unique individual coming only once,
but as the one entrusted with the task, who, as long as that task
has not been fulfilled in its entirety, must return again and again ;
not as the same person or the identical soul (of course we are not
intended to think of transmigration of souls or anything resembling
it) but precisely as the one continuing the fulfilment of that task,
no matter what else that person or soul may be.

" Prophet " is said here, but what is meant at bottom is that
undivided, entire person who as such receives the message and as
such endeavours to establish that message in life.   Only in
apparent contradiction to this are the words [b] with which the
narrative of Moses' death obviously ended at first ; that thereafter no
prophet arose in Israel like unto Moses " who recognized YHVH
face to face " ; that is, with whom He was in such direct contact
as with Moses.

Here, in order to prevent any misunderstanding of the statement,
the one-time element is separated from the recurrent.   Something,
something paraphrased in these words, does not return ; but what
does return is sufficient for renewal from the Spirit.   Moses is not
the first of the prophets of Israel ; he stands out from that series as
he does from all others ; but the Prophets of Israel, who are men
of the Spirit in the sense of the Word of the Spirit only, continue
his work.   Each of them takes it up afresh ; and every new thing
aims at being no more than restoration.

[a] Deut. xviii, 15.   [b] Deut. xxxiv, 10.

And now Moses ascends Mount Nebo, solitary as he has always
been ; more solitary than he has ever been before. As he is making
his way over the ridge and is mounting to the level summit, he is
reminiscent of one of those noble animals which leave their herd
in order to perish alone.

According to the Bible he was one hundred and twenty years
old ; according to our understanding of the sequence of time the
years were far less in number. In any case he was an aged man.
But as he stands here upon the peak everything within him demon-
strates the soul that has not aged. " His eyes were not dimmed,
and his freshness had not fled " ; that is the speech of a people's
memory.

From Nebo you can see the whole of the Jordan depression and
beyond. When the air is clear you see the snows of Hermon in the
north, and in the West the hills that lie above the Mediterranean ;
it is Canaan. That is what he sees close before him.

On this plateau, " on the heights of the Pisgah ", Israel had once
stood when first it came from the wilderness [a] and saw the Promised
Land lying before it. Now the wandering is at an end.

" So Moses the servant of YHVH died there in the Land of
Moab at the bidding of YHVH." The Hebrew wording admits
of the meaning " by the mouth of YHVH ". This, in turn, was
elaborated by post-Biblical legend, for which the death of Moses
was a favourite theme. But here as ever the Biblical text is far
greater than all expansions ; greater than the picture of death by
the kiss of God is that of the man who has lived by the bidding of
this God, and who now also perishes at His bidding.

" And he buried him in the gorge, in the Land of Moab, facing
Beth Peor " ; that is, facing the spot at which the defection to
Baal had taken place. Although the translation " and one buried
him " is permissible, there can be no doubt that YHVH himself is
regarded as the digger of the grave for His servant ; and therefore
" no man knoweth his grave unto this day ".

[a] Num. xxi, 20.

ADDENDUM: From "The Teaching of the Prophets". (See Note 111)

THE duologue between Joshua and the people, once the later elements (such as Joshua xxiv, 17 and 18a) are excluded, can be recognized as a religious act in dialogue form. Joshua demands that the people should fear YHVH and serve Him " simply and in truth " (verse 14b appears doubtful) ; otherwise they must decide upon and choose " to-day " other gods for themselves ; either the gods of the legendary days of the tribes when the " Fathers " still dwelt in Mesopotamia, or else the gods of the surrounding Canaanite peoples ; " while I and my house shall serve YHVH ".

The people solemnly proclaim that they do not wish to forsake YHVH in order to serve " other gods ". " We too shall serve YHVH because He is our God " (verse 17). This proclamation does not satisfy Joshua, and he warns them that they will not be able to serve YHVH in the way they wish to follow. In that way it is possible to worship other gods but not Him, " for He is a holy God " (verse 19). He is a " zealous " God, who demands absolute devotion and will assuredly consume them for any defection from Him ; no matter whether that defection be partial and casual or whether it be entire.

The people repeat and stand by their declaration. They are prepared to be witnesses against themselves as Joshua requires of them. And now he orders them to put away the strange gods who are in their midst, " and make your hearts to turn unto YHVH the God of Israel " (verse 23).

Only at this point does there appear in the dialogue, as it had appeared at the very commencement of the address (verse 2), this refrain from the Song of Deborah. Only now, after " all the tribes of Israel " have united round the worship of YHVH, does this designation again become legitimate. And to this the people answer conclusively (verse 24) : " YHVH our God shall we serve, unto His voice shall we hearken ". Only now (verse 25) does Joshua " establish a covenant for the people " and " set statute and judgment for them " ; as was told of Moses after the division of the Red Sea (Exodus xv, 25). Nowhere in the Bible save at these two points do we find this phrase, " set statute and judgment for somebody " ; and in neither of these two passages is any information given regarding the content of the things which are set. (It may be supposed that the rules governing the wanderings and journeyings of the desert period were stated there, whereas here they heard the promulgation of the rules concerning the sanctuary of the Covenant, the Festivals and the Assemblies of the Covenant.[1]) And in addition Joshua erects a large stone, a standing stone, as testimony under the terebinth which grows at the sanctuary.

What we are told of here in the form of a dialogue is a historic and vital decision of the people, from which rises the formula " YHVH, God of Israel ", linking the names of the God and the people. Are we to

[1] *Cf.* Buber, Koenigtum Gottes, p. 157 ff.

conclude from this that it must have been the historic hour in which the tribes united by a single act and became Israel, while Israel in turn became linked to YHVH? Is it only at this point that the relationship of faith commences between the God and the people? There have actually been some who have supposed so, and who have expressed the view that " the Covenant of Joshua was really the first, and was the first to be concluded ".[1]

There is no foundation, however, for this opinion. Here nothing of the sacramental character of a Covenant established between God and people is to be found; after the fashion described in the story of the Blood Covenant at Sinai (Exodus xxiv, 8). Here you are not immersed in and imbued with the spirit of the holy occurrence, which is revealed to us as an objective act between those on high and those below, and which fashions a mutual nexus between the nation and God. Instead you feel the spirit of a human group decision which derives from faith; a decision that requires no special sacramental activity and no more than the ordinary symbolic testimony. Here no covenant between Heaven and Earth, and binding on both sides, is to be found, but the bond which the people take on themselves *vis-à-vis* YHVH receives the colour of duties under the Covenant.

In this act Joshua does not function at all " as representative of the people and in its name ", as is supposed.[2] In the Bible the expression " to make a Covenant for somebody " almost always means an action initiated by the superior party or his representative. Even what is before us is only the first of those *renewals* of the Covenant, the nature of which is clearly shown in the case of the " making of the Covenant " by King Josiah (II Kings xxiii, 3). The people who have betrayed or rejected the Covenant once again undertake to fulfil it and perform it; whereas the God, who has faithfully observed the Covenant, does not need to enter into it afresh. He does nothing more than respond, and accepts the renewal by authorizing His representative, in this case the king, to accept it as in force " before YHVH " (similarly to " before the God " in Joshua xxiv, 1), and to fulfil it. (The linguistic form is different in the description of a religious state act such as that to be found in II Kings xi, 17, where the king has to be confirmed as intermediary between God and people; after the fashion known to us in documents of Ancient Arabia, concerning the renewals of Covenants.)

Here we have to define our attitude to another view, which has been expressed by certain outstanding scholars.[3] They hold that " the great majority of the people did not know anything of YHVH until then, and therefore did not participate at all in the wandering through the Desert ", but " remained within the country " and " only upon seeing the wonderful leadership of the hosts of Moses and Joshua, that is, of the Tribe of Ephraim, did they also turn to the God ". This group is now supposed to have solemnly forsaken its " established religious traditions "

[1] Bin Gurion, Sinai und Garizim (1926), p. 405.

[2] Noth, Das Buch Josua (1938), p. 108.

[3] *Cf.* in particular : Sellin, Geschichte des Israelitisch-juedischen Volkes I (1924) ; Noth, Das System der zwoelf Staemme Israels (1930), p. 66 ff. ; Steuernagel, Jahwe und die Vaetergoetter (Festschrift Georg Beer, 1935), p. 63 ff.

and to have chosen YHVH, thus likewise joining in the Covenantal worship which found its centre at Shechem.

Only in such a way, these scholars hold, is it possible to explain the fact that the People of Israel appear here not as though they had once been present at Mount Sinai, but as a people " the greater portion of whom are still idolatrous, and who still have to remove the false gods from their midst ". And among those gods that have to be removed are likewise numbered " all the gods of the Fathers of Israel ". By those " other gods " which, according to verses 2 and 14, had formerly been served by the Fathers, their own particular gods are meant ; the *elim* which were peculiar to them.

But not only is there no trace in the text of any such division of the people into two (for after all, it is impossible to attribute the phrase " I and my house " to all the tribes which participated in the wanderings through the wilderness, even though the latter may have been few in number) ; not only do all the responses in the dialogue sound as though they are the responses of " the people " but, as the first of these responses, the people declare (verse 16) : " Far be it from us to *forsake* YHVH in order to serve other gods ".

Hence the people had followed YHVH until that time as well ; and Joshua refers to those words in his reply (verse 20). For his own words, " If you forsake YHVH and serve strange gods . . . ", have the implication : you forsake YHVH even if you only worship strange gods *beside* Him. To this the people reply : " No (not so), but YHVH (and He alone) shall we serve." It is impossible to see a late addition in the words " Far be it from us to forsake YHVH ", which actually serve as the main theme of the dialogue. Here it is stated quite clearly that " the people " had followed YHVH until that day *according to their own view;* that is, in their aspect of a complete unit. Yet what follows (verse 19) makes it clear that *in the eyes of Joshua* such service is not regarded as true service of YHVH, since it was not absolute ; it did not satisfy the demand of the " Holy God ", of this " zealous God ".

The meaning of their words to Joshua is : assuredly we recognize YHVH. But the purpose of the words of Joshua to them is : there is no true recognition of YHVH when those recognizing Him recognize other powers as well ; you must decide to whom it is that you wish to cleave, whether to those powers or to Him ; for from this moment you are not entitled to imagine that you may do both things together. It cannot be claimed, to be sure, that in this word " other " Joshua had referred to other gods in the simple sense of *elim* ; for if he had been referring to them, the people could not have denied so energetically that they thought of other gods. What, in that case, was his purpose ? And what, in that case, was the sin of the people against the Covenant, which necessitated the renewal of the latter ?

The people are not at all aware that they are supposed to have served other gods ; for *as a people* they had no other gods. As far as they are aware, they really had no other gods, for with the exception of YHVH they had no god who was *common* to them all. Nor did any single tribe have a separate god of its own ; all of them, as we have seen, participate in the general declaration. But the families have separate gods, family gods, household gods, private gods, the existence of which had not made any impression on public consciousness. These gods are almost certainly in the form of wooden masks. The term *tharaph*, the root of which is found in a text from Ugarit (Ras Shamra), and which is found only in the plural in the Scriptures, seems to have been explained in later texts as something that gradually rots away. It is easier to get on with them, to be sure, than with the invisible spirit. They secure happiness, they increase strength, they foretell the future, recourse may be had to them at all times or under any of the situations which are liable to befall in life ; and the womenfolk bring them to the homes of their husbands from the homes of their fathers. Characteristic of them is the fact that they are nameless gods, that they have no personality, that they enjoy neither mythos nor worship [1] ; they are entirely incidental gods, gods by the by, as it were. They were incidental gods in the cultural regions of Babylon and Syria, among those peoples in whose midst Israel passed along its way. They were brought from " strange parts ". Now they are incidental gods in Israel. And it is in that respect, and in that respect specifically, that they must be " put away ".

How are they to be put away ? The legends of the Fathers contain the following description (Genesis xxxv, 2-4) : All the " strange gods " are handed over to the head of the family, who buries them under a holy tree in the vicinity of Shechem ; and this would appear to be the tree under which Joshua set up the memorial stone. Here too, in the legend, the act of putting away bears the implication that a fresh situation has come about. In the historical story we find a kind of concentration which bears the stamp of history. Here no fundamental distinction can be drawn between religion and politics, just as in general no distinction could be drawn between them in Israel, at the period when the singular qualities of the latter began to assume form. Since these private incidental gods weaken the concentration of the people round YHVH, they prevent the establishment of a unified " Israel ", which could be capable of functioning in history as a unified people. This is made particularly clear in a well-preserved fragment (I Samuel, vii, 3) which linguistically resembles the earlier portion in the narrative of the Book of Joshua. This fragment belongs to a tale dating from the days of the Wars of the Philistines, the remaining sections of which have been reworked again and again. In this tale Samuel commands " the whole house of Israel " to return unto YHVH with all their hearts, to remove from their midst the strange gods (the word " and the Ashtoreths " is a later addition), to " prepare " their hearts for YHVH and to serve Him *alone*. The corresponding action on the part of Joshua is an expression and outcome of his experience while he had been leader and general of the people ; no matter whether all the tribes were under his command, as would appear from the Biblical account, or only a smaller group.[2] Up to this point the conquest of the country

---

[1] Kaufmann quite correctly points out this fact (History of the Hebrew Religion I, p. 675 and elsewhere) ; but he identifies the *baalim* with the *theraphim* without any reason for doing so.

[2] *Cf.* Alt, Josua (Werden und Wesen des Alten Testaments, 1936), p. 1 ff.

had been only partially successful, because there was not any real and vital national unity in existence as yet. The lives of the tribes were largely restricted to family interests, and remained subject to the family gods. The people could not exist in history as a unit and a reality unless they became, absolutely and entirely, " the people of Yhvh " ; unless Yhvh became absolutely, entirely and indisputably the " God of Israel ".

It was this that was the crux of the matter here, as it was to be later on in the Song of Deborah. The association of the tribes upon which Joshua stamped an organic form can have had its centre nowhere else than in the sanctuary of Yhvh ; and the forms of its gatherings could not have been any except those of the festivals of Yhvh.

NOTES

[1] Usener, Der Stoff des griechischen Epos. Sitzungsberichte der Wiener Akademie der Wissenschaften, philologisch-historische Klasse CXXXVII (1897), p. 4 f. (reprinted in Usener, Kleine Schriften IV, p. 201 f.).

[2] Herzfeld, Mythos und Geschichte. Archæologische Mitteilungen aus Iran VI (1933), p. 102 ff.

[3] Jacob Grimm, Gedanken ueber Mythos, Epos und Geschichte. Deutsches Museum 1813, III, p. 53 (reprinted in Jacob Grimm, Kleinere Schriften IV, p. 74).

[4] B. Jacob, in a study on " The Childhood and Youth of Moses, the Messenger of God " which reached me only after the completion of this book (Essays in Honour of the Very Rev. Dr. J. H. Hertz, 1942), p. 250, declares that there can be no question of a legal adoption in the Biblical narrative. That the report, however, of the child being brought to the daughter of Pharaoh and becoming as her son (Exodus ii, 10) indicates that Moses was brought up to maturity by the Princess, cannot well be disputed. Incidentally, the passage in II Samuel vii, 14, quoted by Jacob, where God says that Solomon will become His son, is clearly a metaphor drawn from the sphere of legal adoption ; compare the analogous formula in Psalms ii, 7.

[5] Sethe, Die Totenliteratur der Alten Aegypter (1931), p. 9.

[6] A good, although still incomplete, review is given by Jirku, Die Wanderungen der Hebraeer (1924). Since that time certain important facts have become known without, however, considerably changing the general picture.

[7] Speiser, Ethnic Movements in the Near East in the Second Millennium B.C. (1933).

[8] Toynbee, A Study of History III (1934), p. 14.

[9] Ed. Meyer, Geschichte des Altertums I, 2, para. 340.

[10] Cahun, Introduction à l'histoire de l'Asie (1896), p. 48.

[11] Cf. Buber, The Teaching of the Prophets (Hebrew, 1942), p. 30 f. ; also von Rad, Das formgeschichtliche Problem des Hexateuchs (1938), p. 3 f. (" The rhythmical and alliterative character of the beginning is particularly archaic.")

[12] Lewy, Ḫābirū and Hebrews, Hebrew Union College Annual XIV (1939), p. 616, interprets : " A disloyal servant who rose against his master ". To me, however, this does not seem to follow of necessity from the fact that in the texts, as was actually the custom in all literatures, a servant is compared to a dog. A runaway dog does not rise against its master.

[13] Cf. in particular Landsberger, Ḫabiru und Lulaḫḫu (Kleinasiatische Forschungen, I, 1930), p. 327.

[14] Cf. Buber, Koenigtum Gottes, 2nd Ed. (1936), p. 73 ff. ; Buber, The Teaching of the Prophets, p. 29 ff. Haller in " Religion, Recht und Sitte in den Genesissagen " (1905), p. 32, justly remarks : " Since the God concept of the legend of the Fathers contains all these characteristics, not only a considerable uniformity, but also the character of the real God of the nomads, must be ascribed to him. It is therefore scarcely thinkable that so lively a memory of the requirements of nomad life should be nothing more than a literary costume, which could also have altered the God idea."

[15] Radloff, Aus Sibirien, 2nd Ed. (1893) I, p. 517.

[16] Grimme, Althebraeische Handschriften von Sinai (1923), p. 95.

[17] Lowie, An Introduction to Cultural Anthropology (1934), p. 53.

[18] Strzygowski, Asiens bildende Kunst (1930), p. 578.

[19] Hasebroek, Griechische Wirtschafts-und Gesellschaftsgeschichte (1931), p. 1.

[20] Mauss, Critique interne de la légende d'Abraham. Revue des Études Juives lxxxii (1926), p. 39.

[21] B. Jacob, Das erste Buch der Thora (1934), p. 376.

[22] Despite the similar Babylonian and Canaanite terms for "warrior, fellow-warrior, man sworn to war", it seems to me that this meaning should be adhered to as being the original one.

[23] We find this verb with the meaning of the parental bringing-forth in Genesis iv, 1 and, in rather more attenuated fashion, in Deuteronomy xxxii, 6. In an epic text of the Ras Shamra the spouse of the highest God is described by this very term as the "bringer forth" of the Gods. (It must, however, be noted that this meaning is being contested by Levi della Vida, El 'Elyon in Genesis XIV, 18-20, Journal of Biblical Literature, lxiii, 1944, p. 1 ff.)

[24] Cf. Westermarck, Ritual and Belief in Morocco (1926) I, p. 35 ff.

[25] Thus, for example : Peet, Egypt and the Old Testament (1922) ; Jack, The Date of the Exodus (1925) ; Musil, The Northern Hejaz (1926) ; Garstang, The Foundations of Bible History, Joshua-Judges (1931) ; Oesterley and T. H. Robinson, A History of Israel, I (1932) ; Yahuda, The Accuracy of the Bible (1934) ; cf. also Yahuda, The Year of the Exodus (Hebrew), The American Hebrew Year Book, vii, 1944, p. 126 ff.

[26] Thus, for example, Wardle in H. W. Robinson, Record and Revelation (1938) ; Albright, From the Stone Age to Christianity (1940) ; J. Kaufmann, History of the Religion of Israel (Hebrew) IV (1942).

[27] R. Kittel, Geschichte des Volkes Israel I, 5-6 Ed. (1923), p. 366.

[28] Thus, for example, Frazer, Folklore in the Old Testament (1919) II, p. 438 ff.

[29] Lord Raglan, The Hero (1936), p. 178.

[30] Yahuda, op. cit., p. 60 ff.

[31] Yahuda, op. cit., p. 65 f.

[32] In the article already mentioned B. Jacob also indicates, p. 253, that there is a play upon words here. It is his opinion, however, that the name was actually given to the child with this specific sense by the linguistic advisers of the Princess, who were presumably familiar with Hebrew ; and that thereby they wished to express the hope that "he himself is to draw his people out of the waves of death " ; where " waves of death " has to be regarded as a popular simile and poetic speech. I cannot concur in this view. The passage from Isaiah in particular proves that the idea behind the name is not the metaphorical waters of death, but the actual waters of the Red Sea.

[33] Cf. Buber und Rosenweig, Die Schrift und ihre Verdeutschung (1936), p. 39 ff., 58 ff., 64 ff., 68 ff., 72 ff., 116 f., 126 f., 152 f., 211 ff., 249 ff., 262 ff.

[34] Cf. Phythian-Adams, The Call of Israel (1934), p. 144 f., who points out that in the country of the Masai on the Congo a volcano is called " The God mountain ". The author, however, does not notice the fact that the Masai have obviously been influenced by Biblical traditions in the shaping of their mythology.

[35] Gressmann, Mose und seine Zeit (1913), p. 30.

[36] Gressmann, op. cit., p. 21. From this statement, which cannot be supported from the text, the author draws the conclusion on p. 442 f. that : " An inner experience such as that enjoyed by the prophets who left writings, or by Jesus, is excluded ab initio ". That is, it is " not testified to anywhere ". Gressmann's addition, namely that an experience of the kind runs counter to " the spirit of antiquity ", is quite incomprehensible to me. It is impossible to understand Zarathustra, for example, without positing some actual religious experience ; and Moses even less. Cf. also J. Kaufmann, History of the Religion of Israel (Hebrew) II, 1 (1942), p. 48 f.

[37] Gressmann, op. cit., p. 22.

[38] Cf. Isidore Lévy, La légende de Pythagore de Grèce en Palestine (1927), p. 137 ff.

[39] B. Jacob, Mose am Dornbusch, Monatsschrift fuer die Geschichte und Wissenschaft des Judentums, New Series, XXX (1922), p. 17. Special reference should be made at this point to Jacob's as yet unpublished commentary on Exodus.

[40] Cf. Schmoekel, Das angewandte Recht im Alten Testament (1930), p. 8.

[41] I have given a detailed criticism of this thesis in my work, "Koenigtum Gottes", 2nd Ed., p. xxxi ff.

[42] Montgomery, Arabia and the Bible (1934), p. 10.

[43] Gressmann, op. cit., p. 434.

[44] Cf. Buber, The Teaching of the Prophets, p. 36 ff.

[45] Cf. Kaufmann, op. cit., II, 1 p. 279 ff.

[46] That early tribal gods are also creators is known to us from countless myths, of which the Polynesian and North American are particularly characteristic. For the myth-makers the land of the tribe means the entire earth, since it alone affects them directly.

[47] God, using the same choice of words, says to Moses (Exodus xxxiii, 19) that He will call out the name of YHVH before him; and it is told with the identical wording (xxxiv, 5) that He does so.

[48] Cf. Buber, Koenigtum Gottes, pp. 84, 235 ff., and the literature referred to there; Buber-Rosenzweig, Die Schrift und ihre Verdeutschung, pp. 201 f., 207 f.; Buber, The Teaching of the Prophets, pp. 26 f., 35, and the literature referred to there; more recently A. Vincent, La religion des Judéo-Araméens d'Eléphantine (1937), p. 46. Among the literature that reached me after the completion of this book the article of Montgomery, The Hebrew Divine Name and the Personal Pronoun HU, Journal of Biblical Literature, LXIII/2, 1944, p. 161 ff., is noteworthy. It refers to II Kings ii, 14 and Jeremiah v, 12.)

[49] Nicholson, Selected Poems from the Dīvāni Shamsi Tabriz (1899), p. 126 f., 282.

[50] Mowinckel in a letter to Rudolf Otto, printed in R. Otto, Das Gefuehl des Ueberweltlichen (1932), p. 326 f.

[51] L. Koehler, Theologie des Alten Testaments (1936), p. 234.

[52] This should be read : wa-thiga.

[53] Among certain Arab tribes of the Sinai Peninsula and the South Egyptian desert, this is done by the mother or sister of the circumcised boy placing the severed foreskin on her toe and keeping it lying there as long as possible (G. W. Murray, Sons of Ishmael, 1935, p. 176); in this way the practice is also of use to the women of the tribe.

[54] So Ed. Meyer, Die Israeliten und ihre Nachbarstaemme (1906), p. 59; Ed. Meyer, Geschichte des Altertums II 2, 2nd Ed. (1931), p. 206; Weill, Le séjour des Israélites au désert (1909), p. 66; Gressmann, Mose, p. 56 ff.; Loisy, La religion d'Israel, 3rd Ed. (1933), p. 91 f.; most recently Beer, Exodus (1939), p. 38 f. Similarly already Mauss, Essai sur le sacrifice, L'année sociologique II (1899), p. 134.

[55] Rudolph, Der "Elohist" von Exodus bis Josua (1938), p. 7.

[56] Volz, Das Daemonische in Jahwe (1924).

[57] The considerations adduced against Aaron having been the brother of Moses are of weight, but not convincing.

[58] Jaussen, Coutumes des Arabes au pays du Moab (1908), p. 366.

[59] Pedersen, Passahfest und Passahlegende, Zeitschrift fuer die alttestamentliche Wissenschaft, New Series XI (1937), p. 167.

[60] Gressmann, Mose, p 120.

[61] That she is called "the sister of Aaron" here, and is also mentioned elsewhere together with him, may well be explained on the basis of an old clan tradition, which can no longer be precisely apprehended by us, according to which the older members of the family constituted a group on their own; to which the clan-member adopted by the Egyptian woman, or more strongly Egyptized for other personal reasons, did not belong.

[62] The material speaking in favour of this has been best collected in Phythian-Adams, The Call of Israel, p. 166 ff.

[63] *Cf.* Buber, Koenigtum Gottes, p. 131 f., also Galling, Die Erwaehlungstraditionen Israels (1928), p. 6 : " Here speaks the unbroken national consciousness of the whole people. This can most easily be thought of in the era of David."

[64] *Cf.* Buber, *op. cit.*, p. 63 ff.

[65] *Cf.* Eichrodt, Theologie des Alten Testaments I (1933), p. 95 f.

[66] The verse does not consist, as is usually supposed, of two phrases but of a single one ; the second, " Who is like thee " is only an intensifying reiteration (*cf.* verse 6). It should be understood as : Which among the protective gods, O YHVH, is so glorified in holiness as thee, dread in praiseworthy works and performer of wonders !

[67] *Cf.* A. Kaiser, Wanderungen und Wandlungen in der Sinaiwueste (1928), p. 21 ff. ; Bodenheimer and Theodor, Ergebnisse der Sinai Expedition 1927 (1929), p. 54 ff.

[68] J. Hehn, Siebenzahl und Sabbat bei der Babyloniern und im Alten Testament (1907), pp. 6 ff., 93. *Cf.*, however, H. and J. Lewy, The Origin of the Week and the Oldest West Asiatic Calendar, Hebrew Union College Annual, XVII (1942/3), p. 16 f.

[69] Colson, The Week, an Essay on the Origin and Development of the Seven-Day Cycle (1926), p. 3 is right in observing that the early forms of the sequence of weeks have nothing to do with the phases of the moon.

[70] Doughty, Travels in Arabia Deserta I, chapter 13.

[71] The contrary views of Jastrow, The Original Character of the Hebrew Sabbath, American Journal of Theology II, 1898, p. 323 ff., are not convincing. The hypothesis that the Sabbath was originally a day of fasting is also unfounded. (The arguments in favour of it can be found in Webster, Rest Days, p. 259 f.) The view of Nilsson in Primitive Time-reckoning (1920), p. 333 ff., that the Sabbath was originally a market day, is wrong in assuming the late (although pre-exilic) development. The authors of the article mentioned in note 68, H. and J. Lewy, assume that the seven-day week (after the failure of an attempt at calendar reform under King Josiah) developed out of the original fifty-day unit of Ancient Orient only in the time of Ezra ; the valuable article, containing in particular important indications of the connection of the Babylonian septenary system with the number of winds, failed, however, to convince me of the late origin of the seven-day week.

[72] Hehn, *op. cit.*, p. 130.

[73] Wellhausen, Rede zur Feier des Geburtstages Seiner Majestaet des Kaisers und Koenigs (1900).

[74] *Cf.* Buber, Koenigtum Gottes, p. 47 ff.

[75] *Cf.* Buber, *op. cit.* p. 4 ff.

[76] It seems that Joshua's original name Hoshea was expanded to Yehoshua upon his adoption into a narrower YHVH association.

[77] Lobeck, Ueber die Symbolik des Szepters, in : Auswahl aus Lobecks akademischen Reden, published by Lehnardt (1865), p. 71.

[78] Musil, Arabia Petraea III (1908), p. 377.

[79] *Cf.* Buber, Koenigtum Gottes, p. 284.

[80] Budde, Religion of Israel to the Exile (1899), p. 25.

[81] *Cf.* the texts of Rabbinic and Karaite exegetes compiled by Bin Gorion in Sinai und Garizim (1926), p. 222 ff.

[82] Oesterley and T. H. Robinson, Hebrew Religion (1930), p. 112.

[83] Budde, *op. cit.*, p. 22 f.

[84] Gressmann, Mose, p. 161 ; *cf.* Gray, Sacrifice in the Old Testament (1925), p. 208.

[85] Budde, *op. cit.*, p. 24.

[86] Budde, Die Altisraelitische Religion (1912), p. 132. The Septuagint reading " and Jethro offered " (*wa-yaqrib* instead of *wa-yiqaḥ*) is based on a defective technical grasp of what took place.

[87] See the commentaries of Ibn Ezra and Rashbam.

[88] On community sacrifice or " total sacrifice " among the Arabs see Wellhausen, Reste arabischen Heidentums, 2nd Ed., p. 120.

[89] Albright, From the Stone Age to Christianity, p. 195.

[90] Eerdman's assumption, in : Alttestamentliche Studien II (1901), p. 44 ff., that the Kenites were craftsmen settled at the oases, many of whom, and particularly the smiths, went to live with the nomads for longer or briefer periods, calls for some qualification ; in no case should this semi-nomadic type be described as " town-dwellers ". Eisler, Das Qainzeichen und die Qeniter, Le Monde Oriental XXIII, 1929, p. 59 ff., offers suggestions worthy of notice, particularly regarding Kenite activities as ore-smelters, but tries to prove too much.

[91] Buber, Koenigtum Gottes, p. xliv.

[92] It is in no way " unnatural " (Gray, Sacrifice in the Old Testament, p. 207), but is the Oriental fashion of speech, for Jethro to offer his advice in such a manner that he first formulates that part of Moses' experience which he afterwards recommends him to continue. For this reason it is baseless to assume with Gray that there was an earlier version of the story in which Moses had not previously had this experience, but that he learnt this from Jethro as well. Is it really likely for the tale originally to have run that Moses now learnt from his father-in-law that he had " to be before God for the people " (verse 19).

[93] In passages such as Judges vi, 15, I Samuel x, 19, the word elef means not " thousand " but racial association, gens, in accordance with the original meaning of the root " to associate " (cf. the noun elef., herd).

[94] Phythian-Adams, The Call of Israel, p. 76,

[95] Volz, Mose, 2nd Ed. (1932), p. 84 ; cf. also Staerk, Zum alttestamentlichen Erwaehlungsglauben (Zeitschrift fuer die alttestamentliche Wissenschaft, New Series, XIV, 1937), p. 8, and von Rad, Das formgeschichtliche Problem des Hexateuchs, p. 36.

[96] Buber, Koenigtum Gottes, p. 112 ff. ; cf. also Quell, article $\delta\iota\alpha\theta\acute{\eta}\kappa\eta$ in Kittel, Theologisches Woerterbuch zum Neuen Testament II (1935), p. 123.

[97] Gressmann, Die Anfaenge Israels (Die Schriften des Alten Testaments I, 2), 2nd Ed. (1922), p. 60 ; cf. Gressmann, Mose, p. 185.

[98] Eissfeldt, Einleitung in das Alte Testament (1934), p. 260.

[99] Cf. Buber, Koenigtum Gottes, p. 126 ff. Regarding the interpretation in detail cf. Staerk, Zum alttestamentlichen Erwaehlungsglauben, p. 8 ff.

[100] Cf. the excellent exposition in Baudissin, Kyrios als Gottesname im Judentum III (1927), p. 379 ff. (See p. 398 ff. in particular for the attribute of justice.)

[101] Cf. Buber, Koenigtum Gottes, p. 140 ff.

[102] Ibid., p. 132 ff., 273 ff. ; cf. also Gunkel, Einleitung in die Psalmen (1933), p. 208.

[103] Eichrodt, Theologie des Alten Testaments I, p. 96.

[104] Cf. Buber, Koenigtum Gottes, p. 69 f., 93 ff., 211 ff.

[105] On Gideon see ibid., p. 3 ff. I have demonstrated the unity of nucleus of the Samuel story in my as yet unpublished work, " The Anointed" (passages from which have appeared in the Hebrew Historical Quarterly Zion IV, 1939, pp. 1 ff.).

[106] On the age of the first constituent cf. Steuernagel, Der jehovistische Bericht ueber den Bundesschluss, Theologische Studien und Kritiken LXXII (1899), p. 349 f. ; on that of the second cf. Baentsch, Exodus-Leviticus-Numeri (1903), p. 213 f., Gressmann, Mose, p. 182.

[107] Cf. Buber, Koenigtum Gottes, p. 254 f.

[108] Cf. T. H. Robinson, The Crises, in H. W. Robinson, Record and Revelation (1938), p. 141.

[109] Noth, Das System der zwoelf Staemme Israels (1930).

[110] Sellin, Geschichte des israelitisch-juedischen Volkes I (1924), p. 98 ff. ; Noth, op. cit. p. 69 f.

[111] In view of the importance of the subject, I append above (p. 202) a translation of the relevant passage from my Hebrew work, "The Teaching of the Prophets".

[112] Volz, Mose, pp. 77, 88 ; cf. also Caspari, Die Gottesgemeinde von Sinaj (1922), p. 168.

[113] Noth, Die israelitischen Personennamen (1929), p. 191 f., 208 f.

[114] Cf. Sachsse, Die Bedeutung des Namens Israel (1922), p. 91.

[115] Cf. Buber, Koenigtum Gottes, pp. 219, 224 ; Baudissin, Die Geschichte des alttestamentlichen Priestertums (1889), p. 55 ff. ; Baudissin, art. Priests and Levites, in Hastings' Dictionary of the Bible IV, p. 69 f. Van Hoonacker, Le sacerdoce lévitique dans la loi et dans l'histoire (1899) understands " servers of the people in the procedure of the God cult " ; but that is a strangely complicated concept. In that case one would expect simply " the lads " instead of the " lads of the Children of Israel " ; as correspondingly for Joshua (Exodus xxxiii, 11) and Samuel (I Samuel iii, 1).

[116] " The occasion described here is unique ; and so, in some respects, is the ritual." Gray, Sacrifice in the Old Testament, p. 200.

[117] Cf. Buber, Koenigtum Gottes, p. 111 ff.

[118] Op. cit., p. 123 f.

[119] Buber, The Teaching of the Prophets, p. 118.

[120] Baudissin, " Gott schauen " in der alttestamentlichen Religion (Archiv fuer Religionswissenschaft XVIII, 1915), p 217.

[121] Buresch, Klaros (1899), p. 89 ff. ; the passage on the Decalogue is found on p. 116.

[122] Wellhausen, Skizzen und Vorarbeiten I, Die Composition des Hexateuchs p. 96.

[123] Alt, Die Urspruenge des israelitischen Rechts (1929), p. 52 ; cf. Rudolph, Der " Elohist " von Exodus bis Josua, p. 59 : " a conglomerate of little value from the Book of the Covenant, which is in no way source material ".

[124] B. Duhm, Israels Propheten (1916), p. 38.

[125] Beer, Exodus, p. 162.

[126] Hoelscher, Geschichte der israelitischen und juedischen Religion (1922), p. 129.

[127] Steuernagel, Einleitung in das Alte Testament (1912), p. 260.

[128] Beer, op. cit. p. 103.

[129] Budde, Religion of Israel to the Exile, p. 33 : " both superfluous and impossible ".

[130] Mowinckel, Le décalogue (1927), p. 102, is of the opinion that unlike the Decalogue the moral elements " seem to be lost within a long series of ritual and cultic commandments " ; but a glance at the text shows that the ritual and cultic commandments constitute less than half in the Egyptian, and only a small fraction in the Babylonian.

[131] Bruno Gutmann, Die Stammeslehren der Dschagga (3 vols , 1932 ff.).

[132] Mowinckel, op. cit. p. 101.

[133] Nowack, Der erste Dekalog (Baudissin-Festschrift, 1917), p. 395.

[134] Beer, Moses und sein Werk (1912), p. 26.

[135] Cf. J. Kaufmann, History of the Religion of Israel, II/1, p. 77. He connects Aaron with these influences.

[136] With regard to the powerful influence exerted particularly by the " Faustian " element in the Moses saga on Goethe, cf. the fine essay by Burdach, Faust und Mose (Sitzungsberichte der Koeniglich Preussischen Akademie der Wissenschaften, philosophisch-historische Klasse, 1912).

[137] Mowinckel, op. cit. p. 75.

[138] Wellhausen, Reste arabischen Heidentums, p. 102.

[139] Chantepie de la Saussaye, Lehrbuch der Religionsgeschichte, 4th Ed. (1925), I, p. 89.

[140] Thus, *e.g.*, Edvard Lehmann, *ibid.*, I, p. 33 ; *cf.* also Florenz, *ibid.*, I, p. 294 ;
Hempel, Politische Absicht und politische Wirkung im biblischen Schrifttum (1938),
p. 14 ; also Gressmann, Mose, pp. 203, 207, 211. In my book, "The Teaching of the
Prophets", I have dealt with the matter in detail in the chapter, "The God of the
Fathers" ; *cf.* also Koenigtum Gottes, p. 73 ff.

[141] Lagrange, Études sur les religions sémitiques, 2nd Ed. (1905), p. 507 ; *cf.*
Février, La religion des Palmyréens (1931), p. 37 ; *cf.* also Rostovtzeff, The Caravan-
gods of Palmyra (Journal of Roman Studies XXII, 1932), p. 111 f.

[142] Schrader, Die Keilinschriften und das Alte Testament, 3rd Ed. (1903), p. 29.

[143] Haller, Religion, Recht und Sitte in den Genesissagen, p. 23, is of the opinion,
to be sure, that YHVH "detached himself from stone, tree and spring and linked
himself with the person of the shepherd", but also remarks : "Or is the process
to be regarded as reversed, so that Yahve was originally a protective spirit that wandered with the shepherds and gradually, as the nomads began to settle, became
established at a fixed habitation ?" Gunkel noted in his copy of Haller's book
that stationary god and settled worshippers as Canaanite are faced by "wandering god and wandering nomads as *Israelite*". It must, however, be added that this
god does not sleep in the tents of the nomads like the *theraphim* fetishes, but from time
to time withdraws to the spacious heavens, which are inaccessible to men ; Jacob's
vision of the gate of Heaven is a primordial constituent of the tradition. (That
it is therefore impossible to "have" this god may hence have been one of the
chief reasons for the women of the tribe to take the *theraphim* about with them.)

[144] According to Lods, Israel, p. 531, the people imagined YHVH with an aerial
and therefore invisible body, "susceptible d'apparaitre sous des formes diverses".

[145] For the relation between imagelessness and invisibility *cf.* Max Weber,
Gesammelte Aufsaetze zur Religionssoziologie (1921) III, p. 170, who sees the relation otherwise but as no less close : "A god whose cult has been imageless since immemorial time had to be normally invisible as well, and also had to nourish his specific
dignity and uncanny quality by means of that invisibility".

[146] Mowinckel, *ibid.*, p. 103.

[147] Mowinckel, *ibid.*, p. 60.

[148] Mowinckel, Psalmenstudien II (1922), p. 224.

[149] Mowinckel, Le décalogue, p. 100.

[150] Eissfeldt, Hexateuch-Synopse (1922), p. 275 *.

[151] *Cf.* Koehler, Theologie des Alten Testaments, p. 238 : "The fact that in the
Biblical decalogue any such commandment as 'Thou shalt not lie' is absent,
awakens all kinds of thoughts".

[152] Gunkel, Die israelitische Literatur (Die Kultur der Gegenwart I/7, 1906), p. 73.

[153] Gressmann, Mose, p. 477.

[154] *Cf.* Buber-Rosenzweig, Die Schrift und ihre Verdeutschung, p. 176 ff. ;
Staples, The Third Commandment, Journal of Biblical Literature LVIII (1939),
p. 325 ff.

[155] *Cf.* Procksch, Der Staatsgedanke in der Prophetie (1933), p. 5.

[156] J. M. Powis Smith, The Origin and History of Hebrew Law (1931), p. 8 f.

[157] Hempel, Das Ethos des Alten Testaments (1938), p. 183.

[158] Volz, Mose, 2nd Ed., p. 25.

[159] Volz, Mose, 1st Ed. (1907), p. 93 f.

[160] Caspari, Die Gottesgemeinde von Sinaj, p. 159.

[161] Sellin, Geschichte des israelitisch-juedischen Volkes I, p. 72.

[162] Volz, Mose, 2nd Ed., p. 78.

[163] L. Koehler, Der Dekalog (Theologische Rundschau I, 1929), p. 184.

[164] Rudolph, Der "Elohist", p. 47.

[165] *Cf.* Ganszyniec, Der Ursprung der Zehngebotetafeln (1920), p. 18. (The
little study contains interesting material, from which, however, unwarrantable conclusions are drawn.)

[166] *Cf.* Eerdmans, Alttestamentliche Studien III, p. 69 f.

[167] Morgenstern, The Book of the Covenant I (1928), p. 34, argues against the originality of the tradition of the Tables that the description " Tables of Witness " is late, and is only found in the Priestly Code. But Exodus xxxii, 15, in general, is not attributed to P.

[168] Morgenstern, *loc. cit.*, adduces the absence of any such tradition as his chief argument against the witness character of the Tables. But it seems reasonable to assume that Solomon, with his cult policy which aimed at immobilizing the Ark and its contents in order to withdraw the political coloration from the *melek* character of YHVH, would have no objection to ordering the removal of all traces of such a tradition (*cf.* Klamroth, Lade und Tempel, 1933, p. 60 ; Buber, The Teaching of the Prophets, p. 78 f.).

[169] Hans Schmidt, Mose und der Dekalog (Gunkel-Festschrift), p. 90.

[170] L. Koehler, Der Dekalog, p. 179.

[171] Wellhausen (Die Composition des Hexateuchs, p. 89), followed by many others, has regarded the word as " most strikingly " Deuteronomic ; but this can have a meaning only if the end of the Song of Deborah is mutilated ; which has been done by some for no other reason than the use of this word. The turns of phrase which it is customary to regard as Deuteronomic, and hence as late, derive naturally from the history sermon (*cf.* Koehler, Der Dekalog, p. 169) ; which collected its basic phrases from verbal and written tradition, while admittedly depriving them of their original weight by incorporating them in the rhetorical sequence. The fact that Exodus xxxiv, 7 does not mention the haters and the lovers does not prove anything, since here almost half of the sentence, including the entire positive section, has been omitted. This appears to be an extract from the Decalogue section, introduced here for elucidatory purposes.

[172] A. Klostermann, Der Pentateuch II (1907), p. 515.

[173] Jepsen, Untersuchungen zum Bundesbuch (1927), p. 25 ; *cf.* S. A. Cook, The Laws of Moses and the Code of Hammurabi (1903), p. 155.

[174] *Cf.* Ring, Israels Rechtsleben im Lichte der neuentdeckten assyrischen und hethitischen Gesetzesurkunden (1926), p. 148.

[175] Schmoekel, Das angewandte Recht im Alten Testament, p. 65.

[176] *Cf.* Eerdmans, The Ark of the Covenant (The Expositor, 1912), p. 415 f.

[177] It is not correct, as supposed by Benzinger, Jahvist und Elohist in den Koenigsbuechern (1921), p. 12, that the plural would be suitable here because there are two images. Nobody would say of two images which are placed at two different spots, " These are thy gods ".

[178] Albright, From the Stone Age to Christianity, p. 230 : " Conceptually there is, of course, no essential difference between representing the invisible king as enthroned on the cherubim or as standing on a bull ".

[179] Reichel, Ueber vorhellenische Goettterculte (1897), p. 37.

[180] Oppenheim, Der Tell Halaf (1931), p. 85.

[181] *Cf.* inter alia Malten, Der Stier in Kult und mythischem Bild (Jahrbuch des Deutschen Archæologischen Instituts XLIII, 1928), p. 101 ff. ; where, however, it becomes particularly clear that the concept of the god-carrier can develop into that of the incarnation of the god. The historical way is the reverse, from the bull " as the abode of a demon or a god " to the bull as a god-carrier and divine attribute ; but in such developments popular atavisms are frequent. Eissfeldt, Der Gott Bethel (Archiv fuer Religionswissenschaft XXVIII, 1930), p. 15, justly points out that precisely the same weather-god, who is imagined as standing on the bull, is also himself portrayed as a bull ; however, it should be borne in mind that since the purpose of Jeroboam was primarily to introduce the " true " and legitimate YHVH cult, he could not permit himself to go too far.

[182] Obbink, Jahwebilder (Zeitschrift fuer die alttestamentliche Wissenschaft, New Series, VI, 1929), p. 269.

[183] Hempel, Jahwegleichnisse der israelitischen Propheten (Zeitschrift fuer die alttestamentliche Wissenschaft, New Series, I, 1924), p. 101.

[184] *Ibid.*

[185] R. Kittel, Geschichte des Volkes Israel I, 5/6th Ed., p. 374.

[186] *Cf.* Eichrodt, Theologie des Alten Testaments I, p. 47; Albright, From the Stone Age to Christianity, p. 203.

[187] Caspari, Die Samuelbuecher (1926), p. 476.

[188] *Cf.* inter alia Reichel, Ueber vorhellenische Goetterculte, p. 3 ff.; A. B. Cook, Zeus, I (1914), p. 135 ff.; S. A. Cook, The Religion of Ancient Palestine in the Light of Archæology (1930), p. 21 ff.; Dibelius, Die Lade Jahves (1906), p. 60 ff.; Hans Schmidt, Kerubenthron und Lade (Gunkel-Festschrift), p. 132 ff.

[189] *Cf.* inter alia Dibelius, *op. cit.*, p. 96 ff.

[190] Musil, The Manners and Customs of the Rwala Bedouins (1928), p. 571 ff.; Jaussen, Coutumes des Arabes au pays du Moab (1908), p. 173 f.; relevant material from various accounts of journeys can be found in R. Hartmann, Zelt und Lade (Zeitschrift fuer die alttestamentliche Wissenschaft XXXVII, 1917/18), p. 217 ff.; Seligman, Sacred Litters among the Semites, Sudan Notes and Records I (1918), p. 265 ff.; and Morgenstern, The Book of the Covenant I, p. 88 ff.; *cf.* also Lammens, Le culte des bétyles et les processions religieuses chez les Arabes préislamites, Bulletin de l'Institut Francais d'Archéologie Orientale XVII (1920), p. 38 ff. Recently, the subject has found a comprehensive presentation, based upon thorough comparison of the ethnological material in Morgenstern, The Ark, the Ephod and the Tent of Meeting, Hebrew Union College Annual XVII (1942-43), pp. 153-265, XVIII (1944), pp. 1-52. Unfortunately the learned study does not appreciate the place and the value of the historical, the happening but once, in the history of religion. History of religion and history in general exists only if, and as far as, we distinguish between the happening but once and the recurring, the first being a fashioning, so to say, of the latter.

[191] A conjecture of this kind can be found in Eissfeldt, Hexateuch-Synopse, p. 52 f.

[192] *Cf.* Klostermann, Der Pentateuch II, p. 492 f.

[193] Thus already Ibn Ezra in his commentary. Eerdmans, Alttestamentliche Untersuchungen III, p. 74 f. remarks : " All of a sudden there is talk here of a tent which had never previously been mentioned "; but the reference in xviii, 7 clearly appears to have been sufficient for the redactor. *Cf.* also van Hoonacker, Le sacerdoce lévitique, p. 146, and Hertzberg, Mizpa (Zeitschrift fuer die alttestamentliche Wissenschaft XLVII, 1929), p. 171.

[194] Regarding the composition of the conversations see Buber and Rosenzweig, Die Schrift und ihre Verdeutschung, p. 262 ff.

[195] Whether these are " secondary" in their context (Eissfeldt, Hexateuch-Synopse, p. 274*), is not relevant to our question regarding the genuine character of the biographical tradition.

[196] *Cf.* Buber and Rosenzweig, *op. cit.*, p. 273.

[197] R. Kittel in the earlier and more comprehensive editions of his Geschichte des Volkes Israel I, p. 309 f.; *cf.* Sellin, Das Zelt Jahwes, Kittel-Festschrift (1913), p. 168 ff.

[198] Genesis xxv, 27, should be compared for the meaning of the construction : " To sit in the tent " means here to visit it again and again, " according to one's habit " (Caspari, Die Samuelbuecher, p. 59).

[199] *Cf.* Dibelius, Die Lade Jahves, p. 21 ff. His proofs do not seem to me to have been overthrown by Hans Schmidt, Kerubenthron und Lade, p. 143 f.

[200] *Cf.* also Klostermann, Der Pentateuch II, p. 73 ; Boehl, Exodus (1928), p. 167 ; Torczyner, Die Bundeslade und die Anfaenge der Religion Israels, 2nd Ed (1930), p. 38.

[201] Dibelius, *op. cit.* p. 115.

[202] *Ibid.*

[203] The second saying should not be emended, as Torczyner proposes, so as to read, " Be mounted, Yʜvʜ ", instead of, " Wend homewards, Yʜvʜ ". The victorious leader of " the myriads of units of Israel " is now called upon to return to His heaven (and to cover and protect His people from thence ; until the latter need His direct leadership once again).

[204] *Cf.* Torczyner, *op. cit.*, p. 15 ; Dhorme et Vincent, Les Chérubins (Revue biblique XXV, 1926), p. 485.

[205] Dibelius, *op. cit.*, p. 100.

[206] *Ibid.* p. 117.

[207] *Cf.* Galling, Biblisches Reallexikon (1937), p. 343.

[208] According to Numbers xiv, 44 the Ark, and hence the Tent, is unequivocally to be found within the camp. From Numbers xi, 26 and xii, 4 it has to be assumed that the camp consisted of a circle of tents, in the centre of which the Tent of God is to be found ; and that people therefore " went forth " to it.

[209] Caspari, Die Samuelbuecher, p. 476.

[210] W. Andrae, Das Gotteshaus und die Urformen des Bauens im alten Orient (1930), p. 11 ff., 21 ff. ; *cf.* Rost, Die Vorstufen von Kirche und Synagoge im Alten Testament (1938), p. 36.

[211] This verse must be reckoned as part of the older kernel, which may well be ascribed to the time of David, of the address of God, afterwards reworked in sermon-style. *Cf.* Rost, Die Ueberlieferung von der Thronnachfolge Davids (1926), p. 68 ff. When Wellhausen (Prolegomena zur Geschichte Israels, p. 46) holds that the reading of the parallel passage in Chronicles (I, xvii, 5) " from tent to tent " is based " on an entirely correct understanding ", he misses the connection between the speech of Nathan and the tradition which stands firm by the unity of the Tent (*cf.* Sellin, Das Zelt Jahwes, p. 172 f., on the Chronicles text).

[212] R. Hartmann, Zelt und Lade, p. 225.

[213] *Cf.* Buber, The Teaching of the Prophets, p. 158 f.

[214] This does not in any way mean that during the battle Yʜvʜ sojourns upon the Ark ; there is certainly no contradiction between His relation with the Ark and His advancing before the vanguard of Israel (Judges iv, 14). He displays His presence by His appearance over the Ark, and repeatedly stays there as it is His throne ; but meanwhile He advances against the foes and also supplies heavenly hosts to participate in the battle. Yet it should not be assumed, as is done by J. Kaufmann (History of the Religion of Israel II, p. 83, 351 ff.) that only the moving forward of the Ark compelled Yʜvʜ, in a kind of higher " sympathetic magic ", to depart from heaven and, riding upon the heavenly cherubim, to attack the foes of Israel. Such a verse as " I went about in tent and habitation " cannot be explained by any such provision for action at a distance.

[215] This is clearly the nature picture in Exodus xvi, 10.

[216] That is presumably the proper way to imagine the natural background of Numbers ix, 16.

[217] Gressmann, Mose, p. 268.

[218] Goldziher, Abhandlungen zur arabischen Philologie (1896), p. 15 ; Hoelscher, Die Propheten (1914), p. 99.

[219] Robertson Smith, The Prophets of Israel (1897), p. 392 ; *cf.* Goldziher, *op. cit.*, p. 74.

[220] Musil, Miszellen zur Bibelforschung (Die Kultur XI), p. 10.

[221] Doughty, Arabia Deserta II, Chapter 5.

[222] Musil, The Manners and Customs of the Rwala Beduins, p. 400.

[223] Wellhausen, Reste arabischen Heidentums, p. 135.

[224] *Cf.* Guillaume, Prophecy and Divination among the Hebrews and Semites (1938), p. 125 ; an ominous croak of raven is " seen " by those who are seers.

[225] *Cf.* inter alia Mowinckel, Psalmenstudien III (1929), p. 9. " The gift of the seer is in all probability genuinely Israelite ".

[226] Jepsen, Nabi (1934), p. 117.

[227] *Cf.* Hempel, Gott und Mensch im Alten Testament, 2nd Ed. (1936), p. 165.

[228] *Cf.* Gressmann, Mose, p. 137 ; Gressmann, Die Anfaenge Israels, p. 81.

[229] *Cf.* Buber and Rosenzweig, Die Schrift und ihre Verdeutschung, p. 33 ff., 131 ff., 160 ff., 279 ff.

[230] *Cf.* Buber, Koenigtum Gottes, p. 167 f. ; Buber, The Teaching of the Prophets, p. 60.

[231] *Cf.* Buber, Koenigtum Gottes, p. 173 f.

[232] On the relation between *ruaḥ* and word *cf.* Buber, The Teaching of the Prophets, p. 61. J. Kaufmann in particular has recently indicated the emissary element of the Israelite religion, in his " History of the Religion of Israel ".

[233] Mowinckel, The " Spirit " and the " Word " in the Pre-exilic Reforming Prophets, Journal of Biblical Literature LIII (1934), p. 199 ff. ; Mowinckel, Ecstatic Experience and Rational Elaboration in Old Testament Prophecy, Acta Orientalia XIII (1935), p. 264 ff.

[234] *Cf.* Masing, The Word of Yahweh (1936), who, however, does not keep *ruaḥ* and word apart ; Duerr, Die Wertung des goettlichen Wortes im Alten Testament und im antiken Orient (1938), p. 22 ff.

[235] Jepsen, Nabi, p. 119 f.

[236] Hempel, Gott und Mensch, p. 271.

[237] I agree with the view that a tribe called Kushan, associated with Midian (Habbakuk III, 7) is meant here ; and that the end of the verse is a gloss. The word, however, is certainly not to be taken as meaning, after Gressmann (Mose, p. 272 f., Die Anfaenge Israels, 2nd Ed., p. 96) that Zipporah was abused here with the secondary sense of " negro woman " (and hence also the Kenite god YHVH as " negro god "). The strange Ethiopians dwelling on the edge of the world are, to be sure, a subject of metaphor and simile for the Biblical writers ; but there is no feeling of abuse in the use made of their national name.

[238] *Cf.* Bacon, The Triple Tradition of the Exodus (1894), p. 175 ; Harold Wiener, Essays in Pentateuchal Criticism (1909), p. 99.

[239] *Cf.* J. Kaufmann, History of the Religion of Israel, II/1, pp. 46, 122.

[240] *Cf. e.g*, Musil, Manners and Customs, p. 400 ; Guillaume, Prophecy and Divination, p. 122 ff.

[241] *Cf.* Alt, Der Gott der Vaeter (1929) ; Boehl, Das Zeitalter Abrahams (1931) ; Buber, The Teaching of the Prophets, p. 29 ff.

[242] *Cf.* Dillmann's Commentary *ad loc.*

[243] *Cf.* de Groot, Numeri (1930), p. 128 : " without there having been any division between the two ".

[244] *Cf.* Holzinger in Kautzsch, Die Heilige Schrift des Alten Testaments, 4th Ed., *ad loc.*

[245] Thus Smend, Die Erzaehlung des Hexateuch (1912), p. 230.

[246] *Cf.* Buber, Koenigtum Gottes, p. 133.

[247] The interpretation given here is the only suitable one in this connection.

[248] A division of sources which separates XXIII, 23 and XXIV, 1 (as, most recently, Rudolph, Der " Elohist ", p. 121 f.) is something I cannot agree to ; they point to one another in the same way as XXIII, 23 and XXII, 7.

[249] In the oldest popular saga of the evil wizard Balaam, the late effects of which have been retained in Numbers xxxi, 8, 16, and Joshua xiii, 22, his demon should have been the inspiring one (*cf.* Loehr, Bileam, Archiv fuer Orientforschung IV, 1927, p. 88 ; Rudolph, *op. cit.*, p 10).

[250] Rudolph, *op. cit.* p. 105.

[251] Kuehtreiber, Bericht ueber meine Reisen (Zeitschrift des Deutschen Palaestina-Vereins XXXVII, 1914), p. 11.

[252] *Cf.* Woolley and Lawrence, The Wilderness of Zin (1914), p. 58 ff.

[253] Woolley, *op. cit*, p. 71.

[254] *Cf.* A. Klostermann, Geschichte des Volkes Israel (1896), p. 69.

[255] Garstang, The Heritage of Solomon (1934), p. 177.

[256] Gressmann, Die Anfaenge Israels, 2nd Ed., p. 106.

[257] von Rad, Das theologische Problem des alttestamentlichen Schoepfungs-glaubens, in : Wesen und Werden des Alten Testaments (1936), p. 139.

[258] Galling, Die Erwaehlungstraditionen Israels, p 65.

[259] Alt, Der Gott der Vaeter, p. 57.

[260] *Ibid.* p. 41.

[261] *Ibid.* p. 46.

[262] Buber, The Teaching of the Prophets, p. 40.

[263] *Cf. ibid.* p. 36.

[264] The Arabs of Sinai, to be sure, use the name *qadeis* for a spoon-shaped wooden vessel which they employ when drawing water out of an almost empty well (Woolley and Lawrence, The Wilderness of Zin, p. 53). This name is held to come from a word in the Hedjaz dialect. But it can be explained properly only as a folk-etymology of the name of the place, not as genuine etymology. Phythian-Adams, in The Call of Israel, p. 196, assumes quite incorrectly in this connection that the name has nothing to do with sanctity.

[265] Rhodokanakis, Die Bodenwirtschaft im alten Suedarabien (Anzeigen der Wiener Akademie der Wissenschaften LIII, 1916), p. 174.

[266] von Rad, *op. cit.*, p. 139.

[267] *Cf.* Jirku, Das israelitische Jubeljahr (Reinhold-Seeberg-Festschrift, 1929), p. 172 ff.

[268] Pedersen, Israel, its Life and Culture I-II (1926), p. 544.

[269] *Ibid.*

[270] Alt, Die Urspruenge des israelitischen Rechts, p. 65 ; *cf.* also von Rad, Das formgeschichtliche Problem des Hexateuchs, p. 31 f.

[271] Menes, Die vorisraelitischen Gesetze Israels (1926), 39.

[272] Pedersen, *op. cit.*, p. 480.

[273] Alt, *op. cit.*, p. 65 f.

[274] Fenton, Early Hebrew Life (1880), p. 67 ff. ; Kennett, Ancient Hebrew Life and Custom (1933), p. 77 ; Alt, *op. cit.*, p. 66.

[275] *Cf.* Musil, Arabia Petraea III, p. 293 f.

[276] Jirku, *op. cit.*, p. 178.

[277] Alt, *op. cit*, p. 66.

[278] Alt, *op. cit.*, p. 67.

[279] Ed. Meyer, Die Israeliten und ihre Nachbarstaemme, p. 80 f.

[280] Kugler, Von Moses bis Paulus (1922), p. 42 ff. ; Kennett, *op. cit.*, p. 77.

[281] *Cf.* inter alia Baudissin, Die Geschichte des alttestamentlichen Priestertums, p. 35.

[282] Thus Gressmann, Mose, p. 261 f.

[283] *Cf.* Gray, Sacrifice in the Old Testament, p. 249 f.

[284] The article "Levi" by Hoelscher, in Pauly-Wissowa's Real-Enzyklopædie des klassischen Altertums XII, p. 2155 ff., is most comprehensively based, but is nevertheless an unsuccessful attempt to view the Levites as the ancient priestly order of Kadesh, by whom Moses was supported. *Cf.* Gray, Sacrifice in the Old Testament, p. 239 ff, on the complexity of the problem. Albright's assumption, in Archæology and the Religion of Israel (1942), p. 109, that the Levites were " a class or tribe " which as such exercised sacral functions (even in pre-Mosaic times), and which increased both naturally as well as through children who were dedicated to the service of YHVH, is satisfactory in certain respects, but still does not offer any adequate solution of the problem. And that Moses as well as Aaron were Levites

" by virtue of their priestly function ", presupposes a professional priesthood on the part of Moses, which must be questioned.

[285] *Cf.* Rost, Die Vorstufen von Kirche und Synagoge im Alten Testament, p. 7 ff., 32 ff. ; on Numbers xvi f., pp. 10, 14, 90. The double sense of *edah* in our section is not given consideration here.

[286] *Cf.* Buber and Rosenzweig, Die Schrift und ihre Verdeutschung, p. 217 ff.

[287] The last attempt of which I am aware to prove that Moses was a priest, in Gray's Sacrifice in the Old Testament, p. 198 ff., is one that I likewise cannot regard as successful.

[288] This is inter alia the thesis of J. Kaufmann, History of the Religion of Israel, II/1, p. 342 ff.

[289] Thus, *e.g.*, Bacon, The Triple Tradition of the Exodus, p. 190 : " Certain prominent individuals aspire to the priesthood and raise rebellion against Moses ".

[290] To complete what follows *cf.* Buber, Koenigtum Gottes, p. 140 ff.

[291] *Cf.* the chapter on Hosea in my book, The Teaching of the Prophets.

[292] *Cf.* Buber, Koenigtum Gottes, p. 65 ff., 204 ff. and the literature cited there ; Buber, The Teaching of the Prophets, p. 67 ff.

[293] Buber, The Teaching of the Prophets, p. 69.

[294] *Cf.* Buber and Rosenzweig, Die Schrift und ihre Verdeutschung, p. 58 ff.

[295] *Cf.* Pedersen, Canaanite and Israelite Cults (Acta Orientalia XVIII, 1939), p. 6 : " Aliyan Baal is the bull-god whom we know from the Old Testament ", he " represents fertility ".

[296] *Cf.* Buber, Koenigtum Gottes, p. 282, note 19, for textual analysis.

[297] *Cf. Ibid.*

[298] Alt, Josua, in : Wesen und Werden des Alten Testaments, p. 13 ff.

[299] Bin Gurion, Sinai und Garizim.

[300] Meek, Hebrew Origins (1936).

INDEX

CPSIA information can be obtained
at www.ICGtesting.com
Printed in the USA
BVHW072351150620
581358BV00004B/85